CHINESE POLITICS ILLUSTRATED

The Cultural, Social, and Historical Context

Lance L P Gore

Bowdoin College, USA

World Scientific

NEW JERSEY • LONDON • SINGAPORE • BEIJING • SHANGHAI • HONG KONG • TAIPEI • CHENNAI

Published by

World Scientific Publishing Co. Pte. Ltd.

5 Toh Tuck Link, Singapore 596224

USA office: 27 Warren Street, Suite 401-402, Hackensack, NJ 07601

UK office: 57 Shelton Street, Covent Garden, London WC2H 9HE

Library of Congress Cataloging-in-Publication Data
Gore, Lance, 1958–
    Chinese politics illustrated : the cultural, social and historical context / Lance L.P. Gore.
        pages cm
    ISBN 978-9814546744
    1. Political culture--China. 2. Political participation--China. 3. China--Politics and
government--1949–   I. Title.
    JQ1516.G67 2014
    320.951--dc23

                                                                2013051171

British Library Cataloguing-in-Publication Data
A catalogue record for this book is available from the British Library.

In-house Editor: Dong Lixi

Typeset by Stallion Press
Email: enquiries@stallionpress.com

Printed in Singapore by World Scientific Printers.

CONTENTS

LIST OF TABLES

LIST OF FIGURES

LIST OF BOXED ESSAYS

ACRONYM

ACFIC	All-China Federation of Industry and Commerce
ACFTU	All China Federation of Trade Unions
CCP	Chinese Communist Party
CEC-CEDA	China Enterprise Confederation and China Enterprise Directors' Association
COD	Central Organization Department
CPPCC	Chinese People's Political Consultative Conference
GO	General Office
KMT	Kuomintang (the Nationalist Party)
NPC	National People's Congress
PBSC	Politburo Standing Committee
PRC	People's Republic of China
PC	People's Congress
SOE	State-owned Enterprise
SPC	State Planning Commission

ACRONYMS

A STORIED PRELUDE[1]

After supper, Secretary Chang went for a walk on the streets of D city. It was hot. Walking out of the door was like entering a furnace.

When he came to a quiet street in a remote area, he saw on the roadside a farmer's tricycle truck loaded with watermelons; on the ground there spread a bamboo sheet. A boy clod with dirt sat on it, eating a steamed bun. A woman with plain clothing stood by the tricycle, sweating and looking at the people passing by. Besides her was a man in grey shirt wet with sweat on the back. There were a few map-like sweat marks on the shoulder as well.

They smiled broadly when they saw Secretary Chang approaching. The woman talked in a sweet voice, "Come on and taste our watermelon, all red and sandy meat, very fresh and thirst-quenching." The man picked a melon from the truck and cut it open. Indeed, red meat with black seeds, very tempting.

Secretary Chang said, "What a melon! They must be selling very well." The woman replied that there were too few pedestrians on this street. It would take three to four days to sell their load of watermelons. "Why don't you go to the center of the city?" said Secretary Chang, "There are more people there." The husband shook his head like a hand drum: "Watermelon farmer's trucks are not allowed to enter the downtown area." The woman asked, "Brother, where do you live? Let him deliver to you, no matter which floor you live." The boy on the ground also shouted repeatedly, "Uncle, please buy some!"

Hearing the child's voice, Secretary Chang felt his heart warming up. He also answered repeatedly, "Alright, alright, uncle will buy." He took out a 50 yuan note from his pocket and said to the man, "I will buy only

---

[1]Story by Liang Haichao, "Secretary Chang Sells Watermelons," from Wang Yaowen *et al.* 2011. *Being an Official (youguan zaishen)*. Nanjing, China: Jiangsu People's Press.

30 yuan of melon. Take the remaining 20 yuan and ask your woman and kid to take a bath in a hotel and have a bowl of noodle. It is so hot; how could you let your boy eat only steamed bun? Let me help you to tend the stall and sell the watermelon for a while."

The woman burst out in laughter, "You know how to sell watermelons, big brother?"[2] Secretary Chang also laughed: "My family used to be watermelon farmers too." The woman was afraid of losing this business and agreed with many thanks.

At this time, a fat man and a thin guy came along. The fat man was shaking his T-shirt to stir up the air to cool him down. They came to the melon stall and stared for a long time before asking, "Secretary Chang, what are you do…?" When Chang realized that they had recognized him, he said "These are relatives from my native village. Since I happen to have some spare time, I am helping them sell melons for a while."

The fat man opened his mouth but nothing came out. He and the thin guy did not know what to do: to stay or to leave. Secretary Chang said, "Go on with your walk." The two felt like they had gotten amnesty. They repeatedly said alright and they would return soon. Indeed, before long the two came back. Claiming that they had guests at home, each purchased 100 pounds of watermelon. The farmer wanted to deliver for them but they called a cab to take the melons. A few minutes later, cars came one after another. They belonged respectively to the bureau chief, the section head, the chairman of the Union, the township director and so on. They surrounded the small tricycle truck. Some said that they had been thinking of shopping for watermelon but did not know where to find good ones; some said their work unit had just finished a conference that afternoon and wanted to celebrate; still others said that they wanted to make some small contribution to poverty relief. Secretary Chang and the farmer could barely keep up. The "customers" did the weighing and loading themselves. Some bought 100 pounds and some 300. The truck load of watermelons was sold out in less than 10 minutes.

At the beginning, the farmer was worried that somebody might not pay or may short-change him. What happened was exactly the opposite. A bagful

---

[2] "Big brother" here does not carry the English connotation. It is commonly used to address someone with higher status and of similar age. It implies closeness.

of watermelons was worth about 20–30 yuan but the buyers gave him a 50 yuan notes. 100 pound watermelons were about 50 yuan but the buyers gave him a 100 yuan note each. They all refused the change. More and more "customers" came. Those who were not able to buy complained to the farmer that he should have brought more. Secretary Chang said to those colleagues who were unable to buy, "Thank you everybody. This year, all the watermelon farmers that have come to our city are my relatives. If you need watermelons, please go to their stalls to buy."

The result was that evening all watermelons were sold out in the city.

7.4 Petitioners can be seen outside government buildings in many cities. They are a salient feature of contemporary Chinese politics. Both the Party and the government have "letters and visits departments" specialized in dealing with citizen's petitions. In keeping with the Confucian tradition the Chinese people often prefer petitioning the government to litigation. Rapid socioeconomic transformation has created numerous conflicts that outstrip the capacity of China's archaic political systems plagued by corruption.

After Secretary Chang sent away those cadres who came to buy watermelons, the woman and the boy came back from dinner. When the woman saw the empty truck, she got anxious, asking her husband, "Where are our melons? Are they confiscated again?" The man told her that Secretary Chang had sold all the melons. The woman was in shock for a long time before she cried out.

A few days later, the county had a new policy — allowing watermelon farmers to sell their produce in the downtown area.

After the summer, at a routine flag-raising ceremony in the county party committee compound, one hundred or so melon farmers appeared at the gate. The guard thought they were petitioners but at eight o'clock, they lined up and, very seriously, bowed three times to the rising red national flag.

This short story raises a host of questions and puzzles about Chinese politics. It paints the life in China for the ordinary people in vivid color and details. For beginners, the highest public official in a Chinese city is not the mayor. It is instead the secretary of the municipal committee of the Chinese Communist Party (CCP). Similarly, the top leader of China is not the President or the Premier; it is the General Secretary of the ruling CCP. So whenever you go to China, remember the real boss in a state-owned corporation, a university, a government department or any organizations in the public sector is the party secretary, not the CEO or top administrator. As shown in this story, the power and influence of a municipal party secretary is unimaginable in the West. The casual act of Secretary Chang helping the family of a watermelon farmer on his daily after-supper stroll launched the entire cadre corps of that city into a buying frenzy. As a result, the watermelons were sold out overnight in that city. This story makes one wonder how much and what political power can do in China?

We are taught from very young age that "absolute power corrupts absolutely" and we have all heard about the rampant corruption and pervasive repression in China and the wanton violations of human rights by the Chinese government. This story, however, reveals much more things about Chinese politics. Party secretary Chang seems a caring person who showed genuine concern for the welfare of the peasant family. His ability to mobilize the entire government (even without saying a word) and to change public policy like flipping a switch is remarkable. The length those cadres were willing to go in order to please Secretary Chang is equally remarkable. The gratitude the 100 or so watermelon farmers expressed in the form of patriotism (by saluting the national flag) is perhaps more puzzling for outsiders. Careful readers will also notice the enormous urban–rural income gap. There are many other memorable details: the petrified pair who came across Secretary Chang selling watermelons, the overpayment for watermelons, the humble peasant woman being moved to tears etc. These are important dimensions of power in Chinese politics that we will not normally be exposed to but are critical to understanding the epical transformation undertaken in China and its implications for the rest of the world. Stories like this makes China less of a strange beast to be either feared or admired. After all, it consists of real human beings who share a great deal with you and me. Looking at the giant leap China is making through the small steps its ordinary citizens are taking is what this storied textbook about.

Where Did China Come from and Where Is It Going?

China today is a bundle of contradictions to an outside observer. There are several major puzzles about the rise of China. For example, it has a vibrant market economy presided over by a communist polity and, as many studies have shown and as we can see from the stories in this book, the Chinese economy took off not in spite of the communist institutions but in large part because of them; the Chinese markets are highly competitive and dynamic despite the continued dominance of "public property rights" and pervasive state interventions. Above all, the ruling CCP poses a puzzle that challenges many of the received wisdoms in political science; it also causes a great deal of confusion and apprehension in the world at large about the rise of China: Can it still be called a communist party? How does it adapt to a marketized and globalized economy? How long can single-party rule be sustained or when will it collapse? And, with the CCP in charge, how will China behave when it becomes the largest economy in the world and its military strength achieves parity with that of the United States?

To resolve these and many other puzzles requires understanding the internal dynamics of China's political, economic, and social developments and the forces driving them. The stories in this book provide us an opportunity to gain some in-depth understanding of the workings of the Chinese system. They offer us a front row seat to watch the everyday drama of Chinese politics as the actors themselves experience it and understand it. Through them, readers can feel the pulse of China, get to know the country not as a monstrous abstract but as concrete individuals who have joys and sorrows just as you and I. Their lives are likely to be different from ours but it is in the study of these differences that we can truly understand China. This micro-understanding of China, which cannot be gained from a conventional textbook of political science, in turn, should help to demystify China. Hopefully, these stories and essays will help readers, be it students of Chinese politics and society, entrepreneurs, policy makers, journalists, and ordinary citizens who are interested in China, to deal with China and the Chinese people more effectively.

However, as the Chinese saying goes, "looking at the leopard through a tube," which is equivalent to the English saying "seeing the trees but not the forest", these stories are like the spots on the fur of a leopard that one sees through a tube. They must be put into a larger context to make better sense and become helpful in understanding the larger issues of Chinese politics. The first three Study Units lay out the three contexts of contemporary Chinese politics — the cultural and historical context, the context of the "Great Chinese Revolution" (that started in the second half of the 19th century and is still on-going today), and the structural context (namely, the political system). They allow us to understand the deeper meanings of the ongoing transformation of China and appreciate the politics in the stories. These three contexts and the five topical essays in Part III of the book provide the basic analytic framework, within which we will examine the major reform measures, uncover the genesis of the Chinese economic "miracle" and understand the problems bedeviling China today. Above all, we will sort out the social and political consequences of the economic "miracle" and its implications for the future of China.

The rest of the Study Units, in conjunction with the textboxes and the boxed essays throughout the book, address some salient issues in Chinese politics as well as in political science, such as political culture, ideology, corruption, mass protests, elite politics, state–society and state–market relations, policy and decision making, political participation, the political economy of development, power succession, political change and so on. The book seeks to be thought-stimulating by constructing an implicit dialogue between the wisdom of Western political science and the real world politics unfolding in a non-Western cultural setting.

To the Instructor: Why and How to Use This Textbook?

During many years of teaching contemporary Chinese politics in a liberal arts college in America, I felt a pressing need for a textbook that is at the same time entertaining, enlightening, as well as educational. The conventional textbooks on the politics of a country outside the Western culture tend to be demanding on the imagination for students who have no experiences living or traveling in the country under study. My classes are often automatically divided into two groups with contrasting views on a range of culturally sensitive issues, based upon whether the students have personal experiences in China or in East Asia in general. I find a sense of realism makes a world of difference in the effectiveness of teaching and in the way the students absorb the reading materials. It is the rich imagination of the younger generation that this book appeals to in conveying that sense of realism, which in turn facilitates a quicker, better, more sophisticated and in-depth understanding of contemporary Chinese politics and society.

Like everybody else, college students understand the finer nuances of politics in a different culture and society by invoking their personal experiences growing up in their own culture and society. Real stories and imageries from their own lives are vehicles for their interpretation of course materials. They are also influenced by perceptions shaped by the mass media and other casual encounters. However, neither is a reliable guide for understanding the complexity and intrigues of Chinese politics. The Western media, or any other media for that matter, typically report the politics of a different cultural, social and ideological context with selection biases. What to report and how to report are influenced by the nature of the assignments and the dispositions of the reporters. Their reporting is further filtered by editors who are obligated by their business sense to maximize the ratings. This is often translated into reporting things their audiences like to hear and expressing views that are easy for them to understand or accept. The sound bytes of domestic politics are matched by the stereotypes of a foreign country. The media business thus does not serve as a reliable guide. But it nevertheless influences public opinions and hence the predisposition of the students. Nowadays, many American colleges and universities require their students to take at least one "non-Eurocentric" course to better prepare them for the globalized world. Such courses, however, are often taught by professors who have limited direct exposure to the culture and society they are teaching about; the textbooks they use are seldom entertaining and are often immersed in Western political discourse. These factors limit the students' ability to comprehend alternative political arrangements and appreciate political dramas based on different cultural assumptions and institutional arrangements.

This book redresses this problem through "storytelling." It carefully selects a group of short stories from the huge volume of political fictions — a very popular genre nowadays in China based closely on real-life stories — to bring out the salient features as well as the intricacies of Chinese politics being played out in the contemporary Chinese cultural and social context under tremendous historical inertia, and as the political actors experience them in daily life. Apart from the pedagogical objectives, another purpose of this book is to entertain: it illustrates Chinese politics as if a theatrical performance. In a sense, the students are offered the ringside seats to watch a game unfolding on the stage of Chinese politics. To put it differently, the book attempts to substitute the sense of realism of the target culture for one based on the source culture. We know that in the print media, literature is the best way to peep into a different culture and quickly gain a sense of realism from it. The richness of literary presentation is unmatched by any academic theorizing. Literature also surpasses the audio and visual media in the depth of presentation. It is multi-dimensional and gives students the necessary space to make their own judgment and form their own interpretations. In contrast, a conventional textbook typically makes such judgment for them.

Each story illustrates in multiple dimensions one or several topics listed in Part II. For example, the story above illustrates power relations, Chinese political culture as manifested in today's structural context, poverty, the urban–rural income gap, the rural roots of the CCP regime, state–society relations, elite politics and so on. At the end of each short story (or a section of a longer one), there are provided a few Chinese proverbs exemplary of Chinese cultural wisdoms, various suggested assignments, exercises and classroom activities for educators to choose from. For example, the following relate to the story above:

Proverbs:

— The sky is high and the emperor far away. (天高皇帝远)
— Being a public official and yet unable to stand up for the people, I'd rather go home to sell sweet potatoes. (当官不为民作主, 不如回家卖红薯)

Questions:

1. Like all the short-short stories in this book, exaggeration is used to make a point about Chinese politics. What is the main point the author is driving at?
2. Secretary Chang is the top leader of this county-seat city. How does he relate to the farmer (ordinary people) and other public officials of that city respectively? How do you describe Secretary Chang's feeling for the watermelon farmer family? Where do you think such feelings come from?
3. How do you describe state–society relations as reflected in the story?
4. Why did the fat man and the thin guy feel like they had gained amnesty when Secretary Chang told them to go on with their walk? What do you think they had done before they came back?
5. What does the story tell you about the Chinese political culture?
6. What caused the watermelon farmers to salute the national flag? Were you the farmers, would you have done such a thing and why?

Suggested Exercises and Assignments:

1. Use the story as a script and enact the whole event with your class-mates. Tell each other how you feel in your roles as the party secretary, the farmer and his family members and the cadres.

2. Find some details in the story that indicate the income gap between rural farmers and cadres in the cities. Estimate how large the gap is and find statistical data (there are many sources: the UN, the World Bank, the Chinese National Statistic Bureau websites etc.) and see if you are right.
3. Paraphrase the story from your memory and write it down. Compare what your memory captures with the original text. What is missing and what does your memory pick up? Compare yours with some of your classmates' versions to see if there is a pattern of hit and miss.

You probably notice immediately that some of the questions are open-ended and some of the exercises will require some research. These are all part of the design to stimulate thinking and promote active learning.

This book is, however, not just stories. It also covers major areas of academic inquiries into contemporary Chinese politics.[3] The "three context" readings and the topical essays at the end of the book provide the basic structure that connects everything into a coherent knowledge base that students may take with them. Each of the 11 Study Units addresses a particular topic with a combination of stories, textboxes, boxed essays, reading/discussion questions, and various assignments. Each unit outlines the learning objectives, provides the relevant questions and suggests exercises and other activities for the attainment of the objectives. A list of suggested readings is also attached to each study unit for the convenience of the readers who want to pursue further study on a particular topic in that unit.

This book can be used in a variety of ways. One suggested course plan is to devote the first half of the course time to story reading that is organized around the questions and activities suggested at the end of each story. As such, the students will develop a sense of realism, accumulate large number of questions and form their own opinions on many issues on Chinese politics and political science in general. The second half of the course is used to sort out

---

[3] Because of the limitations of the stories, some areas such as foreign relations and foreign policy are not covered.

these questions and opinions and develop a systematic under-standing of Chinese politics. The 11 "Study Units" are designed for that purpose. However, the coverage of some study units is much more substantial than others, e.g., the first three units on the three contexts of Chinese politics. They require more class time. The same is true with the topical essays.

A second suggested plan is to start with the three contexts (Study Units 1, 2 and 3), driving them home with a combination of lectures, documentary films or other visual aids, supplementary readings and the questions and activities suggested at the end of the study units. This will provide a systematic albeit rather abstract knowledge base of Chinese culture, history, and the political system. The second part of the course will launch into story reading, allowing students to make sense of the stories with the knowledge base they have already built up. The third part addresses specific topics in Chinese politics and key concepts of political science by following the remaining study units. Finally, the essays provide a venue for more in-depth analysis of Chinese politics.

Alternatively, this book, especially the stories, can be used in conjunction with existing textbooks on the market. The ways to integrate the lessons are completely at the discretion of the instructors.

Because of the peculiarities of a storytelling textbook, the course materials drawn together in the Study Units do not follow a sequential pagination as do the chapters in a conventional textbook. Instead, each unit draws materials from various parts of the book. Compared with other textbooks, the reading load of this book should be lighter, in part because of the stories. Most stories are short and the explanatory textboxes are concise; hence inten-sive reading is recommended. The readings for the "three contexts" and the topical essays are more challenging but many points they make are illustrated in the stories. The assignments in this book also involve active learning: the students will be responsible for finding out for themselves particular historical events, key terms and institutions, and key historical figures and events. They will be making extensive use of the resources on the internet, searching for basic knowledge, visual aids, and alternative theories and interpretations of a particular event or phenomenon. The students are also encouraged to collaborate in such endeavors, compare notes and debate their findings. As mentioned above a main objective of this textbook is to give students enough room to formulate their own views, judgments, theories, and assessments of various issues in Chinese politics, as well as of political science concepts, theories, and models in general.

This author did all the translations required in this book. The style of translation is liberal, with a focus on pedagogical objectives. Some plots from the original works have been omitted if they do not directly serve our objective or if they were considered distraction. All the textboxes, highlights, and footnotes in the stories are added by this author. Although all the stories are in the realist tradition, some do involve exaggeration or idealization on the part of their authors. The students are warned against these things either in the prelude to the story or in the reading questions that follow it. But overall, the stories faithfully illustrate the everyday reality of Chinese politics, typical actions of Chinese politicians, the basic political structures and processes, power distribution, the underlying cultural assumptions, the rituals and the interactive dynamics among various types of people in the Chinese society. However, unlike mature Western democracies where a sense of permanency prevails, China changes rapidly and is in the process of a fundamental transformation. By the time this book is out in the market, some phenomena depicted in the stories may have evolved or faded away. For instance, corruption today is found on a much grander scale and with more sophisticated schemes. Nevertheless, in terms of pinpointing the root causes of corruption and the weaknesses of the political system these stories remain relevant. Recent developments in state–society relations and patterns of elite politics, the ever-increasing impact of globalization, the rise of the social media etc. are dealt with mostly in the topical essays. In general, the educational objective is achieved when the students can confidently comprehend the essays.

The textboxes or highlights serve primarily as a reading guide. They are numbered by the Study Unit they belong to. For example, the textbox in the above story pertains to study unit 7. The boxed essays address more general issues of political science in addition to defining key terms in Chinese politics and history. The proverbs (included those appearing in the stories that are highlighted) expose the students to the more enduring elements of the Chinese culture and mindset. The book can be used either as a stand-alone text or as a companion to a conventional textbook by pairing the suggested study units with the corresponding chapters in the latter.

The Chinese put their surname before the given name. This book follows this cultural practice instead of reversing the order as commonly done when Chinese names are rendered in English. Therefore, when a single name is used such as Chang, Sun or Lu, they may not be the given names as assumed by English readers. For example, the person by the name Sun Yat-sen can be referred to as Sun or Yat-sen. The former is a formal designation while the latter a diminutive one. The reader has to refer to the order in which the full name first appears to decide which is the case.

ACKNOWLEDGEMENTS

From conception to eventual publication, this book took 12 years to test-drive, take shape and maturate. This long process led to the accumulation of debts by a long list of people. It is impossible to thank them all, but my first and foremost gratitude goes to my undergraduate students at Bowdoin College and my graduate students at the Fletcher School of Law and Diplomacy of Tufts University, who read both the Chinese and English versions of some of the stories. They were the most enthusiastic endorsers to this innovative project and unconventional textbook. Their questions, comments, discussions and debates in and outside the classroom are the basis of all the reading questions, exercises, and other assignments built into this textbook. I also owe a debt to my daughter, Victoria, for her reactions and feedback, and for soliciting feedback from her classmates at Boston University. My son, Adam, also helped with typing my hand-written translation, during which he also provided me with many fresh insights. All together these young scholars enabled me to think about Chinese politics from different perspectives and enriched my understanding of it.

The initial idea about such a textbook was explored with Elizabeth Perry of Harvard University. My colleagues at Bowdoin College, in particular Craig McEwen, Paul Franco, Nancy Riley, Shu-chin Tsui, Songren Cui, John Holt, Henry Laurence, Belinda Kong, among many others, generously shared their views and injected their teaching experiences and expertise into this project. Professor Wang Gungwu of National University of Singapore, an eminent historian of China and Southeast Asia, read through the entire manuscript and provided valuable comments and suggestions from both scholarly and pedagogical perspectives. John Copper of Rhodes College, Wenfang Tang of University of Iowa,

xxx   *Chinese Politics Illustrated*

and Kjeld Erik Brodsgaard of Copenhagen Business School read part or the entire manuscript and contributed many good suggestions. Michael Heng, commissioning editor of World Science Publishing, gave this book project the final push to publication while it was left at a corner of my bookshelf, neglected from all my other research and writing projects. Dong Lixi of World Scientific guided the editing and production process with great skill and effectiveness. Her attention to details greatly improved the quality of the manuscript and, at times, I felt that she was more devoted to the project than I. That said, I am solely responsible for all the shortcomings that remain. I am equally hopeful that my future students, my fellow teaching professionals who adopt this text and their students will continue to improve it. For the book will then take on a life of its own and become our common project.

PART I

THE STORIES

STORY 1: COMPUTER ASSIMILATION OF FINANCE BUREAU CHIEF[1]

Guo Zhenghai

Upon graduation from college, Zhou Dewei was hired as a clerk in the financial department of a company. He was a good learner, motivated, and upright as a person. His friends always said that if he entered public service he would certainly be a good official. Zhou also believed it. As the saying goes, "The soldier who does not want to become a general is not a good soldier." The greatest dream of his was to become a finance bureau chief of the government someday by working hard and conscientiously.

One day, he found an online game while surfing the internet. It had a special program that allowed anyone to experience being a government official — all it took was to fill in your name and the position you wanted. Zhou was excited about it. After registration, he entered his username. In the space for "Position" he put in without hesitation "Finance Bureau Chief." Instantly the screen exploded with flowers, fireworks, and a line: "Congratulations! You have been officially appointed as the director of the financial bureau by the authorities!"

After the celebration, a line appeared on the screen: "How are you, Director Zhou? The municipal water bureau chief Wang would like to invite you for dinner tonight. Do you want to go?" At the bottom of the screen there was a hint: You have always had a good relationship with Director Wang. If you agree to go, please click on "Yes" and if you do not, click "No."

---

[1]From Wang Yaowen *et al.* 2011. *Being an Official (youguan zaishen)*. Nanjing, China: Jiangsu People's Press.

As old friends it would be unnatural not to go; Director Wang would think that I am conceited. I should go. After thinking about for while, he clicked "Yes."

In the evening, Director Wang came early and waited for him in a private dining room of the city's most luxurious King's Hotel, together with a few others. Zhou moved the mouse to make the virtual trip to the dining room. Upon arrival, Director Wang introduced the other people to him: this is President Liu; this is Manager Zhang, and this is Boss Wei. The computer screen flashed another question: "If they make toasts to you, will you drink?" Well, such question raised in such a setting, Zhou Dewei felt that the programmer was silly — a drink is a must when old friends meet. He clicked "Yes" without hesitation.

Amidst toasting and drinking, another question appeared on the screen: "Director Zhou, you are very drunk now. After dinner, Director Wang wants you to visit the nightclub; will you go?" The virtual Director Zhou was drunk but the real one was clear-minded. I wanted to be a good public servant even in my dreams; how could I set foot in such places? He pressed "No." Immediately a big thumb up appeared on the screen and a sweet voice said, "Director Zhou, you are really a good official." It made Zhou very happy.

After dinner another line jumped on the screen, "Director Zhou, Deputy Mayor Liu, whose portfolio includes financial matters, called asking you to give the green light to an investment project. The paper works for this project are not complete yet. Will you give the go ahead? Hint: Deputy Mayor Liu played a big role helping you to secure your promotion to financial bureau chief."

This is a tough one. If I reject it, I may well offend my direct boss, to whom I owe so much. I want to give the nod but the paper works are incomplete. As Zhou was wondering what to do another timely hint jumped up, "Director Zhou, Deputy Mayor Liu called again, complaining that you are too slow at work." It looks that he has no choice, and he clicked "Yes."

"Director Zhou, someone came to your home to seek your help on some matter. That day you happened to be out but your wife accepted a 20,000 yuan diamond ring. Your wife married you against strong objections from her parents and you pledged to her that you would achieve success to give her a good life. Now, how will you deal with this diamond ring?"

Zhou felt that the ring should be returned but clicked "Keep" when he thought about the sacrifice his wife had made for him.

"Director Zhou, the children of many other leading cadres at the same rank as yours have gone abroad to study. You also want very much to send your child but cannot afford it. *As if sending coal to someone in a snowy day*, somebody gives you a sum of money, stating clearly that this is a gift. Will you accept it?" Since it is clearly stated that the money is a gift, not in exchange for some favor, accepting it is not against the law nor in violation of the party discipline. He clicked "Yes" again.

"Director Zhou, it's almost the Lunar New Year now. Other cadres at the same rank as yours all pay visits to their superiors, bringing presents. Will you send presents also?" Zhou knew that he must go with the flow even if he is reluctant at heart. Once again, he clicked "Yes."

"Director Zhou…" Zhou Dewei was mesmerized playing the virtual finance bureau chief and answering the questions. Suddenly, the computer flashed, "Your game is over. Do you want to know the result?"

Zhou pressed "Yes." Consequently, an extra-large handcuff appeared on the screen, sparkling with cold light.

1. Political Culture

Political culture is defined by the *International Encyclopedia of the Social Sciences* as "the set of attitudes, beliefs and sentiments which give order and meaning to a political process and which provide the underlying assumptions and rules that govern behavior in the political system." It encompasses both the political ideals and operating norms of a polity. Political culture

(Continued)

(Continued)

is thus the manifestation in aggregate form of the psychological and subjective dimensions of politics. A political culture is the product of both the collective history of a political system and the life histories of the members of the system and thus it is rooted equally in public events and private experience. Political scientist Daniel Elazar identified political culture as one reason that different states enact different policies to deal with similar problems.

Political culture differs in different nations. Some national political cultures are characterized as "individualistic," "moralistic," "traditionalistic," etc. Individualistic political culture often emerges from capitalist market economy where individuals have to make life choices based on their comparative advantage at the marketplace. Such political culture favors a limited role for the government and is distrustful of bureaucracy. A moralistic political culture emphasizes the collective over the individual. It regards government as a force to advance public interests, which can also play a positive role in the lives of citizens. Politics tends to evolve around real issues rather than abstract ideals. Corruption is less tolerated because government officials are expected to play a morally exemplary role for the public. Bureaucracy is viewed favorably as a way to achieve the public good. Traditionalistic political culture embraces established rules, rituals, authorities and the patterns of role expectation among individuals of different statuses. A central role of the state is to maintain the established order. Politicians come from society's elite, especially established families. They have paternalistic obligations to the people who offer their loyalty, obedience or compliance in exchange for protection. Ordinary citizens are not expected to participate in politics or even want to vote in elections. Politics tends to be competition between rival factions within the elite rather than between class-based parties.

(Continued)

(Continued)

The dominant political culture of China is informed by Confucianism with an emphasis on the family metaphor (*see Boxed Essay 7 on page 197, Confucianism*). It is both traditional and moralistic, but is also increasingly infused with elements of individualistic political culture that insists on individual rights because of inroads into the market economy and capitalism.

Proverbs:

— Sending coal to someone on a snowy day. (雪中送碳)
— A fall into a ditch makes you wiser. (吃一堑, 长一智)

Reading Questions:

1. The author describes Mr. Zhou as "a good learner, motivated, and upright as a person." Do you agree with the choices he made in the game? In your cultural context, would you describe him as a decent guy? Why and why not?
2. If you were playing the same computer game, would you make different choices? If so, please think carefully and give your reasons.
3. Hoping to be a good public servant, why did Mr. Zhou end up in jail? What went wrong, if any, in his logic of thinking that led him to the unexpected as well as unintended outcome?

STORY 2: SON OF YELLOW EARTH

Xi Jinping[1]

This is an autobiography of Xi Jinping, General Secretary of the Chinese Communist Party and President of China. It tells the story of how a communist was hardened by the experience of a life of extreme poverty and hardships with the peasants. Xi Jinping's father, Xi Zhongxun (vice premier of China then), fell away from Mao and was stripped of all his positions. His disgrace affected his family, including his son, who was exiled from Beijing to northern Shaanxi where his father used to conduct revolutionary activities. The story sheds light on a great many things that happened during the Cultural Revolution and how people's lives were changed because of it. More importantly, it sheds valuable light on the values, convictions and character of China's new top leader.

The writing is colloquial (probably dictated rather than written) with mixed up pronouns and time line. The translation has kept the original style largely intact but re-paragraphed it for clarity.

In January 1969, I was sent to settle down in the village of Liangjiahe in Wenan township of Yanchuan county, Shaanxi province, as "the children of black gang."[2] I was only 15. I felt lonely at first, having left the capital city, been thrust into an unfamiliar environment and surrounded by distrustful eyes. But then I thought, having raised my parents the Loess Plateau would also accept a naïve kid like me with her broad bosom. So, I tried sincerely to mingle with the

---

[1]Source: *Study Forum* (Central Academy of Socialism), No. 9; available at: http://www.zysy.org.cn/portal/xywh/xuexiluntan/nine/webinfo/2013/01/1353295998883149.htm (last accessed 10 September 2013). The memoir is also available on many Chinese websites.

[2]During the Cultural Revolution, the term "black gang" (*heibang*) was used to refer to "capitalist roaders," i.e., those who preferred capitalism to socialism. It is revealing that Xi Zhongxun, father of Xi Jinping, later became a pioneering reformer as the party chief of Guangdong province who initiated many market-oriented reforms in the early post-Mao era.

5.5 The rural commune in Mao's era did not pay the farmers' wages. A workpoint system was used instead: a day's work was kept on record as workpoints. Usually, a strong and skilled male adult earned 10 workpoints per day; a woman usually earned 8 points and child laborer 6. When crops were harvested, the farmers would be paid in kind according to the workpoints he or she made. However, a minimum ration was given to everybody regardless of whether they worked or not.

peasants and consciously accepted the hard life as a way to build character.

In the few years there, I overcame four major difficulties. The first was flea. I had never seen a flea when I lived in the city, but at Liangjiahe one almost slept on a blanket of fleas during the summer. The whole body became swollen from scratching the flea bites. But after two years, I got used to it. I slept soundly despite the fleas. The second difficulty was food. In the past, I ate fine rice and flour but now I had to eat roughage of various kinds. But before long I could swallow the food and began to enjoy it. Even today, I am fond of the food of rural northern Shaanxi. Take sauerkraut for example, I will miss it if I have not had it for several days. The third is labor. When I first started doing farm work, I earned 6 workpoints a day, less than what women earned. Two years later, I earned the full 10 workpoints accorded to a strong male farmhand and became a skilled farmer. The fourth difficulty was to change my mind set. This was most important. I have learned the peasants' honest and practical ways and their spirit of hard work.

Meanwhile, the folks gradually treated me as one of them. I lived and worked among them and there was no distinction between us. They were frank with me and let me become a barefoot doctor,[3] a book keeper, and an agricultural technician. They elected me to be party secretary of the production brigade when I was 20 years old.

[3] A "barefoot doctor" was a villager with minimum medical training who treated ailments of the villagers on site. This barefoot doctor medical care system significantly improved health in rural areas. It was dismantled in the Dengist reform era. Later, the basic healthcare system in rural areas has to be rebuilt from scratch.

Together with the commune members, we dug wells, built dams, repaired roads and increased production in order to change the look of our hometown. I have determined that this is my second hometown.

When I returned to Liangjiahe in 1993, some folks mentioned to me the blacksmith shop I started

> *7.6 The masses — the ordinary people — are often idealized in the communist ideology, which holds that they are the real history makers. The reality, however, is that the masses have no real leverage over the cadres and hold the latter accountable. Cadres easily turn into a privileged class.*

for the village and that I led them in building the first biogas digester in Shaanxi province which the villagers used for lighting and cooking. However, what I remembered was that they had helped and protected me selflessly and, in particular, that their pure, honest and down-to-earth character had affected me deeply and edificated my soul.

When I first came to the Yellow Earth as a 15-year old, I was perplexed and lost; when I left at 22, I had firmly established my life's purpose and was full of confidence. As a servant of the people, my root is in the plateau of northern Shaanxi. For it planted a firm belief in me: to do practical things for the people!

No matter where we go I will always be the son of the Yellow Earth.

The ancient poet Zheng Banqiao wrote a famous poem called "bamboo growing from the rocks":

Clinging to Aoyama and never let go
sinking roots in the cracks between rocks.
Becoming ever stronger with thousands of hardships,
standing firm against wind blown from all directions.

I want to change a few words to make the poem a testimony to the profundity of my experience in the countryside:

Clinging to the grassroots and never relaxing,
for I am rooted in the masses;
Becoming ever stronger through thousands of hardships,
regardless of the direction the wind blows.

The grassroots are closest to the masses and the best place to build character. Seven years of living in the countryside have benefited me tremendously; they allowed me to forge deep bonds with the masses and laid the foundation for my growth and progress.

I was influenced by my family from a young age in the area of building comradeship with people around. My father often taught me about solidarity and required us to be the ones who sought and forged unity with others. *"Do not do to others what you don't want them to do to you"; "To help others is to help yourself."* In his words, when doing something one must consider not only whether he himself is willing or not but also whether others are willing or not; for you cannot be self-centered when you live among the people. Later on, when we lived collectively with others, we developed deeper understanding of the truth about solidarity that my father talked about. Whether it is a boarding school, or living in the countryside, or at the workplace, I have a deep feeling that things go well when you can unite others and they do not go well when you cannot. When I was in northern Shaanxi, hundreds of miles away from family and relatives, all I relied on was comradeship with others.

In this regard, I have had my share of setbacks and lessons. I was compelled by circumstances to go to the countryside when I was very young. I did not pay attention to the issue of unity because I did not plan to stay for long. Every day, others went to work in the mountains but I was very casual about work. The folks did not have a good impression on me. I went back to Beijing after a few months and was then sent to the old revolutionary base in Taihang Mountain.[4] It was here that my maternal aunt and her husband had brought my mother to join the Revolution. They are the people I respect very much. My uncle used to tell me his activities during the December 29th Movement when he was still a college student at Northeast University, and how he later came to Taihang Mountain. He told me that at the time we were looking for opportunities to join the masses and today who would you rely on if not the masses? My auntie also said, we always went to the villagers and it is not right that the young people of today are afraid of going.

---

[4]One of the base areas of the CCP in northern China during World War II.

Besides it is not easy staying in the city. Why are we here — to let them treat us like fugitives every day?[5]

Every year then around the National Day there would be a clearing up of the "backflow population."[6] But then they would not allow us to return (to the countryside) after the clear-up. Instead, they locked us up in the police station — each time for 4–5 months. What's more, while inside they did not allow you to stay idle. You had to do heavy manual labor. The drainage pipes in Haidian District were all laid by us. After I returned to the countryside, I followed their advice and tried to mingle with the masses. A year later, I got used to life there. I worked together with the masses and overcame the difficulty of hard labor. When people saw the changes in me, they began to treat me well. More and more people came to visit me. My house gradually became the center of that place. That was around 1970. Every evening people came in droves, young and old. When they came in, I would put up for them a show of storytelling about things both ancient and modern, foreign and domestic. They loved the chitchatting of an urbanite about things they did not know. Gradually, even the party secretary would consult me on various matters. He said that young people were well-informed, know more than he did. In this way, I gained respect in the village. I was then only 16 or 17 but the village elders would come to consult me when something came up. Nowadays, some writers describe how miserable life was for the educated youth but my feelings are not at all like that. I felt miserable only at the beginning, but when I got used to local life, especially when I was integrated with the masses, I felt that my life was fulfilling.

My maturation and progress started in northern Shaanxi. One of my biggest gains was to get in touch with reality and gain confidence in myself.

Around 1973, we concentrated on the university entrance exams. However, people from family backgrounds like mine had no hope of being admitted at the time. Later on, I went to Zhaohe

[5] People without *danwei* were called fugitives or "blind wanders" (*mangliu*).
[6] Namely, people who had been sent to the countryside but returned to the city without permission.

5.2 Socialist education was CCP's effort to indoctrinate the peasantry with socialist ideology and change their way of thinking and behavior. It also served to correct the mistakes rural cadres made, address people's grievances and solve their conflicts. The latter was called rectification.

Brigade of Fengjiaping Commune to participate in "socialist education." Engaging in socialist education was interesting. At the time, I was a member of neither the Youth League nor the Communist Party. The secretary of the county Youth League committee was also an educated youth from Beijing, from Tsinghua University High School. He called me to Zhaojiahe Brigade that he was in charge of and said to me, you stay here to carry out the "commune rectification"; whatever the outcome I'll accept it. If it is good then it's your achievement but if it's bad I'll be the one responsible. I was only 20 then. During the rectification, a 30-year old man became the new party secretary (of the brigade). The outcome of the rectification in that village was good and the masses trusted me. They requested that I stay on and work in that village. However, Liangjiahe Brigade wanted me back. To stay on and work for the village party branch committee raised the question of party membership. All together I wrote 10 applications to join the Party but was turned down each time because of my family background. This time, the commune once again sent my case to the county party committee for consideration. The county party secretary said that because of the complicated clan conflicts in that village, it would be difficult for a native to deal with them and therefore as an outsider he (Xi Jinping) would be needed to take charge of the village. They further deliberated if there was a conclusion drawn for my father's case? They decided there was none, and therefore, this should not prevent me from joining the Party. I was admitted into the Party and was made the brigade party secretary. The previous party secretary was reassigned as the chairman of the revolutionary committee.

Prior to this, it also took a great deal of trouble for me to join the Youth League. I wrote eight applications. After I wrote the first application, I invited the brigade party secretary to my cave dwelling. I made him a dish of scrambled eggs and two hot steamed buns. After the meal, I said to him "Isn't it time for you to deliver my application?" He said, how could I, since they (higher officials) said you are an "educatable child."[7] I asked him what is an "educatable child"? He said those above said you did not make a clean break (with your father). I asked him, where is the verdict? There must be a verdict as to exactly what problems one has; what is the verdict for my father? Have you seen the Central Document (about his case)? He said "not really." Well then, he delivered the application. He told me when he came back that the commune party secretary scolded me that I was stupid — how dare you to deliver for such a person? I said what kind of person am I? What did I do? Did I write or shout counterrevolutionary slogans? I am a youth seeking progress.[8]

3.1 The Communist Youth League is the CCP's auxiliary organization among younger people. It recruits youths between 14 and 28 and grooms them to be future CCP members and cadres. Its nationwide organization structure parallels that of the CCP. Many top leaders of the Youth League move on to become important leaders in the CCP and form the so-called "Youth League faction" in the Party. General Secretary Hu Yaobang and Hu Jintao, Premier Li Keqiang etc. are all considered members of this faction.

What's wrong with that? I was undaunted. After a few days, I wrote two more applications and asked the party secretary to deliver to those above. I repeated it till I wrote the eighth application. I did not feel bitter or lack of self-esteem. I had but one belief that there would be less bad persons inside the Party and the Youth League if there were more good ones. I'll join regardless, unless you do not let me.

---

[7]That is, kids with undesirable family backgrounds. They were discriminated against.
[8]"Seeking progress" means making effort to join the Party, the Youth League etc. in China.

Finally, my eighth application was approved. Of course, it was after the Youth League secretary of the commune lent his support for me. He came to my place, stayed and chatted with me for five days. We became diehard buddies. It was he who burned all the "black material" in my dossier after he took over as the county Youth League secretary.

On that occasion he took me to a small ravine and we sat on a rock. Then he told me, I have brought all the black material about you. I asked what's for? He said, to burn it. I said, do you dare to do such a thing? One could lose his head for it. He said of course I dare; I think the material was not sent by your school. As a middle schooler then, my material should be sent by the August 1 Middle School but instead it was sent by the Central Party School. Because my mother was at the Central Party School then — after my home was ransacked (by the Red Guards) my family moved to the Central Party School. While living on the Party School campus my stubbornness and refusal to be bullied off-ended the Rebels. They

4.3 In China, every urbanite (especially cadres and party members) used to have a personal dossier on file with the authorities. It contained evaluations written by his or her superiors and records of awards or penalties etc. The dossier followed the individual wherever he or she went. "Black material" referred to the negative records or evaluations. These often determined the fate of a person.

blamed everything bad on me, believing I was behind it. I was singled out (for mass criticism) by Cao Yi'ou, the wife of Kang Sheng,[9] as family member of the "black gang." I was not 15 yet at the time. They said I deserved to be shot one hundred times. I thought being

---

[9]Kang was a radical during the Cultural Revolution allied with Mao and the "Gang of Four" — Mao's wife Jiang Qing, Zhang Chunqiao, Wang Hongwen and Yao Wenyuan who were purged after Mao's death. Kang, however, died before Mao to escape the fate.

shot once is no different from being shot one hundred times; what's there to be afraid of? However, they didn't even send me to the police. They only threatened me that the machinery of dictatorship[10] would persecute me and said that they'd give me another five minutes (to repent). Then it was reading "Quotations from Chairman Mao" (the Little Red Book) every night staying up late. I said I don't care where to go as long as I can sleep well. They took me back when we reached the door of the police station. Finally they decided to send me to a juvenile detention center because it was running a class for the children of "black gang." However, all spots were filled and I had to wait a month or so to get in. In December 1968, Chairman Mao's latest instruction was issued: "Educated youth should go to the countryside to be re-educated by the poor and lower-middle peasants."[11] I immediately signed up at the school to join the movement of "going up to the mountains and down to the countryside," stating that I was answering the call of Chairman Mao. They found out that I was going to Yanan — practically an exile, and let go of me.

After so many twists and turns of the "Cultural Revolution" and "Going to the Mountains and Countryside Movement," finally this village needed me and could not do without me. At the time, I felt I was lucky to have come to the countryside. Had I been a worker or this or that,[12] I would have been subject to mass criticism everyday because those places were being rampaged by the Cultural Revolution. In northern Shaanxi, there were also "mass criticisms" — to criticize Liu Shaoqi, Deng Xiaoping and their agents in the Northwest: Peng Dehuai, Gao Gang, Xi Zhongxun, Liu Lantao, Zhao Shouyi and so on. I was the one who had to read the newspapers during mass criticisms.[13] Very few locals were

---

[10] Namely, the police, the military etc. "Dictatorship" refers to "the dictatorship of the proletariat" in Marxism.
[11] At Mao's time, the education level was low; anyone with a middle school education would be considered an "educated youth."
[12] That is, any non-farming jobs.
[13] The official party newspapers carried Chairman Mao and the Party Center's policy lines and instructions. At the village level, people did not receive Central Documents. They used newspapers instead.

5.4 The "Little Red Book" is a compilation of the "quotations from Chairman Mao." It was said to have the magic power of solving any problems in life. During the Cultural Revolution people were encouraged to read and memorize Mao's quotations. Study sessions and competitions were held to promote it.

literate. I read aloud everyday and soon became indifferent to it. But the local folks were very understanding. After all, this used to be the base area of my father. My father used to be the chairman of the Soviet of the Border Region of Shaanxi and Gansu when he was only 19 years old. With this background, many people protected and helped me; this plus that I was strong-willed allowed me to survive the period.

Therefore, my growth and progress started from the seven years in northern Shaanxi. My two biggest gains from that period of my life are: first, I know what is reality, what is "seeking truth from facts", and who are the masses. I have benefited from these gains all my life ever since, even today. When I first came to the countryside, there were many beggars coming to our doors. We used to drive them away and unleash the dogs after them. In the minds of us students, beggars were "bad elements" and "hobos." We did not know then that those were a time of "fat January, skinny February, and half-dead March and April."[14] Every household lived on chaff food and wild veggies for half a year. The wives and children would go out begging to save the grain for strong laborers in the family so that they could do the spring plowing. We learned this only after living in the countryside for some time. I was very emotional about this knowledge gap between us and the peasants.

Secondly, the experience has built up my self-confidence. As the saying goes, *the knife is sharpened on a grinding stone and a man is made through hardships.* Hardships can strengthen the will power of

[14]Here it means dwindling food stock. In January, the peasants still had food but by March and April, before the harvest of wheat, they were starving.

a person. Seven years of hard life in the countryside was a great exercise for me. Later in life whenever I ran into difficulties, I would think of that period. How could I not carry on now when I could work under those extremely difficult conditions? The difficulties now are no comparison to the difficulties then. This spirit is very important to a man. One should have the determination and audacity to face challenges no matter what difficulties he runs into. He should have faith, stay calm under changing circumstances, and strive forward against difficulties.

Proverbs:

— To be a blacksmith your body must be strong and sound (打铁还需自身硬)[15]
— Set yourself as the standard. (以身作则)

Reading Questions:

1. Why Xi Jr. calls himself "son of the Yellow Earth"? What does "Yellow Earth" symbolize?
2. Why was Xi Jinping sent to a remote, mountainous countryside with extreme poverty?
3. Why does Xi treasure his experience of hardships? Is he reasonable?
4. How would you describe Xi Jinping's personality?
5. How do you describe the upbringing in the Xi family? Is there any similarity with yours?
6. Why do you think Xi was so insistent in joining the Communist Youth League and the Communist Party under those difficult conditions?

Suggested Exercises and Assignments:

1. Find out what is "December 29 Movement" and its historical role in China.

---

[15]Xi used this proverb in his acceptance speech after the 18th Party Central Committee confirmed him as the General Secretary on November 15, 2012. The point he was making is that the CCP must rid itself of corruption if it is provide strong leadership.

2. Find out why Mao wanted urban school youths to live in the countryside.
3. Go online and find out the content of the Little Red Book.
4. Write an outline of Xin Jinping's early life history described in this story and its time frame.
5. Find several people from Mainland China and ask him or her about the Cultural Revolution.
6. Find on the internet a picture of the cave dwelling of northwest China on the Loess Plateau.

2. The "Sent-down Movement"

The "Up to the Mountains and Down to the Countryside Movement" (or simply "sent-down movement) was a policy instituted in the late 1960s and early 1970s. As a result of the anti-bourgeois thinking prevalent during the Cultural Revolution, Mao Zedong decided in 1968 that the urban "educated youth", mostly middle or high school graduates, should be sent to remote mountainous areas or farming villages to be "re-educated" by the peasants. Over seven years millions of urban youth, including China's current top leader Xi Jinping, packed up to resettle down in rural and border areas, often pressured to go by great fanfare as described by Kim Yet (Story 7). Most of them were rebel Red Guards who were raking havoc in the cities. The Red Guards had risen up at his beck and call but Mao soon found that they were out of control. The stated objectives of the "sent-down movement" was to keep urban youths from being "spoiled" — developing bourgeois lifestyle, ideas and way of thinking, by keeping them close to the working masses. However, a major motive of Mao was to use the movement to quell unrest by removing the source of chaos. More importantly perhaps it also helped to relieve the pressure of finding employment for middle and high school graduates. Many fresh high school graduates, who became known as the Rusticated Youth of China, were forced out of the cities and effectively exiled to remote

(Continued)

(*Continued*)

areas of China. In the stories of this book, the "sent-down move-ment" apparently achieved its educational purpose for Xi Jinping but to Kim Yet, it was an educational in addition to a personal disaster for the majority of the "sent-down youths." A whole generation of young people lost their opportunity to attend university. When they were allowed to return home, they lacked the necessary skills for non-farming jobs. For example, the majority of the janitors in Kim Yet's Downtown District were these returned youths — no longer young by then. Therefore, the "sent-down youths" are frequently referred to as China's "lost generation." It is an irony that President Xi, who suffered so much during the Cultural Revolution, retained fond memories of it and attempted to resurrect some aspects and practices of Maoism after he became CCP's General Secretary in 2012.

STORY 3: INTEGRITY
AT RETIREMENT[1]

Tian Dongzhao

This story is set in late-1990s. It tells in vivid details the process in which a righteous communist cadre is compelled to adapt to the changes in the large socioeconomic environment by his family's depressing prospect of a life in retirement. It also highlights some of the most important channels of corruption that have continued to this day. Although the amount of bribery involved is peanuts by today's standards, the process and the structural sources of corruption are still relevant.

I

They were comrades in arms who disagreed on very few things. As a result, life for them was like still water, with neither storms nor excitements. One day, Lu Haoyu said to his wife, "We have been married for so many years, and I have yet to experience your famous 'iron lips'. Why don't we fight over something?"

Qi Yun replied, "I am sort of unusual in this regard. Words pour out like fountain only when I am backed up against the wall and have to do it. My mouth is clumsy if I am not in such a situation and therefore I cannot pretend to quarrel or fight a war of words."

"Then I shall be patiently waiting," said Lu Haoyu with a laughter, "to experience it when you are backed to a corner."

What Lu did not expect was that after nearly 30 years of marriage of harmony when he was about to retire and begin the final stage of his life in peace, frictions between the two finally surfaced. Qi Yun became opinionated about his being a clean official. Debates

---

[1] Story from Guan Shannen *et al. The Tao of Careerism in the World of Officialdom.* Beijing: Zhongguo Xiju chubanshe, 2002, vol. 2.

followed. Currently the two disagreed on their son's wedding. It was quite obvious that a verbal battle was in the making.

Lu Haoyu looked at Qi Yun, recalling how she stepped onto the podium and argued victoriously against her opponents 30 years before during the Cultural Revolution. He said to himself, this time it looks indeed that I will finally experience the ferocity of her iron lips. A quiet smile sneaked up from the corner of his mouth. From that smile Qi Yun could tell that she must have looked like a rooster in a cock fight, and couldn't help laughing at herself.

Laughter relaxed the atmosphere but could not resolve the issue. Lu Haoyu realized how difficult it was to convince his wife but felt that he could back down no more. He must face the difficulty.

"Qi Yun," said Lu Haoyi, as calmly as he could. "We are not the same as the rank-and-file. We are the family of the municipal party secretary. We would set a bad example if we make too big a deal out of our son's wedding."

A flicker of sarcasm shone on the face of Qi Yun and quickly vanished like lightening. "Your Highness, Mr. Secretary. Haven't you paid enough attention to your exemplar role ever since you became a leading cadre?"

Lu Haoyu said with a bitter smile, "Look Qi Yun. We have lived in harmony and with such good chemistry for so many years. Now that we both are old, what kind of wrong medicine have we taken that we become so quarrelsome and could not even discuss our son's wedding calmly?"

"Circumstances have changed — and extremely fast. It's no exaggeration that the changes are epical. There wouldn't be such difficulty between us if we had both gone with the tidal flow. How could there be no friction between us if one of our rear ends is too heavy to move forward?"

"Well," said Lu, extending his neck. "I am behind the tide? Let me ask you, my dear wife, to be lavish on our son's wedding is vanguard now?"

"I couldn't say that it is vanguard but it is the tide, absolutely! Nowadays, people throw banquets and invite guests on baby's full month, the one hundredth day, as well as the birthday. More reason to do it when their sons and daughters get married. They invite whoever should be invited; even those who should not be invited are invited under various pretexts. The only difference is that the ordinary people do it openly while the big shots do it quietly; or little people collect small sums of money while big shots harvest a fortune."

A faint smile climbed up Lu Haoyu's face. It was clear that he had found some ammunition and was about to launch a counter-attack.

Qi Yun quickly caught the message in her husband's facial expression and said, "You should not regard collecting money and presents as something to be ashamed of. There is no shame if everyone does it. I may as well elaborate on it in greater detail. For instance, if each guest brings 100 yuan as wedding present, we could make at least 500 yuan per table at the wedding banquet. 10 tables would fetch 5000 and 20 tables 10,000 yuan. This is the going rate for the small potatoes when they gather their small money. Of course, these presents have to be repaid in kind but it can be done slowly over a long period of time. The interest on the money could cover it. Therefore, it is net profit, no matter how much is collected. As for the big shots, the going rate is much higher, ranging from a few hundreds to a few thousands or even over ten thousand yuan per guest. A big fortune is made in each such event. It's an open secret although people do not talk about it in the open."

Instead of receding, the smile on Lu's face intensified. "Would you please, my dear lady, tell me whether we are big shots or small potatoes? In other words, if we did it would we earn a big or a small fortune?"

Qi Yun smiled unapologetically and replied, "I'll *speak as frankly as if the skylight is open*. On this matter we are no exception. In Donghua City, we are the big shots and the No.1 personality. As to the size of the fortune, well, we do not pressure or force people to do it and we do not have to worry about if it is too big or too small. How about that? Is that a satisfactory answer?"

Lu Haoyu shook his head with a bitter smile. "Qi Yun, you are really open and honest."

"So what? Do you think I am talking to the municipal party secretary? No, I am talking to my husband. I can say anything I want. How could we be a couple if we hide things from each other and could not speak honestly?"

Lu Haoyu fixed his eye on Qi Yun. After a brief silence he said, "Since you are so open and honest, I'll return in kind and tell you all my thinking. Three years ago, we disciplined a cadre — the deputy magistrate of Sanhe county, for lavishing on his parent's funeral. Do you still remember? You issued orders to reprimand others but now you are doing it yourself. How do you explain it? More importantly, I am wary of those who, under the current social environment, are watching closely the leaders of the city, *like flies seeking out the cracks on the shell of an egg*. Doing this could give them the opportunity to engage in big briberies. When the wedding is over, I, Lu Haoyu, would become overnight a corrupt cadre who has taken enormous briberies. How could we do such a foolish thing?"

Qi Yun tilted her head sideways and said, "The more you talk about it the more confused I become. We are planning our son's wedding; what does that have to do with corruption? Who is to determine it: the Party Discipline Commission or the Procuratorate?"

"It's the masses," replied Lu Haoyu. "They have a scale in their hearts and they know clearly what we do and what we say. Those who regard the masses as fools are not much better than idiots."

"The masses?" said Qi Yun sorrowfully. "If what the masses say count there would not have been corruption. Let me give you another example of your old classmate and our mayor Huang Shanbai, who held his son's wedding three years ago. He told people that he had too many relatives and had to arrange at least 15 tables for the wedding banquet. As a matter of fact, he had 54. He did it by spreading it over three days and held them in different restaurants. That is not all. A few days later, he went together with his son and daughter-in-law to his native village, where he held another 49 table banquet at two different times. Putting it all together he had 103 tables. Even if we assume that the guests brought only the usual amount he would have pocketed 500,000.

But he is the mayor. How could anyone bring only 100 yuan? You can imagine how much he would have collected. Did the masses know about it? Did they talk about it? Of course, because I learned all this from the masses! But what is the use? The leaders of the provincial party committee did not say that he was too extravagant, let alone that he is corrupt. Did you, the highest official in the city, say

> *7.7 Democracy is not a product of Western civilization. It is rooted in the basic human needs and sense of justice. Demanding a say in matters concerning oneself is only natural; it may lead to different forms of democracy.*

anything at all? He is still the mayor. On the contrary, many praise him for his flexibility and for his extensive *guanxi*. In contrast, you have been clean since your first job and continue to be so. Do the masses know about it? I'll bet they know, and I also have heard many praises for you. But what's the use? Do any of the leaders in the provincial party committee listen to what the masses have to say? Do any of them appreciate your integrity and have publicly recommended you? None. Just as nobody talks about Mayor Huang's corruption, nobody speaks about your integrity either. In other words, under the present political system, public opinion matters little. It would matter when the people like you are elected. When would that day come? The reality you face now is that you are going to retire next year. You need to wake up!"

"Iron lips indeed!" exclaimed Lu. He knows it was futile to carry on the debate. It's obvious that to convince her was going to be extremely difficult. He must try another method. He picked up that day's newspaper and began reading the co-ed piece. After finishing one paragraph he said, "Let's discuss it another time." This is his cliché. Whenever a decision was difficult to make because of differences of opinions at the standing committee meetings, he would say, "Let's discuss it another time" and dismiss the meeting. This became a habit that he applied even to his wife.

Qi Yun laughed and said to herself, "No problem at all. You can run but you cannot hide. I'll see what new tricks you'll come up with." She picked up the remote control and began watching TV.

Reading Questions:

1. Comment on the role of public opinion in Chinese politics.
2. What changes were China going through as felt by Qi Yun? Do you think these are changes for the better or worse? Are they inevitable?

II

The following evening they resumed their discussion. This time their son Lu Wei and daughter-in-law Nie Xiaofang joined in. After graduation from college, Lu Wei declined the government-assigned job[2] and went alone to Shenzhen to try out his entrepreneur's leg. Four years later, his career still did not take off. He had to come back. He joined a coal transport company on a temporary basis. Fortunately, his fiancé Nie Xiaofang was still waiting for him. Love had obviously lifted the burden of career failure. Therefore, he was in relatively high spirit. Following the order of his father he brought Xiaofang home to discuss their wedding.

Naturally, Qi Yun was happy to see Xiaofang. She cooked a few dishes to treat her daughter-in-law to be. After dinner, Lu Wei pulled Qi Yun over to sit on the couch, while urging his father, "Dad, hurry up!"

Liu Haoyu was lighting a cigarette. He had reduced his smoking to only one cigarette a day after dinner, following his doctor's advice and Qi Yun's wish. He stuck to the rule strictly. Upon hearing his son, he came and sat on the sofa, with that cigarette between his index and middle fingers.

Liu Wei began the discussion by saying, "Mom, dad, what do you have in mind about our wedding? We hope your plan reflects our own wishes, or at least not contradicting ours."

---

[2] Towards the end of the 1990s, the government ceased to assign jobs for college graduates, but before that college graduates were virtually guaranteed a job upon graduation.

"A family also needs democracy," said Lu Haoyu. "We should listen to their opinion because it is their life's event after all. Well, please tell us your ideas first."

Qi Yun looked at her son closely, worrying that he might ruin her plan.

"Our opinion is that we should make it simple, a few thousand yuan spent on a honeymoon trip to the Suzhou and Hangzhou region will do."

Lu Haoyu immediately showed his support of the idea, "Do something new with a new way of doing it, good idea!"

Qi Yun said, "A honeymoon tour and a wedding ceremony are not contradictory. I agree too. Let's do the wedding at home first and then the honeymoon tour."

1.3 Wedding night carnival (闹洞房) is a folk custom widespread in northern China. In fact, after they left the newlyweds, some young guests would return to eavesdrop on the couple's first night together and spread jokes the next day. The custom serves a social function in rural China.

"Mom," said Lu Wei. "I know that we don't have a lot of money. Why should we spend it on both? Let's save one."

Qi Yun wanted to say, "You little fool! The money collected from the wedding will pay for the tour. How can you say spending on both?" But she could not say it in Xiaofang's presence. Instead she said, "It's a major event in your life that takes place only once in a life time. Whatever spending is necessary, we should spend it."

"No," said Lu Wei, "we'll only go on the honeymoon trip and nothing else. This is the opinion of both of us. Ask her if you don't believe me."

Nie Xiafang indeed did not like going through the ceremony. The local custom was that on the wedding day there was no distinction in generation, age, gender etc. Anybody could do anything out of the ordinary at the banquet table in day time or in the new couple's bedroom in the evening. People played all sorts of mischief on the newly wed. They forced the bride to kiss the bridegroom's uncle, or the father-in-law to carry the bride on his back and circle around the room three times with the mother-in-law watching the show. She must also sip a mouthful of vinegar and say, "It's very sour!"

Xiaofang despised as well as dreaded all this. Now that Lu Wei wanted her opinion, she immediately turned to Qi Yun and said, "Mom — since we are getting married soon, I'll call you mom from today on."

This "mom" in advance warmed the heart of Qi Yun. She held Xiaofang's hand in her own, rubbing it gently and said, "Since you call me mom in advance, as mom I also must do my duties. No matter how much it will cost us I'll see to it that this is done in such a way that people are impressed and you are happy."

"Mom, you really want me to be happy?"

"Foolish girl, how can mom lie to you?"

Nie Xiaofang said, "Then please do it according to our wish."

"No problem," said Qi Yun. "Isn't it a honeymoon tour that you want? Let's hold the wedding first and you are on your way as soon as it's done."

"You are only half right, mom. To let us be happy you should do whatever we like, not what we don't like. I don't like ceremonies, banquets etc."

Lu Wei concurred, "Yes, Xiaofang is sick to death about those things. Please spare us of them, mom."

"If you grant our wish, mom," Nie Xiaofang said, while rocking Qi Yun's arm, "I would sleep well tonight and have sweet dreams."

All the while, Lu Haoyu was watching in silence. He now broke the silence and joined the conversation. "In my opinion, we should go with the children's wishes." Then he added, "For parents, there is no better thing than children's sound sleep. In comparison, nothing else matters. Don't you agree?"

Qi Yun was in an extremely difficult position now. She could not speak frankly what she had in mind. The planning of her son's wedding was much more than a wedding ceremony alone. It concerned whether this family could carry on normally after her husband retires and whether they could have a worry-free life in retirement. But she ran into such stiff resistance. It would not be that difficult if the objection came from her husband and son — she could use extensive reasoning to convince them. She was very confident on that. However, faced with the eager plea of Nie Xiaofang, she was at wit's end. She could not make her case as she could to her son and husband. Now with six eyes of the three fixed on her, she had no place to escape to. After a brief pause, she threw herself back against the couch and said reluctantly, "alright, do as you wish."

"Thank you mom!" Nie Xiaofang was very happy.

"Dad is indeed very smart," said Lu Wei. "He said there would not be any problem if Xiaofang did the plea. It did turn out as he expected."

Qi Yun found something was not right and asked quickly, "Your dad smart? Why do you say that?"

Lu Wei laughed and said, "Mom, to tell you the truth, to get the consent you just gave, dad called both of us to his office and discussed the matter for almost a full hour."

"Oh!" Qi Yun's face changed a little.

"Thank you, mom, once again," said Nie Xiaofang.

"I also thank you, mom. Now that a happy ending is achieved, we two would like to go and see a movie."

Qi Yun barely maintained a smile when she saw Xiaofang off to the door. Then she turned back with a completely changed face. She threw herself into the couch and said to her husband, "Haoyu — no, Secretary Lu — you are indeed smart!"

Lu Haoyu asked, with a feigned innocence, "What is the matter?"

"What is the matter?" said Qi Yun, "You are indeed a politician. Your skills at political maneuver are not bad at all!"

"Do you mean the fact that I called Weiwei[3] and Xiaofang to my office to discuss the matter?"

"What discussion? Why couldn't you come home to discuss it together?"

"I happened to have some time and gave them a ring."

---

[3] Nickname for Li Wei.

"No. Your 'discuss it another time' was a delay tactic. It's manipulation. It's clandestine plotting and alliance building. I am the bad apple of this family and hence you form a united front to deal with me!" She abruptly got up and went into the bedroom in visible anger.

Lu Haoyu sat alone for a while, then got up to pace back and forth in the living room. When he finally also went into the bedroom, he saw Qi Yun was already in bed facing the wall, with anger radiating from the back of her head.

Lu Haoyu said, looking at the back of her head, "Qi Yun, don't you think you made too big a deal out of this incident?"

Qi Yun was silent.

Lu Haoyu went on, "You were quite tolerant before. How can you now become so narrow-minded? Come on. Turn around and let's do a heart-to-heart talk. It won't do you good to keep it to yourself. We can untie any knot."

"What's there to talk about? Let's discuss it another time." She then pulled the quilt over her head.

Lu Haoyu said to himself: she also said "let's discuss it another time." Obviously she was deeply resentful to the "Let's discuss it another time" that I said yesterday.

There was no talk that night.

Qi Yun was silent the next day, but her facial expression showed neither anger nor happiness. It looked so calm as if nothing had happened. However she remained silent, as if she turned dumb overnight. On the third day Lu Haoyu was about to go on a official trip to inspect several poverty relief programs, Qi Yun made breakfast but did not eat before she went grocery shopping at the morning farmer's fair with a bamboo basket. Lu Haoyu left her a note before he left home.

Lu spent three days in the countryside and returned to office at 5 pm of the third day. The clock indicated 6 when he finished browsing the three days' news papers and reading a few letters. He then hurried home for dinner.

Qi Yun sat on a small stool, scaling fish. Her face completely returned to normal. It looked no different from it used to. When she saw Lu Haoyu, She sat up and said hello.

"Yes, I am back." Lu responded.

"I've prepared hot water in the bathtub. Go wash youself."

"You go first. I am in no hurry," said Lu.

"I am not going to take a bath today. It's prepared for you."

Lu was puzzled, "How did you know when I came back?"

"You went to read newspapers in your office at five; so I knew that you would be back by six."

Lu was even more surprised, "How did you know I was reading in my office? Do your eyes see things 10,000 miles away?"

"It's the age of information," said Qi Yun. "It's nothing out of the ordinary."

Lu Haoyu went into the bathroom. After carelessly washing his face, he came out, still drying his face with a towel, to announce, "My weather forecast for today is: cloudy to sunny."

Qi Yun said, "It has never been cloudy."

"Not a word in a whole day, can you say it's not cloudy?"

"I did not talk because I didn't feel like to," said Qi Yun. "I did not talk because it's not yet the time to talk. Didn't I say 'Let's talk about it another time'? What's there to talk about if the timing is not right?"

Lu Haoyu said, "Is it to say the time to resume the discussion has come? Very well then, let's talk."

"Not now," said Qi Yun, "After dinner."

When they finished dinner, the two sat in the living room. Qi Yun turned on the TV to let her husband watch the news. Then she turned down the volume to the minimum and began, "Let's set the ground rule first. Either of us should not become too emotional. The other evening when you united against me, I kept cool. I was silent because I was afraid of losing control. It should be like this today too. No matter what comes up, we mustn't get agitated."

Lu Haoyu laughed, "Sound as if it is so serious. Do you really think I am so narrow-minded that I will leap on my feet upon hearing what you have to say?"

"All right then," said Qi Yun. She fetched a piece of paper from the bedroom and passed it to Lu Haoyu. On it was written "Zhao Xin of Guanlong county three, Li Dongmin at Siuhe county four."

Lu Haoyu read it several times over but still could not understand it. He asked, "Who are Li Dongmin and Zhao Xin? What do the number 3 and 4 mean?"

"They learned about our Weiwei's wedding," replied Qi Yun, "and sent their present no matter we hold the formal ceremony or not. Three means 30,000 and four means 40,000."

Upon hearing this, Lu Haoyu almost leapt onto his feet. "70,000 for only two people?"

Qi Yun nodded, "There's also one antique object." She pointed to the corner stand. On the second shelf, a little lion crouched. She took and put it on the tea table. "This is brought by Zhang Ziyi at Coal Transportation Company. He said it was given to him by a friend. He has had it examined in Beijing; it is authentic. It's made of white jade in late Ming Dynasty, with a market worth of 38,000 at the time. Earlier this year he took it to Beijing once again and it has appreciated to 65,000. He said he had nothing else appropriate for Weiwei's wedding; a lion is a symbol of luck. Placing it in Weiwei's bedroom may bring them good luck."

"Anything else?"

"No more," said Qi Yun

"The three put together worth 135,000, is that correct?

Qi Yun nodded, while looking at Lu Haoyu; a sign of nervousness was worn in between her eyebrows. She added "What could I do? They left as soon as they dropped the presents, and had long disappeared into the crowd in the street when I put on my shoes to go after them."

Lu Haoyu walked a circle in the room, and asked when he came back to Qi Yun, "Didn't you deal with such matters very well in the past?"

"The past is the past; the present is the present. Time changes everything. I admit that I've changed and I am no longer what I used to be. Why do I have to change? Let's sit down, Haoyu, and I'll tell you everything without reservation."

Lu Haoyu did not sit down. He asked, "where is the 70,000?"

"It's not safe to leave it at home. I deposited it in the bank."

"Where is the deposit book?"

"I folded it inside one of the books on the shelf, but I forgot which one," said Qi Yun.

Lu Haoyu knew the bookcase in the study has five shelves from floor to ceiling and is filled with several thousand books. It wouldn't be easy to find it. Obviously, this is a pretext. She did not want to give it to me.

"Can you sit down and listen to what I have to say? Will you please?"

Once again, Lu Haoyu did not sit down with her. He made his way to the study, sat on the swivel chair, and began staring at the ceiling. In the last couple of years, Qi Yun had grown increasingly dissatisfied with him. He had worried that she might eventually accept briberies people brought to their house all the time, and force him to accept it. Now she finally has done it. What should I do? Taking a clear stand against it or give in?

Qi Yun followed him to the study. She grabbed a chair and sat in front of Lu Haoyu. Once again, she wanted to explain.

Lu asked, "How did other people know about Weiwei's wedding? Especially this Zhao Xin and Li Dongmin. They are from the countryside. How did they learn it so fast?"

"My guess is that," said Qi Yun, "Zhang Ziyi learned it from Weiwei. As to the other two, it may have something to do with me. You know that since the paper work for my retirement was completed a month ago, I haven't been back to my *danwei* for a month. The day you went down to the countryside I went back, and had a brief conversation with Ruilian. She asked about Weiwei's wedding. I told her it would take place soon. Li Dongmin is Ruilian's brother, who in turn is a friend of Zhao Xin's. That's all."

Lu Haoyu asked, "You leaked the news on purpose, didn't you?"

"I don't want to defend myself on this. On purpose or not, the reason behind is the same. After you listen to me carefully, you will agree that it matters little whether I did it on purpose or not."

Lu Haoyu did not listen to her, for he suddenly remembered that the secretary of the provincial Youth League is in town, and he should pay him a visit at his hotel. He went to the living room to place a call to his chauffer.

Reading Questions:

1. How do people make money through wedding banquets?
2. What are some of the guises that people use to conduct briberies? How would you deal with them if you were an upright official in China?

III

It was not until he returned from the hotel did Lu Haoyu listen to Qi Yun's explanation. Qi Yun insisted on telling it when Lu Haoyu was ready to listen — avoidance was not a solution. He made himself a cup of tea, took out a pack of cigarettes and was about to open it. Cutting down on smoking was done under Qi Yun's oversight. Therefore, the latter gave him only one; the rest was put away.

Lu Haoyu lit up the cigarette and sucked in a mouthful. Then he began, "Qi Yun, your action has brought me a huge difficult problem to deal with — you've completely broken my peace of mind. We've been through thick and thin for so many years together. It's not easy at all! In all this, your help is invaluable. However, I've never expected that when we are almost there — when we are about to successfully dot the i's and cross the t's — you changed. You did such a thing and also want to drag me onto your boat. Do you really now recognize only Brother Greenback,[4] not your husband anymore?"

Qi Yun said, "Haoyu, you are only half right. I do recognize Brother Greenback. However, this is not to say that I no longer recognize my husband. I want my husband to know Brother Greenback together with me. That's because today's society belongs to Mr. Greenback, without whom you are going nowhere."

---

[4]The original is "Brother *Kongfang*." Ancient Chinese money was minted as a round disk with a square hole in the middle. *Kongfang*, meaning "square hole," is another way to say "money."

Smoking slowly, Lu Haoyu adjusted his posture to one of listening attentively. He knew that once Qi Yun opened her chatbox, one rarely had a chance to speak.

Tucking her face in between two hands, Qi Yun looked at Lu Haoyu for a moment and began, "You said that I've changed. I admit that I have. However, we should say it is the society that has changed first. I only follow it. For many years, our society was characterized by low pay, low consumption, but with security. A family like ours is especially secure — the husband is an official at the prefecture level and the wife is ranked at the section level working on the enterprise management team. In retirement or not, we did not have to worry about life; we had more than enough food and clothing and comfortable housing; we enjoyed free medical care and our children would be guaranteed a job. In a word, we were secure and worry-free. We've led such a carefree life all these years. But now things are very different. Everything has changed. Consumption level is high and prices of everything keep on going north. In the past, it cost only 8 cents to send a letter, but now it's 80 — exactly a ten-fold increase. Public housing is privatized — sold to the residents. You must pay a much higher rent if you don't want to buy it. Under these conditions, you are an ordinary person even if you are still in office, aren't you? After so many years, our saving is a meager 70,000. When Lili and her husband were laid off we gave them 20,000. Weiwei is getting married and the house needs at least some repair work and remodeling. You tell me how much will be left? Therefore, we have an extreme mismatch between our political stature and our financial condition. Politically, you are No. 1 in the city, but financially you are at the bottom among the ordinary citizens. Who do you think you are? Currently, you are numb on financial issues, but that's because you are excited on the political side. Once you retire, you'll find that you are in fact only a miserable common citizen."

"Of course, it is not that I don't want to live a life of an ordinary citizen; I've never thought of joining ranks with the privileged. The problem now is that after you retire next year can we continue our life as ordinary citizens? Haoyu, I know that you are too busy to think about it carefully, but I did and my conclusion is that we cannot even sustain a life as ordinary citizens. There are three reasons.

"The first is housing. Under the current housing reform program, all public housing is to be sold to individuals. The official residence for Standing Committee members is not for sale. We can't afford it even if it is. But we need a flat that belongs to us, say a three-room flat. One is our bedroom, one for your study. The children also need a place to stay when they come home. I'm not asking too much, am I? But do the math to see if we can afford it. The second concerns the kids. Children

1.4 In the Chinese tradition, children are supposed to take care of their parents in old age. Reflecting this necessity, filial piety is one the highest virtues in the Confucian ethic-political ideology. Social security for retirement is established only recently.

are the insurance against aging; if they are well to do and support us, that's their responsibility. As parents however, it is also our responsibility to support them if they are laid off and could not support themselves as a result. The Lily couple are already laid off; Weiwei has a job now but it's hard to say about the future. When that comes, will we have the resources to do our duties as parents? The third is also the most terrifying — that we are too old and suffer from many ailments. Nowadays, even the salaries of active government officials are not guaranteed, let alone the medical care of retirees. Perhaps yours is guaranteed, but what about mine? Perhaps small medical services are covered. What about major illnesses that cost more than 10,000? The deputy director at the Cultural Bureau, Liu San suffered from kidney failure. He went to Beijing for examination and was told that he needed a new kidney. The cost was 100,000 yuan. His *danwei* did not have the money and there was no way his family could pay for it. He died last September. There is also old Cao at the Sports Commission, the one who organized the ball party at the arena. He suffered from heart problems. The specialists in Beijing determined that he needed a by-pass. The cost was astronomical for him; he had to come back and stay at home. I heard the day before yesterday that he was about to pass away; the doctor has served the notice. These two would have survived had they had 100,000–200,000 at hand. Now looking back at us, if we ran into such situation there's no doubt that I would have only one way to go — to die. Now talking about you, can you really guarantee to pay for medical services? Would you dare to say that the Bureau of Senior Cadres will foot the bill without a problem?"

At this point, Qi Yun felt a little thirsty. She picked up her husband's tea cup and drank from it. She continued after refilling the cup. "Haoyu, you accused me of only seeing Brother Greenback, not my husband! Now you tell me how can anyone manage not recognizing Brother Greenback? How can we carry on if we do not have 300,000 or 500,000 in our hand? These are our worries and they are big ones too, not small ones. If we go on like this, we won't be able to buy an apartment and others would interpret it as though we are misers, and say that we prefer money to life. You can only end up in such miserable situation when you insist on being clean and pure."

Qi Yun felt she had let out all that was necessary. She then lay back on the sofa to take a rest. However, her mind did not stop sorting out the points she just made to see if any one needed further elaboration.

Lu Haoyu kept an expressionless face. He asked, "you've said so much, but did you forget the main issue?"

"What issue?"

Lu Haoyu said, "Being so generous on money, it can't be that these people expect nothing in return."

Qi Yun nodded, "In this age there is no one-way traffic between people anymore. To put it negatively it's called making use of one another. To put it positively, it's called helping each other."

"What help do they want from me?" asked Lu Haoyu

Qi Yun said, "Zhao Xin is currently the township director and he wants to become the township party secretary. Li Dongmin is the first deputy director at the propaganda department of the county party committee. The GO director of the county is about to

10.5 Chinese officials are in general not well-paid but enjoy a large package of fringe benefits. In simple math, clean officials like Lu Haoyi cannot afford to buy an apartment with the savings from their legitimate income. However, all officials are assumed wealthy with illegitimate incomes. That is why Qi Yun is afraid that others may regard her family as misers.

be re-assigned and he wants that job. Zhang Ziyi's son is the deputy commissioner at the municipal Economic Commission; the commissioner is about to retire, and he wants to succeed him. The first two cases are a piece of cake for you. A couple of phone calls to the party secretaries of the two counties will do. The last one has to go through the municipal party committee meeting, but since you are the "first hand," you can veto nominees of others; they can do nothing about it. However, even if a couple of people are against your nominee, you still can push it through with a vote. The minority must go along with the majority even if with a bitter smile."

Lu Haoyu said, "You are worthy of the name of a talented domestic aid. You have even worked out the details for me. I should really thank you a lot."

Qi Yun looked at her husband from the corner of her eyes and said with a sigh, "You are being sarcastic. I know I pose a difficult problem for you and you are hurting in your heart. I have said all I had to say, Just food for your thought. I will not push you and will say no more tonight."

True to her word, Qi Yun spoke nothing about the subject. Lu Haoyu paced back and forth in his study till Qi Yun called him from the bathroom to take a bath. She had prepared the water.

Lu Haoyu had slept relatively well, but that night his sleep was ruined by the 70,000 and the antique lion. He did not sleep till midnight and woke up at almost 2 O'clock. He turned back and forth in bed till 4 am when he fell asleep again. He dreamed of a river, perhaps the one near his native village. The water was only up to the belly button. He was together with several familiar faces.

The next morning after he got up, Lu Haoyu turned the dream in his head and felt that it was full of symbolic significance. Now the money and antique were in your wife's hand; they were waiting for you to return the favor in kind. Isn't it that I am already in the water? The river in his dream symbolized his fall in real life. He wished that the symbolism were clearer, but he went nowhere. He reached neither the other bank nor returned to this land. The dream instead dwelled in the middle of the river.

After breakfast, Lu Haoyu went to work on foot. It took about a quarter of an hour from home to office walking slowly. He had always walked to work. He ran into Ren Qishan, the former general office director of the municipal party committee. He used to be the oldest director at the department and retired in the fall of the year before. He carried a sword on his shoulder and a grocery basket in his hand. He greeted Lu Haoyu from a distance. "Secretary Lu, are you substituting a car ride with a walk?"

"I'm not an early bird, therefore I have to substitute morning exercise with a walk to work. Isn't it closer for you to go home from the west than from the east? Why do you take the longer route that took you here?"

"It's all these stuff to blame."

"I see. You went to the market on your way from morning exercise. You *kill two birds with one stone.*"

"I have no other choice," said Ren Qishan. "My original plan was to do my sword exercise for an hour. However, the burden of life ruined my plan, forcing me to do only 40 minutes before I had to hurry to the market. You probably don't know the trick here, but you probably will understand after you retire. At the peak hour, there are too many people in the morning market who drive the price up. After 7 pm and before the market closes, it is no longer that crowded. Prices come down at this time. For example, in peak time, tomato is 50 cents a pound, but now it's only 45. Normally, I buy a dozen or so pounds each time. That will save me 50 cents. To save this 50 cents your timing must be right. You won't be able to cut down the price through bargaining but if you are too late, they are all gone and you won't have vegetables on your table today. Look, people become shrewd after retirement, more so than a housewife."

Lu Haoyu had become very sensitive to the word "retire." He could not help asking "This has to do with retirement? What percentage do you draw?"[5]

"The percentage is not the main issue. The most important factor is the political devaluation of pension that came with your no longer being in power. As they put it, money no longer lasts as it used to," said Ren Qishan.

"How come?" asked Lu Haoyu.

"Very simple; when you are in office, one yuan can buy 1.3 or even 1.5 yuan worth of goods and services. Take for example a basketful of apples. Let's say the fair market price is 50 yuan, but the staffer you send to the orchard can bring it back for 40 or even 30 yuan. When they hear that it is for so and so secretary, mayor, or chairman, they will naturally be glad to lower the price while ensuring that you get the best quality. Even if the price is less than desired, your staffer would often put in his own money so as to please you. It is more common that people constantly bring presents of all kinds to your door. By living on this free stuff you have saved your own money. Things are completely different once you retire. Nobody brings you presents any more. People no longer reduce the price for you. Nor does anyone put their pocket money for your purchase, and you can no longer ensure the quality of your purchase. You must spend 50 yuan for a basketful of apples, from which you can find several pounds of rotten ones. In addition, the discontent the masses feel against officials often finds release in the form of revenge after you retire. The county magistrate at Dong Huan once bought a watermelon from a road side stall at 0.8 yuan per pound. Someone asked the peddler, 'You've been selling at 0.6 yuan per pound, how come you sold Magistrate Kuo at 0.8 yuan per pound?' The peddler replied, 'When he was in

---

[5] That is, the percentage of salary that one is paid as pension. Cadres who started working for the CCP before October 1, 1949 usually get to keep their full salaries and most of their benefits.

office he would never personally patronize a stall like ours — people brought him watermelon as presents or he sent his men to buy it for him. Now that he has retired and finally came to us in person; why not seize the opportunity to squeeze him for some extra?' Another peddler said, 'Is there anyone of these officials who has not accumulated hundreds of thousands? Let them pay more — they are rich.' When you put all these factors together, how can this pension not depreciate?"

"People are often blinded by success. When you are in power, it is hard to imagine the situation when you are no longer in power." These words were refreshing for Lu Haoyu. He asked, "Do these include your personal experiences?"

"What do you think! The above are all from my own experiences. You'll feel the same when you retire next year. Generally speaking, the higher your position, the deeper you will feel it. Even more so for those who have maintained personal integrity."

Lu Haoyu said to himself in his heart, *I'm already in the water*.

Ren Qishan went on, "You don't need anyone to tell you this. You will understand it all clearly by just looking at how Secretary Gao was spending the last years of his life in great hardship. This is the common destiny of all those clean officials who refused to take bribes and engage in grafting and embezzlement. Let's march on following his footsteps!" He then walked away imitating soldier's march on goose steps.

The way Ren Qishan walked was very funny, but Lu Haoyu could not laugh. He was dumbfounded and stood there staring blankly for sometime before he walked on. He spent alf an hour to cover a 15 minute walk. He could not get rid of the image of Gao Qili that filled his mind.

Lu and Gao used to be partners. When Gao Qili was the party secretary of Hukou county at Wushan prefecture, Lu Haoyu was the county magistrate. Lu respected Gao highly, not only because Gao was a few years his senior, but also, more importantly, because of his reputed public spirit and integrity. Lu Haoyu took over as the party secretary when Gao was promoted to deputy party secretary of Donghua municipality. Later on, when Lu went a full circle as deputy governor, the governor, and party secretary of the prefecture, and became the party secretary at Donghua municipality, Gao had already retired and went to live in his native village in the countryside. However, his stories continued to circulate among government bureaucracies. Gao married very late; his wife was ten years younger and bore him twin boys. Consequently, at the time of Gao's retirement their sons just finished high school and both succeeded in getting into college. This should have been "double happiness" but Gao was worried. That was the time of high inflation. His pension had to support both his living expenses and the college education of the two boys. On top of all these expenses he must also pay for the medical care of his sick wife. He lived in great difficulties.

To help him, the then party secretary of the city made an arrangement that Huaxia Co. hired him to be its advisor, for which the company paid him 500 yuan a month. However, he quitted after only a month. He felt that he could not accept the pay because he was essentially useless to the company's business. The pay he draws was in fact a giveaway. Secondly, he could not go along with some of the company's practices in business, such as bribery and pretty girls in their PR. His conscience would not allow him to accept the pay. He courageously quitted and went back with his wife to the countryside to live in his native village.

Lu Haoyu felt a tremendous surge of feelings each time he heard these stories about Gao Qili. Twice his plan to visit him in the countryside was disrupted. The first was by a telephone notice from the GO of the provincial party committee that the provincial party secretary was coming on an inspection tour; he had to stay to receive the secretary. The second time, he was already on the way when the road was cut off by flood water after a downpour. He had to return with great regret.

Today when he thought about Gao Qili, he felt that his thinking was much more complex than in the past. He knew his thought was completely shaken up by the "common destiny" alluded to by Ren Qishan.

"Secretary Lu!" the secretary-in-chief Wang Zhongyi was walking towards him, obviously to seek instruction from Lu on some matters. Lu pointed to the building of the Municipal Party Standing Committee and said, "let's discuss in the office."

Reading Questions:

Judging from the ways in which the life of the Lu family has been affected, can you guess what are the reform measures?

IV

After the phone conversation with her daughter Lu Li, Qi Yun sat staring blankly. She did not move for quite a long time. At this time, Lu Haoyu came home from work. "Why are you sitting there like that?" asked Lu while putting away his overcoat on the hook.

Qi Yun turned around with tears sparkling in her eyes. "Lili has been hospitalized for ten days and we knew nothing about it!"

"What's wrong?" asked Lu Haoyu.

Qi Yun said, "Baomin caught a cold and Lili had to transport the goods herself on tricycles. She was hit by a truck on the road. It should have been the driver's fault, but he has *guanxi* in the department of public security. They blamed everything on Lili. You are a leader; you tell me what is this society turning into? Is there justice anymore?"

Lu Haoyu asked, "Is it serious?"

Qi Yun said, "Nothing serious. She's already out of the hospital. But she has accumulated 5000 yuan medical bill. It's just like *having incessant rain when your roof is cracked*. They planned to use the 20,000 we gave them when they both were laid off to open a dry cleaning business. But 5000 was already spent on hospital bills."

Lu felt a relief, "Forget about the money, as long as she is OK."

Qi Yun said, "I want to give Lili another 10,000; We will leave the rest 50,000 to Weiwei. Whatever use they put it to — travel, repairing the apartment, and so on. That's all they'll have — they can keep whatever is left and we will give them no more if they are still short."

Lu Haoyu nodded and said, "All right. Weiwei spent four years in Shenzhen. He did not learn how to make money but how to spend it. It must be made clear to him so that he knows saving."

Qi Yun said, "I've called him. He'll be here soon."

As they were talking, Weiwei came. He said, while taking off the overcoat, "Mom is more commanding than the municipal party secretary. She ordered me to come immediately but did not tell me for what. Here I am at your command."

Qi Yun did not feel like joking. She pointed to the sofa, asking her son to sit down. Then she told him about Lili's injury and how she plans to divide the money, emphasizing their savings for all these years are gone. Dad and mom could help them no more.

Weiwei was unaffected, "Don't worry, mom. It's fine with me even if you gave my sister 20,000. I'm shooting for big money. A couple of thousands is nothing to speak about."

Qi Yun looked at her son, and said, "Since when have you learned bragging?"

Weiwei said, "You say I'm bragging? I'll promise even more. When I make a fortune I'll buy my sister a dry cleaning machine — it is just a few hundred grand. Of course," he moved his eyes to Lu Haoyu, "I will need dad's help and cooperation to earn that kind of money. I'd have come home even if mom had not called me. I have most important news to report to dad, happy news that will completely change our fortune."

Lu Haoyu became wary, guessing that it must be that his son wanted him to help to get some position that he liked. While others bought positions, his son simply asked for it. He felt besieged.

Lu Wei continued, "Dad, it is this: Our corporation has a subsidiary labor service company. Boss Zhang wants to let me lease it, on a three-year contract during which I have to turn in 100,000 each year, and pocket the rest."

Upon hearing this, a different worry rose. Lu Haoyu said, "Let's forget about the 'rest' for the moment. I'm afraid you won't be able to fulfill the 'three years for 300,000 part' in your contract."

Lu Wei said, "It's not easy of course, and because of this Boss Zhang offers me a very favorable condition. Do you know what is it? Can't guess it? He'll give my company 100,000 ton quota of shipping coal each year. And it is cooperative coal![6] You know it well, dad. Because the province does not charge dues on cooperative coal, we can make 25 yuan profit out of each ton of coal. Add it up yourself. 100,000 ton would yield 2.5 million yuan. I reckon that a million should be enough to smooth out the relations with various concerned parties; sub-

> *6.6 As discussed in essay 1, decentralization is the main thrust of the market–oriented reforms in the 1980s and 1990s. Contracting based on public property rights also created opportunities for corruption and rent-seeking, as seen in Li Wei's leasing of the subsidiary of an SOE.*

tract 300,000 required by contract, the remaining 1.2 million would be mine. My plan for these 1.2 million is: 100,000 to aid my sister, 300,000 for you to live comfortably in retirement. The remaining 700,000 is capital for my further development. You see, wouldn't this solve all of our problems once and for all?"

Lu Haoyu remembered the jade lion sent by Zhang Ziyi and understood it all: it's not that his son wanted a position; he was helping another to secure a position because of the goody he has received. It was a deal worked out between his son and others. However, directly or indirectly notwithstanding, it all ended with him — he had nowhere to escape. He deeply felt the dilemma those in high positions had to deal with all the time. He played innocent, "It's an internal affairs of your company; what does it have to do with me? Do you want me to go out to rent storage and secure railway carriages?"

Lu Wei said, "Dad, you don't need to do that kind of things. His Venerable Chairman Mao had a famous saying: There is neither love nor hatred without a reason in the world. The same can be applied more generally — there's nothing without a reason. And relationships among people are that of business exchange — both parties need to get something out of it before a deal can be

---

[6] That is, coal sold to business partners at lower, government fixed price.

made. Having given me such a large benefit, they of course have some favor to ask us in exchange. Even if they did not ask for it, we'd try to repay the debt. This is the rule of the game and everybody knows it."

Lu Haoyu said, "All right. I know what I should do."

Lu Wei was surprised, "I haven't told you all; how do you know it? Go on, how do you plan to return the favor?"

Lu Haoyu said, "The Coal Transport Company has done a good job, made major contributions in taxes and profits. At year end, we will recommend it a medal — advanced *danwei*, and award it with flags or certificates of merit — whatever. In fact, we have been doing this for ages and are quite good at it."

Lu Wei laughed, "My dad has been the party secretary for so long that he has returned to childhood from his old age. What I meant is private deals, not business deals. What use do they have for your flag, medal, or certificate? Let me lay it on the table. His second son Zhang Zhong is the deputy commissioner of the economic commission. The commissioner is about to retire. It will do if you promote Zhang to be the commissioner."

Lu Haoyu shook his head, "Appointments of cadres at the section level and above must go through the Standing Committee. It's not like a cigarette in my pocket that I can give one to whoever I like."

Lu Wei said, "Don't fool me, dad. Unlike other countries, Chinese politics is dominated by the "first hand." In other countries, the president's nominees have to be approved by the two chambers. In China, it's the chief executive that calls the shot. For example, if you do not nod on candidates put forward by others, there

4.2 The "first hand" is also called the "squad leader." In the CCP's parlance, the standing committee is likened to a squad in the military and the first hand is regarded as the squad leader. This way, the absolutism in the military is translated into the concentration of power in the first hand, a major problem of the Chinese political system. It has created many little dictators and is the main cause of corruption.

could never be a decision. However, even if a couple of committee members object to the candidate you put up, it does not really matter, because you can influence the majority to vote on it. What I talk about are major decisions, as to a personnel decision concerning only an individual — say, the head of the Economic Commission — it is a piece of cake for you."

Qi Yun had been listening in silence all the while; her mood brightened up, sunshine radiated from between her eyebrows. This change did not escape Lu Wei, who turned to his mother for support, "Mom, dad is too orthodox; such a good thing and he still could not go along. You must give me a hand."

Qi Yun did intervene, but did not back her son. She said, "Come on, Weiwei. Bother your dad no more. Personnel decisions are not so easy that your dad can promise right away. Had he done so would he have survived as the city's party secretary? That's enough: your job is to explain the matter clearly so that your father understands it. Your dad is a cautious man. Don't bother him anymore. You can go now."

"How can I leave when there isn't a result yet?" said Lu Wei.

"Say no more. You leave now," said Qi Yun. She stood and pushed her son all the way out of the door before she came back in.

Lu Haoyu remembered a parable; a wolf had a farmer lying down on the ground and was about to eat him, when a tiger came and drove the wolf away. It turned around and put its front paws on the chest of the farmer and said to him, "You must thank me for driving the wolf away." The farmer said, "To me, to be eaten by a wolf or by a tiger is the same, why should I thank you?"

Lu Haoyu expected an intense psychological warfare from his wife when Qi Yun returned, but she only said to him, "You go to the

> *3.5 Watching the 7 O'clock News is important for cadres and even some business people. Because all TV programs are controlled by the CCP (via its propaganda department), people obtain clues of likely policy change in Beijing and prepare for it accordingly.*

bedroom to take a rest. I'll cook for you." She then put on the apron and went into the kitchen. She cooked fried rice and steamed fish. After dinner, Qi Yun turned on the TV and called Lu Haoyu, who was in the study. "Come on." The Associated News Cast had begun. "Hurry up." The national news was followed by provincial news and then by city news. It was only after finishing all three did Qi Yun turn off the TV. After she made some green tea that Lu Haoyu loved she sat down beside her husband and began, "Now let's talk about that thing Weiwei spoke about."

Lu Haoyu murmured to himself: She was tactically very skillful — taking a long routine that led to this juncture. The parable once again flashed in his mind: ... then the tiger lifted his paws from the farmer's chest and said to him: "Go and have your dinner." After dinner the tiger said, "Go, play and entertain yourself." After the entertainment, the tiger said "Now it's the time I eat you."

"Yes or no?" Qi Yun asked.

"On what?"

"The matter Weiwei brought up just now."

"OK. Let's discuss it."

"On this matter you should be more proactive."

Lu Haoyu did not respond. Once again, the parable continued through his mind's eye: The tiger said, "Why do you lie down on the ground and not moving? You should be more proactive to let me eat you. ..." His eyes slowly turned till they fixed on Qi Yun's egg-shaped face. This face, the pair of eyes in particular, was what he is used to and still loves to see. But now he compared her to a tiger. At the thought of it he could not help laughing.

Qi Yun leapt to her feet to look at herself in the mirror on the wall, but saw nothing out of the extra-ordinary. She came back and asked, "Why did you laugh? OK. I see. It must be that you saw me taking bribery, greedy and shameless, and think I am less than pigs and dogs; isn't it?"

Lu Haoyu told the truth, "I did not compare you with dogs and pigs. Instead, I imagined you as a tiger." He then told her the parable.

After hearing it, Qi Yun was almost in tears. She said, "Haoyu, for these years we have been a loving couple. I never dreamed that I would suddenly become a tiger in your eyes and want to eat you. I may as well hang myself."

Lu Haoyu sighed and also turned serious, "Qi Yun, it's not you who wants to eat me; it's the evil trend and noxious practices that want to eat me. You are a good person fallen hostage to them."

"I wouldn't have the audacity to face you again if you really regard me as a tiger," said Qi Yun.

Lu Haoyu said, "I had such an imagery association because both you and Weiwei targeted at me."

"Then is the matter Weiwei brought up discussable? Or if I discuss it you'll again see me as a tiger?"

"Tell me what you have in mind."

"I felt it's worth considering. The labor service company is a subsidiary of the Coal Transportation Corporation. The parent company helping out a subsidiary with some coal transport quota is a internal business issue of theirs. The money Weiwei is to earn is neither embezzlement nor highway robbery; it's normal business profit. Nobody can find fault with it. As to you, you are far away from this matter. No one can tie you to it. In my opinion, it's a rare opportunity to make some money and we can't let it go no matter what!"

Lu Haoyu said, "You've only told half the story; you did not even touch the more important half. Doesn't he want me to promote his son? How can you say I will not be tied to it?"

Qi Yun countered, "Zhang Zhong's promotion is entirely a different matter. First, the director of the Economic Commission has reached the age limit and there must be someone to take over; secondly, the successor is not some relative of yours that you brought from outside. It's one of the deputies of the Economic Commission. It's normal that when a "first hand" retires or is reassigned one of his deputies succeeds him. Third, Zhang Zhong's promotion is not what you cook up behind the back of everybody. Instead, it goes through the normal procedure to be decided collectively at the Standing Committee meeting. With these three, what are you afraid of?"

Lu Haoyu said no more. He leaned back on his sofa and closed his eyes as if resting. Qi Yun looked at her husband and went on: "This is not a naked deal. It's indirect, therefore, easier for you to accept in your feelings. If you go along with it, I won't raise any trouble for you, I can even return the 70,000 and the jade lion. We'll return all the naked stuff. What do you think?"

Lu Haoyu made no sound. Qi Yun said, "Go to bed earlier," and then went into the bedroom.

That night Lu Haoyu turned about in bed for a long, long time, unable to get to sleep. He re-ran his life with integrity in every detail. As he did so, he suddenly realized that his integrity was not that pure and uncontaminated. For example, in recent years, leaders from above as well as neighboring cities and prefectures frequently sent him notes asking his favor to take care of the matters concerning certain individuals. He knew very well there was something fishy going on behind the curtains; nevertheless for the sake of giving them face he did what he could to help out. That meant that he had already been involved in the power-money exchange; the only difference was that he did the work while others pocketed the money. He could wash himself of any responsibility in the criminal court, but at the moral court he was already guilty. This realization had a profound impact on him; he now knew that the dam he built around himself was full of cracks.

He abruptly sat up from bed. As a matter of fact, Qi Yun could not go to sleep herself. She turned around and said, "I knew you would not be able to sleep tonight. I did not want to say anymore, but still there are a few words that I have to say."

Lu Haoyu said with a dry smile, "It matters little now how much you say."

Qi Yun went on, "You shouldn't just wait for retirement. Can you manage to get into the People's Congress or the People's Political Consultative Conference? You once said that you had thought about it."

Lu Haoyu let out a barely noticeable sigh. There were only three places as the final destiny of party secretaries of cities and prefectures. The first was to become the vice provincial governors or deputy party secretaries; the second was to enter the provincial People's

Congress or Political Consultative Conference as vice chairpersons; the third was to retire at the legal age to enjoy life in retirement. He could not imagine ending up in the first destiny, and was reluctant to accept the third. He had indeed thought about the second and had planned to get it but had not yet started working on it.

Qi Yun went on, "It's time for you to take action. Nowadays the morality of society is rapidly degenerating. How could we get by without some money in hand?"

3.8 In China's Constitution, the People's Congress is the highest body of authority; however, it often serves as a half-way stop to the full retirement of leading cadres of the Party and government. This is indicative of its real status in the Chinese political hierarchy.

Lu Haoyu said, "Qi Yun, will you please get me some sleeping pills?"

After taking the pill, Lu Haoyu said, "Qi Yun, let me get into the water when there's not another way out. You return those naked briberies; I'll consider the matter of Zhang Zhong. Are you satisfied?"

"I am satisfied, and we don't have to worry about our retirement anymore."

Reading Questions:

1. Describe Lu Wei's scheme to make big money; is it corruption? Why?
2. What is the status of the People's Congress and People's Political Consultative Conference in the Chinese political system, judging from their role in cadres' retirement?

V

Qi Yun was a doer who acted fast. The next day after she prepared lunch and told Lu Haoyu to eat alone, she went out with her handbag directly to Zhang Ziyi's company. She made sure that Lu Haoyu saw it when she was putting the jade lion into her bag, and let him know what she was doing. Lu Haoyu nodded so lightly that only he could feel it.

Zhang Ziyi was waiting in his office, for Qi Yun had called in advance. It was not a small matter that the lady of the party secretary paid him a visit. He dared not sit behind an executive desk on a tall swivel chair and looked down on his visitor, as he normally did. He sat instead on the sofa and said in all politeness, "*Shaozi*[7] is a rare guest of honor; as little brother[8] I'll wash my ears to listen to whatever instruction you have for me."

Qi Yun said, "I'm a retired person and would not dare to issue instruction to a big boss like you. I must thank you for giving Lu Wei a job when he returned from Shenzhen. Old Lu also thanks you. Is it true that he is to lease the Labor Service Company? If so, can he fulfill his contracted responsibilities? I came to ask you because I'm a little worried."

3. *Guanxi*

Guanxi (roughly translated as "connections") describes the basic dynamics in personalized networks of influence and access to opportunities. It is a central idea in the Chinese society. At its most basic level, *guanxi* describes a personal connection between two people in which one is able to perform a favor or service for another in exchange of returns in kind. The two people need not be of equal social status. *Guanxi* can also be used to describe a network of contacts, which an individual can call upon when something needs to be done, and through which he or she can exert influence on behalf of others. In addition, *guanxi* can describe a state of general understanding between two people who realize and pledge to keep their mutual obligations.

(Continued)

---

[7] The literal translation is "elder sister-in-law"; it is commonly used to address the wife of someone respected in the same generation (usually older). The term implies closeness.

[8] *Xiaodi* in Chinese. When used in self-reference the term implies humility and ready obedience.

(Continued)

In planning a course of action or strategy, *guanxi* is an important factor (a resource or the lack of it) to consider.

Guanxi can be regarded as a social capital gained from social connections gathered from extended family, school friends, workmates and members of common clubs or organizations etc. It is customary for Chinese people to cultivate an intricate web of *guanxi* relationships, which may expand in multiple directions, including lifelong relationships. Reciprocity is the key factor to maintaining one's *guanxi* web; failure to reciprocate is considered an unforgivable offense. The more you ask of someone the more you owe them. *Guanxi* can perpetuate a never ending cycle of favors that can become onerous. Like many other relationships, *guanxi* is also subject to the family imagery and follows the rules governing the relationship between family members. However, *guanxi* is informal relationships cultivated individually that fall outside formally defined positions such as between employer and employee, teacher and student, subordinate and superior. The relationships formed by *guanxi* are personal and not transferable. On the positive side, *guanxi* is a kind of social capital that generates net benefits. For example, Chinese small businesses tend to form a network of interconnections for mutual help — Chinese capitalism is sometime characterized as "network capitalism." On the more sinister side, *guanxi* represents the manipulation and corruption brought about by selfish and sometimes illegal utilization of it to gain unfair or immoral advantage over competitors. *Guanxi* is generally exclusive.

Zhang Ziyi was an easy-going person. Although only a couple of years younger than Qi Yun, he addressed her *"Shaozi"* (elder sister-in-law) in each sentence he uttered. He understood how to address people so as to feel close. When he heard Qi Yun's question, he hurriedly explained, "It is all my fault that I did not report the details to *shaozi* and caused you to make a special trip. The quota assigned to the Labor Service Company is somewhat difficult to fulfill under normal conditions. That's why nobody dared to take the contract. However, *shaozi*, you don't have to worry about it when Lu Wei takes it. I plan to allocate some shipping quota coal so that he can not only fulfill the contract but also make some real money."

Qi Yun asked, "Is it difficult to ship coal out of the province? For example, how difficult it's going to be to secure customers. Everything is but empty talk without customers, isn't it?"

> *10.1 There is a widely spread and extreme view, or rather, exaggeration, in society nowadays that all corrupt officials are born corrupt. They become corrupt as soon as in power. They do not know that greediness is not something people are born with. The process of turning corrupt in fact is an extremely painful process. The only difference is in the concrete circumstances of each individual and the resultant varying degrees of the pains they feel.*

Zhang Ziyi said, "Please be assured, *shaozi*. How could I have given it to Lu Wei if it were difficult? Customers and railway carriages are already there. In fact, all he needs to do is to settle accounts with customers. Of course, this is only between you and me. In order to quell suspicion, he will have to make some business trips at the beginning. Do you approve such an arrangement?"

Qi Yun nodded. With this matter nailed down, Qi Yun told him the purpose of her visit. She took out the jade lion and laid it on the table. "After playing with this thing for several days, our curiosity is satisfied. Old Lu said you have taste for antiques and it's better to return it to its owner, a collector."

Zhang Ziyi was caught off guard and could not figure out what she meant. Qi Yun then returned to the topic of shipping of coal out of the province. "In this matter, you do whatever you think appropriate because it is your internal business affairs. It's all business. As to Zhang Zhong's job, we'll do our best. It falls in normal personnel decision making and is also a pure business matter. Isn't it preferable that no personal relations are involved?"

Now Zhang Ziyi understood, he quickly said, "In that case, I should take this thing back. You are right; it's all business to business."

"Very well then," said Qi Yun, "I'll disturb you no more and let you go home for lunch."

When Qi Yun got home, Lu Haoyu was already enjoying his daily allowance of one cigarette after meal. Qi Yun told him the whole thing. Lu Haoyu exclaimed, "It's like what they said, God never endows one a talent without a purpose! I thought that mouth of yours was useful only during the Cultural Revolution. It never occurred to me that it finds usage in corrupt deals 30 years later!"

"All you are good at is to disparate me, 30 years ago and 30 years after," said Qi Yun.

Lu Haoyu did not continue with his jokes. He felt strange to joke on such matters, sort of making fun out of a depressing issue. He stood up to pace back and forth in the hallway, substituting for his after-meal walk outdoors. But he walked only for a little while before he went in the bedroom for his nap at noon.

Lying in bed, it occurred to him that it was his turn to carry on this drama. Despite his reluctance he had no way to turn back now. He now realized how difficult it was to do something that one did not want to do. There is nowadays a widely spread and extreme view, or rather an exaggeration, in society that all corrupt officials are born corrupt; they become corrupt as soon as they hold power. They do not know that greediness is not something people are born with. The process of turning corrupt in fact is an extremely painful process. The only difference is in the concrete circumstances of each individual and the resultant varying degrees of the pains they feel.

Scattered thoughts disrupted his daily routine of a nap at noon. He could not get to sleep. When he saw the clock which indicated only 20 minutes left before he resumed work, he got up quickly. After washing his face, he took up the cup of tea Qi Yun had prepared everyday at this time and started sipping.

At 2 O'clock in the afternoon, Lu Haoyu walked into the Standing Committee building exactly on time. His secretary Li Zhijian, who was just one step ahead of him, opened the door to the inner room for him right away. This arrangement that the leaders used the inner room as an office while staffers used the outer one was made by the previous party secretary. Soon after Lu Haoyu took office, the Secretariat proposed to give both rooms to the leading cadre and find other places for staffers. However, to do this would entail a reshuffling of all rooms in the building. It was said to be the idea of Mayor Huang.

9.1 Here is a case of how a decision is typically made. The key figures of the political establishment try to build a consensus before the matter is brought to a formal meeting for a vote.

The reason given was that with staffers right next door it was inconvenient for leaders to discuss sensitive issues, and it was easy to leak information. However, when the proposal arrived at the desk of the new first hand, Lu Haoyu said with a dry humor, "The staff is a miniature commission of discipline inspection. They keep us honest." The chief of staff was waiting for words such as "Do as you see appropriate," but Lu Haoyu said nothing after that joke, and moved to other issues. The chief of staff decided that Lu liked the existing arrangement, or at least was not against it. He hence shelved the proposal. It was said the underlying tension between Huang Shanbai and Lu Haoyu originated from this. Huang later on said to the chief of staff, "Does that imply that we are engaged in corruption? Go ask him won't we have one more door keeper if we collude with the staffers?"

Lu Haoyu entered the inner room. Before he had time to sit down, the phone rang; it was Xu Bing seeking instruction as to when should they get together or "knock heads" to discuss personnel matters. The so-called "knocking heads" here referred to an informal meeting of the first hand, the mayor, the deputy party secretary in charge of personnel and the director of the organization department.[9] If the four reached a consensus, the issue would be brought to the standing committee meeting for approval.

---

[9] The organization department of the Party committee is in charge of cadre management. It tracks and investigates cadre performances and make recommendations on appointments and promotions.

Lu Haoyu had no immediate plan to take on personnel issues but he thought of Zhang Zhong's case. He would like to test the water to see where the others stood on this issue, therefore he said, "This afternoon will do, at 3 O'clock."

Xu Bing further asked, "Only the four of us?" He referred to an old rule on the meeting of these four on personnel matters. However, in recent years the meeting had expanded to include all party secretaries and deputy secretaries in some cities and prefectures. That was why Xu Bing asked. Lu Haoyu mainly wanted to see where the mayor Huang Shanbai stood on this matter. The four already included him, hence he replied, "Today we shall follow the old rule."

At 3 pm, the four simultaneously entered the conference room. Around the oval table were a group of chairs. The party secretary sat on the chair at the head of the table. Next to him on his right and left sat the mayor and the deputy party secretary in charge of cadres. The seats of other deputy secretaries and standing committee members extended all the way to the other end of the table. There were altogether nine standing committee members, each having a seat arranged in a fixed order according seniority. In front of each seat was a deck of paper; a black and a red pencil were prepared for note taking. When the secretary, the mayor and the deputy secretary in charge of cadre affairs took their respective seats, the director of the organization department, who came in last, closed the sound proof door behind him. This was a security measure adopted after Lu Haoyu came. However, the sound proof door could not prevent what happened inside the room from leaking to the outside world. News about the party committee meeting spread as it used to, and fast too. Nevertheless, whenever there was a meeting, the door would be closed.

Xu Bing took out a pack of Lotus brand cigarette to distribute around. He gave Lu Haoyu

3.6 Cadres in the Mao era held office till they died. Deng introduced term and age limits: one can only serve at the maximum two 5-year terms in one position and must retire when reaching the retirement age. The age limit differs for different ranks. Generally, the higher one's rank, the longer he or she can serve.

one too, despite the latter adhering to the rule he set for himself —
no smoking during meetings. Xu said it was meant for Lu to "sniff"
on it.

Lu Haoyu took the cigarette and sniffed on it for a while, and
threw it back to Xu Bing. He then began. "We have decided on the
principle of maintaining relative stability of the cadre corps unless
it's absolutely necessary to make changes. Therefore, we haven't
had a meeting on the issue for a long time. This morning, secretary
Xu called me about cadres, and it happened that we have some
time. Therefore, let us do a preliminary discussion. Secretary Xu,
will you please brief us on this."

"We haven't discussed it for half a year now, and have
cumulated some cases. We have eight cadres who have reached
retirement age, two of them have exceeded by three or four months.
Of these eight, three are down in the counties and five in municipal
government organs. Besides there are four section-level cadres that
must be removed: one because of negligence of his duties during
the flood emergency, one for soliciting and the other two for gambling. We must also deal with these people. We now let director
Wang brief us on the details of each."

Wang Yongfu took out a pile of forms and explained in detail
about the eight people, in particular, their dates of birth and the
exact time they reached the retirement age. He then went on to
introduce the cases of the other four's misbehavior, the time, place
and details of their offenses. All of the four's *danwei*'s recommendations included, "strip of all positions."

A brief silence fell when Wang Yongfu finished. In fact, it was
waiting for the first hand to speak first. It had been an unchanging
rule for many years that others spoke only after the first hand set
the tone.

Wan Yongfu had already reported all this to Lu Haoyu last
Monday. Therefore, Lu already had a pretty good idea what to do.
However, his silence was longer than usual, and it was because of
the guilt he felt when personal objectives were smuggled in public
administration. It felt hard to open his mouth and he was uncomfortable all over his body. He deeply felt a heavy burden brought

by self-seeking. To him, this was an entirely new and yet excruciatingly painful experience.

"I'll say a few words," he finally began. "Retiring at the age of 60 is the law of the state. Unless it is a scientist and necessary for him to delay retirement for the sake of continuing a research project, everybody should obey the law. Nobody would disagree with this point, right?"

The other three nodded to indicate concurrence. Lu Haoyu went on, "The four to-be-disciplined cadres, in my opinion, should be put together with other offenders and dealt with in another time. However, one thing that must be determined today is whether such cadres can remain in a leadership position. My own opinion is that gambling and soliciting are serious offenses. Whether they should be stripped of their position should be left to another meeting, but one thing must be clear: such people are not to be allowed to remain in their positions. Any objections?"

Xu Bing and Wang Yongfu nodded their concurrence while Huang Shanbai said, "no objection."

Lu Haoyu said, "Then our agenda today is greatly simplified. Eight retirements plus the four who are no longer to remain in their positions together are twelve vacancies. Who is suitable to fill them is the topic of today's preliminary discussion. Director Wang, what ideas do you have?"

Wang Yongfu said, "I don't have a mature opinion as to who is suitable. We should mainly listen to the opinions of you leaders. However, I have to make one suggestions. This issue should not be dragged on for too long. So many people are fixing their eyes on these vacancies; the competition is extremely intense. People have gone mad to fight for them. It'll save us a lot of trouble if this is nailed down early."

Xu Bing said, "It's not competition; it's corruption."

Lu Haoyu said, "Work hard with competitive spirit and achieve results — that's real competition. Lobbying madly for promotion is in fact corruption." He felt empty after saying that.

Wang Yongfu nodded, "That's true. It was reported that as the director of the Economic Commission is about to retire, his deputies would no longer sit still. Of the four deputy commissioners, only the third has been able to keep cool. The other three are all madly lobbying. Their relations with one another are extremely tense. They bad mouth each other to distinguish themselves. The sooner this can be decided, the earlier they can settle down to work."

"Who is the one not running around making way for himself?" asked Lu Haoyu.

"His name is Zhang Zhong, the son of the chief executive of the Coal Transport Corporation," replied Wang Yongfu.

Lu Haoyu seized the opportunity, "We should seriously consider someone who is not running mad."

To his surprise, Huang Shanbai immediately objected to it. He said, "Zhang Zhong is not suitable. First, 'running' for office has become a universal phenomenon; nobody is completely innocent. Zhang Zhong is not running it because his dad is doing it for him. Shouldn't that be regarded as 'running' too? We must be realistic on this issue. Second, his credentials is not as strong. He has been deputy director for only three years, while all others have had at least five. To promote him over the others will cause even more resentment. Third, this guy is a modernist. He can sing, dance, drive, swim, play bridge and Mahjong, a playboy. Think about how much energy he has left for work."

Huang Shanbai's objection was strong and determined, but it did not surprise Lu Haoyu. The friction between the two had continued for a long time; the origin was on personnel issues. Huang Shanbai took personnel decisions very seriously. He liked to propose his own candidates and was stubborn about it. Initially, Lu Haoyu often gave in to Huang, but since the year before when he heard more and more about how Huang was collecting a fortune, he became alert, and seldom gave in on disputed cadre appointments. This was the root cause of the tension between them. Huang acted like a child following a policy of *an eye for an eye, a tooth for a tooth* confrontation: if you block my candidate I would also be against yours. If you veto one of mine, I would also create difficulties for yours.

Lu Haoyu's purpose was to test Huang's attitude about Zhang Zhong. Now that he had achieved his objective, he did not want to argue with Huang at this meeting. As he was redirecting the topic away from Zhang Zhong, the director of the general office came and said to him, "Secretary Lu, deputy mayor Han is on the phone asking to speak to you."

When Lu Haoyu came back, he said, "Director Wei of the Provincial Department of Transportation is leaving. I and Mayor Huang will see him

> *9.2 Xu Bing is a skillful staffer who knows the mind of his boss and the intricacies of elite politics, being at the thick of it. Staffers who please their bosses usually get promoted and become the next generation leading cadres.*

off. Our meeting has to adjourn. Today, we probably won't have time to resume it. Let's find another time to continue our discussion."

Lu Haoyu went from the conference room to his office, holding his teacup. Xu Bing followed in and sat on the sofa. Obviously he had something to say.

"What's up, secretary Xu?" asked Lu.[10]

"I can see you want to use Zhang Zhong as the director of Economic Commission. Isn't it?"

"Is it because of what I said at the meeting?"

"Here's how I think: It's unlikely that Zhang Ziyi has not mentioned Zhang Zhong to you. If that's the case, it is very difficult for you to refuse because Zhang Ziyi arranged a job for your son Lu Wei. You have to take that into consideration. It's common human relations."

Lu Haoyu asked, "Leaving this consideration aside for a while, how do you think about Zhang Zhong?"

---

[10] Note the different meaning of "secretary" here. In Chinese, "secretary" in Party secretary is rendered *shuji* and that referring to a staffer is *mishu*.

6.4 At the turn of the 21st Century tens of millions of SOE workers were laid off due to the drastic restructuring of the state sector. Local governments were required to put in lots of resources and effort into the re-employment of these people. China's social security systems began to take shape then.

"In the order of seniority, it's not his turn yet. In terms of achievement, he is also behind. The playboy Mayor Huang talked about is also true. However, it is not to say that he cannot be the commissioner. That guy's mind is open and vanguard, and he has new ideas. It's possible he can do better than the more senior guys when we put heavy responsibility on his shoulder. It's clear now that Mayor Huang is going to resist to the very end, but that does not matter. You talk to the deputy secretaries in advance and I'll talk to the rest of the standing committee members."

Lu Haoyu looked at Xu Bing feeling gratitude to this assistant of his. It was not only because of the stable and consistent support he had given him in the past, but also because he provided him with a fashionable argument on the matter of Zhang Zhong. However, he did not carry on the conversation. "We'll talk about this later. I must now hurry to the hotel."

Reading Questions:

1. Comment on the way Zhang Ziyi, CEO of a state-owned company, related to Qi Yun, the first lady of the city.
2. What do you think has made Secretary Lu to cave in to his wife's pressure?

VI

The three day conference on re-employment of the laid-off workers entered the phase of speeches. By 5 pm, all the nine *danweis* that had prepared delivered their speeches. The conference thus ended one hour ahead of schedule. Lu Haoyu asked his chauffeur to drive him to the "Big World of Clothing," which was one of the city's model *danwei*, and the first to deliver the speech at the conference. Fake models were not to be tolerated, especially one right under the nose of the municipal party committee. He wanted to take a look there on his way back. He talked to two dozens of employees there and learned a great deal about the true condition there before he felt more confident. When he finished, the working hours of the day was over. He did not want to have dinner at the conference. He dismissed his chauffeur and began walking home on foot.

"Secretary Lu, I thought you were at the conference." It was a women's voice from behind. He turned around and saw the mayor's wife Liu Guiqing. This women was one year younger than Qi Yun but had retired for several years to help her disabled son run a drugstore. Lu Haoyu knew the store must be in the neighborhood as soon as he saw Liu.

"I'm going home to have my wife's hand-made noodles."

Liu Guiqing was all smiles and joking, "It's what they say, the meal is delicious when the wife is pretty. Sister Qi's handmade noodle is better than the conference meal, isn't it?"

"It is rather uncomfortable to eat with others around the table. Isn't it true also with Old Huang?"

"That's true indeed," said Liu Guiqing. "However, old Huang isn't a family man as you are. He is so much into the conference that I haven't seen him for two days. Today, my daughter came to see him from Yunzhou but was not able to. She had to leave." She paused for a while and went on, "Secretary Lu, we are already in front of our family's drugstore. Take a carton of cigarettes with you to use at the conference."

Lu Haoyu said, "Thank you very much indeed, but I have quit smoking."

"Since when?"

"For over a year now."

Liu Guiqing nodded sympathetically. "You communist cadres are indeed pitiable. Smoking is like wildfire. How can the little you earn each month feed it? A couple of years ago, our old Huang was also determined to quit. Then we started this business that can make several thousand each month. He didn't have to quit anymore. You see, it's our Wanqiu who, with a crippled leg, earns some money so that he can continue to burn his wildfire."

Lu Haoyu had heard from Qi Yun that whenever talking to people this Liu Guiqing would bring up the topic of how profitable her little store was. Qi Yun said, "Others dare not to reveal their wealth but she does. The store is run by a disabled whose father is the mayor. The tax bureau naturally dares not to tax it much. As a matter of fact, she only stocked the store once when it was first opened. After that she never has to, for the cigarettes, liquor, etc that Huang Shanbai accepted as gifts stream to the shelves of the store." Now Lu Haoyu understood the role of their little store. If run as an ordinary store, hers was not much better than others. It was insincere when she bragged how profitable her store was. It was likely a way to cover up lest her family finance was to be audited. However, from the standpoint of cost, the profit was probably true. Selling the same bottle of liquor or a carton of cigarettes, others earned a profit from the difference between wholesale and retail price, but she in contrast had a reliable source of supplies that cost nothing. Every penny sold was profit for her.

4.1 The Chinese communists have often preferred rule by role models to rule by law. Party members and cadres are expected to exhibit exemplary behavior. A successful case attracts onsite meetings of cadres from all over the country to learn from it. In Mao's time, Dazai Brigade and Daqing Oilfield were the most famous models for agriculture and industry respectively. They received hundreds of "onsite study delegations" each year.

Thinking of these, Lu said, "Guiqing, I should really thank you a lot for solving a big problem for me. Currently, there are tons of retail stalls set up by laid-off workers and they all say they earn a meager income. But yours earns thousands or even tens of thousands each month. The key, therefore, is how the business is run. Am I right?"

Liu Guiqing said proudly, "The store is the same; it all comes down to how you manage it."

Lu Haoyu said, "I want to hold an onsite study meeting at you store and let you and your son tell your experiences. In addition, my guess is that you must also have an excellent stratagem on where and how to obtain your store supplies. We'll also invite people from wholesale businesses to help you sum up your experiences. What do you think?"

In a flicker, the smile on Liu Guiqing's face disappeared. She then tried to put up a smiling face but the forced smile really did not look like one. "Secretary Lu!" said she, "For heaven's sake please don't! Our little private store is unworthy for an onsite meeting. I'd rather shut it down if you insist on it."

Looking at the anxiety filled face, Lu Haoyu laughed and walked away, thinking because Huang Shanbai was afraid of being audited some day he got such a store as disguise. Behind this cover he was doing real deals! His thought moved from Huang Shanbai to himself. When he got home, Qi Yun was cleaning the furniture. She greeted him with "you are home." Lu Haoyu answered with an "eh" and entered the study. While taking off his outfit, the scroll hanging from the wall caught his eyes. He sat down on the swivel chair and began reading it attentively. A poem was written on it. It was written by a Minister of Defense of the Ming Dynasty, General Yu Qian, when he was the governor of Shanxi. Yu Qian was extremely powerful then but also clean and kept his integrity. Although at the time paying tributes was customary in society, he went to see the emperor empty-handed and instead wrote this poem, of which Lu Haoyu was extremely fond. He asked a calligrapher friend of his to write it on paper and hang it from the wall in his study as his motto. One does not necessarily see things right in front of him. The scroll had been on the wall for several years, but today it felt like it was the first time he saw it. He read it word by word, chewing on each line to suck in its meaning, and to experience the sublimity of a top-level official who maintained his integrity.

Qi Yun was a good mind reader. When she saw her husband moody, she thought he must have run into some difficulties at the conference. But when she saw him staring at the scroll on the wall, her heart sank: Did he change his mind on Zhang Zhong? She brought him a pile of newspapers in the hope to draw his attention away from Yu Qian's poem.

"Why don't you read these. These are newspapers of the last couple of days. Your secretary brought them here," said Qi Yun. She looked at Lu Haoyu and went back to her work.

Lu Haoyu began turning the pages of the newspapers. He meant to read *People's Daily* first, but when he picked it up, *Southern Weekend*[11] was exposed. He was shocked by the large-sized title that ran from one side to the other, "Qi Huagui, Party Secretary of the City Sentenced to Death; Where Did He Get His 13 Million Assets?" He read in one breath the article that took more than half of a page. His peace of mind was completely shattered. He shouted towards the door of the study, "Qi Yun, come here for a while."

"What's the matter?" asked Qi Yun.

Lu Haoyu said, "I'll show you an article."

Qi Yun said with a smile, "I read newspapers and journals no less than you. This is your comment on me. Now I am retired and have more time to read. When your newspapers arrived, I read them the first. Tell me which article you refer to."

Lu Haoyu raised his voice higher by 8 degrees, "Come on, hurry!" Qi Yun came in. Lu Haoyu put his hand on the article, "Read this article please."

Qi Yun said calmly, "I have. It's about the party secretary of Dongfang municipality of Hainan province. He's got the death penalty for the 13 million he had accumulated."

"You don't seem to be affected," said Lu.

Qi Yun said, "I did read it carefully, but there's nothing in it that can make us nervous. First, Qi Huagui is way too greedy. He demanded money blatantly. In a poor city with only 60 million tax revenue, he extorted 6 million. Secondly, Qi Huagui is too stupid. When you take others' money you must do what they have asked. This is the rule of the game in the small world of officialdom. He

---

[11] *Nanfang Zhoumo*, a relatively liberal magazine published in Guangzhou.

would not have been in trouble had he played by the rule. People spend money on you in exchange for your helping out on what they want. If you do your part, everybody is happy. Why should anyone report you? For reporting you is also to mark their own positions with shame — because it is bought with money. They themselves violated the law and ended with a terrible reputation. Who should be so stupid? Qi's case unraveled from here. Have you noticed that the article mentioned two people, the township party secretary who spent 80,000 to get his brother a position in the Municipal Court. Qi took the money but did not do anything for him. The other is a petty businessman Wang Ping. He wanted a business license to start a fish farm at Xingang. The 50,000 he spent on Qi is also like being thrown into the sea. These people hate him to the bones. Isn't it inevitable that his case was going to unravel from this?"

He had been with his wife day and night for 30 years and one could not say that he did not know her well. However, this woman in front of him was so clear-minded and articulate, remembering the names, positions, and details just after one reading. He could not help admiring her. When women reach 55 they usually become talkative, loquacious, forgettable, emotionally unstable, and confused. But she was no different than 30 years ago.

Qi Yun went on, "Ours is an entirely different matter. First, we are smarter than Qi Huagui. We'll play by the rules and do what they request if we receive a favor. Secondly, we are not as greedy — we are only after some pocket money so that we will not have to worry about retirement and sickness. Third, we have no direct connection with Zhang Ziyi or his son Zhang Zhong on the line of bribery. The only antique has been returned. The direct beneficiary is our son, and what he'll get is not by neither stealing nor robbery — he works for it. One hundred thousand tons of coal cannot be shipped out like blowing dust, can it? What's wrong to make some money? What trouble the father could be in if the son has no problem?"

Lu Haoyu stared at his wife and said "Qi Yun, you speak eloquently, think fast and articulate. You haven't changed a bit on all these. However, I feel on one thing, perhaps the most important one, you have changed. Why don't you sit down, I'll tell you a story, all right?"

Qi Yun sat down as if all ears. Lu Haoyu began, "In the Daoguang years of the Qing Dynasty, there was a government official named Cheng Hong who was sent by the emperor to audit the state treasury. It would have been a dream job for a corrupt official. However, his wife said to him, "Will you please send me and the kids home to the village?" Cheng could not understand and asked why. "Auditing the treasury is a fat job. People would swarm to you like flies; disaster may fall on you any minute. I can't bear to see your head being chopped off.""

"Cheng Hong was a man of integrity, the words of his wife made his mind even clearer. He pledged in the name of heaven that he would never take bribery. At that moment, someone sent him a flower pot. He refused and signaled the person to take it with him. The guy dropped the flower pot in humiliation and panic. Many glittering gold bars littered the floor."

After hearing it Qi Yun said, "You've told me the story before, and I haven't forgotten it yet."

"Did I?"

"The night you were named the county party secretary, you were so happy and so was I. We made love in bed like mad. Afterward, I said you must be exhausted and better to go to sleep. But you were so excited and went on and on. You said, *one fence needs at least three poles to stand it up, and a man three friends to help.* To be a good county secretary, you needed the support from your family in addition to your own effort. Then you told me this story."

"Oh, now I remember," said Lu Haoyu. "But at the time you likened yourself to Cheng Hong's wife."

Qi Yun gave out a sigh, and said, "I now understand what you mean. Perhaps I have changed but the change is not what I wanted — I have to. In Hong Kong and Singapore, they pay civil servants high salaries to reduce the temptation for corruption. But at the same time, they also have special anti-corruption agencies. This indicates that corruption exists even with good salaries. We now have a low salary system. A city party secretary earns only 800 or 900 yuan a month; it's not adequate when in office, let alone in retirement. We have too many things to worry about. Under such circumstances, it's not that I intend to push my husband over the cliff. What I want is to trade for a worry-free life in retirement with a slight adjustment on your part in your self-assessment or self-image, in your goal at self-perfection, and all this is done under the conditions of being absolutely risk-free and not harming your external image. The change in me is just this little. Do you really think that my feelings for you have changed and I no longer love my husband? Tell me, Haoyu, is it?"

Lu Haoyu fixed his eyes on the ceiling in silence for some time, and then said, "Qi Yun, I declare that I once again surrender to you. But I must make it clear beforehand. Only this once; there will not be a second time!"

"No second time. Let's hook fingers." She pulled over he husband's index finger and hooked on it with her own.[12]

After hooking fingers, Lu Haoyu let out a long and deep sigh. Qi Yun's eyes sparkled with tears.

Reading Questions:

1. Describe the business model of the drugstore run by Mayor Huang's wife.
2. Comment on the influence of the cultural legacy of traditional China on Lu Haoyu through the two ancient stories.

VII

After that, Lu Haoyu really put the matter of Zhang Zhong on the agenda in his mind. He worked out three contingency plans, after repeated comparisons, decided on the third one: he would call another informal meeting of the four. Huang Shanbai alone could

---

[12] Hooking fingers is folk way of pledging to stick to a deal or a promise. It is usually done among kids but occasionally carried over to adulthood.

not veto Zhang Zhong's candidacy. He could bring the matter to the standing committee meeting. If the standing committee could not agree either, he would then hand the decision to the deputy party secretary in charge of industry. This plus Xu Bing's support would be sufficient. There shouldn't be a big problem. Taking one step back, even if the motion still could not pass through the standing committee, he would postpone the decision. Generally speaking, it would be easier the second time. In any case, he felt that he was able as well as had the power to have it done. The only thing lacking was the courage and the righteousness he would have had were it not a selfish matter. As a result, he kept on putting off the informal meeting, Monday to Tuesday and then to Friday. He eventually abandoned his own initiative on the matter, waiting for Xu Bing and the others to push it while he himself concentrated on other official business.

One day, when he arrived in the office, the first thing he did was to quickly check the memorandum under the glass on top of the desk. The most urgent business was a conference of all SOEs of the city scheduled in the first half of next month. The subject of the conference was how SOEs[13] could get out of their current plight. He did not have to involve himself in the conference preparation. His main concern was the report he was to deliver at the conference. He was reputed among people under him as a leader not easily fooled. He indeed did not trust doctored figures and sometimes downright fabrications that were reported to him up through the government hierarchy, let alone a report based on these figures. Therefore, he always revised the draft reports his staff prepared, sometimes again and again. To do so, he needed to do research to obtain primary information. As to the report for next month's conference, he planned to do it in two phases. The first phase consisted of a workshop of top managers of several loss-making enterprises. In the second phase, he would spend three days to visit frontline workers and middle-level

---

[13] That is, state-owned enterprises, which suffered massive losses in the 1990s and had to lay off millions of workers during their restructuring (many privatized). Turning around enterprises in red is part of local government's responsibility.

managers and staff. Better sooner than later, he decided he would start the first phase that same day. He quickly drew a name list to have his staffer Li Zhijian to notify these people by phone, and the workshop was arranged between 2 to 6 pm that same day.

He just finished drawing the list when Director Liu of the Bureau of Retired Cadre Affairs called, "Secretary Lu, Secretary Gao Qili is hospitalized. He asked about you. Would you go see him if you have time?"

Lu Haoyu said, "I must go, no matter how busy I am. Which hospital?"

Chief Liu replied, "No. 4 Hospital. He lives in the west wing of the residence building for cadres, room 305."

Lu Haoyu said, "You should arrange someone to stay with him in the hospital."

"Already done. Today is the 5th day and he is expected to get out in a couple of days."

"Good. I'm leaving right now," said Lu Haoyu.

Lu hung up the phone and thought for a while before he called in his staffer Liu Zhijian. He handed Liu the name list, instructing him that everyone on the list must be notified before noon. He then wrote an IOU note and told Liu to borrow 2000 yuan from the accounting office. He took the money and set out to the hospital.

Gao Qili, the retired former deputy party secretary of the city, looked not at all as beaten as one would imagine. He looked no different than when he was in office, a clean-shaved head and still tough and high-spirited. He was pacing alone in the hospital room.

Lu Haoyu entered the room and called, "Old Gao!" They had always addressed each other this way.

> *3.3 China has perhaps the world's most comprehensive statistics reporting system. However, it is controlled by state officials whose careers are affected by the statistic figures reported. They therefore are motivated to doctor the figures.*

Gao Qili turned around, shaking hands with a big smile and said, "You should add a modifier. Old Gao, the peasant rancher of Gaojia Village." He took a chair to let Lu Haoyu sit down, while he sat on another.

"You should lie in bed," said Lu Haoyu.

Gao Qili said, "I had acute enteritis. I'm okay now and plan to leave the hospital tomorrow. I need to go to work as soon as I'm back — no problem at all to sit and talk to you.

Lu Haoyu asked, "How is Old Li? Why didn't she come?"

Gao Qili said, "My wife accompanied me to the hospital. She went back when the Retired Senior Cadre Bureau arranged a caretaker. Those four-legged at home have to eat and drink. She had to go back."

Upon hearing this, Lu Haoyu felt a sadness that hurt. He nodded and said, "Old Gao, you've been back to the village for four years and I haven't visited you once. I feel really ashamed of myself. Lu Haoyu is a high-above bureaucrat! A man like this should have been driven from power long ago."

Gao Qili smiled, "I know you twice wanted to come. One was disrupted by the visit of a provincial leader and the other by a washed away road. There's nothing you could do about it."

Lu Haoyu sighed, and suddenly remembered the money in his pocket. He said, "I wanted to buy something for you, but I'm spoiled by Qi Yun so much that I forgot how to go shopping. Besides, I don't know what you like to eat. I have to leave some money so that you can buy what you like." He then laid the cash on the nightstand beside the bed.

Gao Qili picked it up. After counting it, he shook it in his hand and said, "Old Lu, are you bribing me?"

Lu Haoyu said, "Indeed. I ask you to do something for me."

Gao Qili laughed, "A party secretary of a city bribing a peasant? Don't you turn the rule of bribery upside down? If that is the case, then everybody would compete to retire earlier. All right, what do you want? I'll write a note for you right away."[14]

Lu Haoyu said, "What I want you to do for me is this: buy yourself some nutritious food and drinks to strengthen your health. Then I'll be happy."

Gao Qili laughed loudly, and then put the money back to Lu Haoyu's pocket and sealed Lu's pocket with his hand lest Lu would take it out to give to him again. He said, "Listen to me. Let me finish telling you the reason. I know your financial situation very well. You are not well-to-do."

"I am. I have no problem."

Gao Qili said, "That's a lie. It's only about 1200 or 1300 yuan putting your salary and Qi Yun's together. You live in the city and with the prices so high nowadays, how much you can save? Your son just got a job after returning from the south. He must also get married and start a family of his own. Your daughter and son-in-law are both laid off and you have to support them. How can you be wealthy? If you are wealthy, it must be corruption. If so the more reason that I can't accept the money. Don't you know what kind of man Gao Qili is?"

Lu Haoyu said, "Don't worry. So far I haven't done anything corrupt yet. This is clean money." What he said was true, but he left some ambiguity, and because of this he felt rather guilty.

"It's a joke," said Gao Qili, taking his hand back. "The main reason is that my circumstances have improved dramatically. I don't need it. Talking about well-to-do, I'm really well-to-do now."

"It's a lie too."

"It's not a lie," said Gao Qili. Then he began telling his story after he went back to his village. The original intention of going back to his native village with his wife was just a short stay for relaxation in the countryside, and on the way, borrow some money from relatives so that he could overcome the difficulties he faced then. The couple was arranged to live in a vacant house. The owner

---

[14] Cadres used to throw their weight with such hand-written notes, either to request a favor or authorize something to be done by subordinates.

had moved from the mountains to settle in the low land. The village party committee bought the house. There were four rooms, a pig sty, a walled yard and a gate. It had everything. During their stay, his wife became interested in such a pastoral lifestyle. She said it was quiet, the air was fresh, and it was much more comfortable than living in big cities. Gao Qili shared her feeling — it was far away from the noises and rush of cities and from its consumption. It was comfortable and inexpensive, very nice indeed. He told the village party secretary about this. The secretary's family name was Liu; he was a little bent on the back. The villagers likened him to Liu Yong of the Qing Dynasty and called him humpback Liu. As soon as he heard it, the idea of having the old couple to stay in the village for a couple of years emerged in his mind. He said to Gao Qili, "If you stay here, you will not only be able to escape this or that of the city but also become rich."

Gao Qili laughed, "I don't know farming at all; how could I become rich?"

Hunchback Liu said, "You don't have to farm; you can raise cattle and pigs."

"Although I'm still in good health, but after all I am over 60 now, how could I possibly do it?"

"It's just a matter of fodder and feed," said hunchback Liu. "Feed is easy to arrange. Fodder is not hard either. In the winter, we have plenty of hay. In the spring and fall each of the several hundred people in the village can bring some green grass from the field everyday when they came back from the field. That'll be more than you need."

"No, no, not a good idea," said Gao Qili in a hurry. "How could I add burden on the people?"

"It's not a burden; it's mutual help. You don't know how difficult it has been for the villagers to get seeds, chemical fertilizers, and mulch these days? If you stay in the village you will help us big time since it'll be so much easier for you to go to the county government to get it. In addition, if you can obtain for us some poverty relief fund to start a project or two, within a few years, our village will take on an entirely new look. So you tell me, isn't it what we ought to do to help you a little?"

After some thinking, the couple stayed. The first year, his wife raised three pigs while Gao Qili raised three cows. The second year, pigs increased to five and cows to six. By now, the number of pigs stayed the same but the number of cows increased to 13. In between, the villagers helped him a lot, and he also did many things for them. As part of the poverty relief program, a date processing plant had broken ground.

Lu Haoyu was deeply moved by the story. "I never imagined that you maintained integrity all your life but in the end got rewarded in the countryside!"

Gao Qili said, "Once Chairman Mao declared to the world that China had become a country free from both external and internal debts. Today I can proudly announce that I've repaid the 20,000 loan. The few thousand yuan that I borrowed from relatives will also be paid off by selling two cows as soon as I get back. I will then really become debt free. My two sons have both graduated from college, and are both enrolled in graduate school. I have the financial resources to support them through graduate school. I have also supported five village kids, who had quit school because of poverty, and sent them back to school. Look, do you still think that I need your help? I accept in my heart your kindness and sincerity. When I come back next time I'll certainly go to your home to drink with you. Did I explain it clear enough?"

Lu Haoyu said, "Old Gao, you've said it all such that I indeed can't insist anymore."

"All right, this matter is clear now. Let's talk about something else," said Gao Qili. "Looking back, these four years of my life have taught me a great deal about life. You've read many books. Have you read 'The Mottos of Children Upbringing' written by Wu Zhenli of the Ming Dynasty? A few lines of it are carved in my mind. 'When Heaven wants to bring disaster on someone, it always brings him a good fortune first in order to lure him into conceit. Therefore, rejoice may not be warranted when good things happen. It's a test on one's ability to stay cool. When Heaven wants to bless someone, it always brings him some misfortune in order to warn him. Therefore, fear may not be warranted when misfortune falls.

It's a test on one's ability to cope with it.' Don't you think that these four years of mine fit right in?"

Lu Haoyu nodded, "Yes, indeed. To put in a common saying, 'Good things can turn into bad ones, and bad things good ones.' However, coping is the key on how to turn misfortunes into fortunes. You coped well with it and have succeeded in digging yourself out of the hole."

Gao Qili nodded, adding, "Not only got myself out of poverty, my sons have also learned the value of hard work and thrifty. It's so great!"

Lu Haoyu said, from the bottom of his heart, "Congratulations! Old Gao — Oh I forgot you are a hospitalized patient. Did I interrupt your resting by talking to you for so long?"

"No problem for me. You can leave if you are busy. Don't let this affect your work. However, if you are not busy, please stay a bit longer. I have something to say to you."

"I'm not busy. Please say it."

1.7 Notice the pastoral idealism or escapism, some would say, revealed in this scene?

"It may sound like a joke, or a dream if I may. Nevertheless, I did think about it, but living in a mountain village I had no one to talk to. My wife was with me all the time, but you know she's a housewife with limited education. I could not talk to her very well either. Today I've got hold of you, so I'll let it out. Everything."

"I believe I'm qualified as your confident," said Lu Haoyu.

Before one word was said, Gao Qili seemed already in dreamland, leaning back with his eyes half closed. Then, he began, "Although I live in an isolated village in the mountains and far away from politics, whenever I lie on the warm stove bed my mind is filled with things like cadres, political institutions, the state of the party and party members. I thought that many countries provide government officials handsome pay to discourage the temptation of corruption, but our country does not. To be sure, low salaries are not an excuse for corruption, but worries about retirement are also real and we must acknowledge it. So what should we do about it? Can we maintain our integrity under the condition of low pay? I think we can! Of course, many measures must be taken. I have come up with one. Take our city for example. We can select a place not far from the city, and with good transportation — in other words, it's convenient for retired cadres to go to the city and see a doctor — to build a 'New Village of Worry-free Cadres in Retirement.' The city government puts in some money to build some simple farm houses, two rooms for a family. Any cadre who is in financial plight after retirement can go there to farm a piece of land to subsidize his family. With his pension covering the basics and the income from the land, he should have no worries anymore. They can live on the farm when there is a lot of work to do in the field, and return to live in the city after harvest — a lifestyle so to speak. Thus, they have no retirement worries when they are in office and have something positive to do after retirement. Wouldn't it be wonderful?"

Lu Haoyu said, "In addition, they can keep fit and extend their lives. It's to *kill two birds with one stone*."

"There is another advantage. Think about it, corrupt and greedy officials would not go live there — the money they've cumulated is enough for their children and grandchildren. Those who go there are all good and clean cadres. That would draw a clear line between the two kinds of cadres. The social effects of this small village cannot be overestimated. Like the Jinggang mountain base when the revolution first started, it could light up a prairie fire!"

A nurse came in at the time, who told Lu Haoyu, "Chief of Staff Wang is on the phone for you."

"Tell him I'll be there soon," said Lu. He then turned to Gao Qili. "There is a meeting this afternoon. I must go now." The two shook hands vigorously. Lu Haoyu then said, "Old Gao, your integrity is no less than before. Your idea is very interesting. Unfortunately, I'm retiring next year. If I could work for another three to five years, I would let your dream come true."

"What a pity," said Gao, releasing Lu's hand. "Hurry up, don't let me disrupt your work."

Lu Haoyu turned back at the corner of the hallway and saw Gao still waving. He waved farewell back. Gao showed no sign of disheartening, and precisely because of this, Lu felt heavy in his heart and watery in his eyes.

Reading Questions:

1. How does the municipal government attempt to help the SOEs and their workers? Can city governments in your country do the same?
2. How has Gao Qili maintained his integrity? Is his proposal for retired cadres realistic?

VIII

That afternoon, while Lu Haoyu was chairing the meeting, an event took place at home that made Qi Yun worried. It began with a phone call from Lu Wei. "Mom, I have a rather difficult matter at hand. Would you tell me what I should do?"

"What is the matter?"

10.3 When corruption becomes part of the culture, it is extremely difficult to reverse it. In such an environment, it is also extremely difficult for people like Lu Haoyi to survive.

"There is one guy who is a relative of one of my classmates from college. He has been bugging me all day long, insisting on giving me 50,000 yuan in exchange of me asking dad to promote him. He is now GO director of the oil company, but wants to become the vice chief manager. Do you think we should okay it?"

Strictly sticking to Lu Haoyu's "only this once" principle, Qi Yun immediately told her son, "Weiwei, you know your dad. Never promise a thing like that easily."

"But mom, that classmate of mine won't let me say 'no'. He keeps on writing letters and making phone calls. I just got off the phone with his long distance call."

Qi Yun said, "You mustn't add more problems to your father's. Explain to him that your dad never accepts presents. Tell him to work hard and do a good job so that he can be promoted through the legitimate channel."

Lu Wei said, "You and my dad are both behind times. I've said this numerous times but you wouldn't listen. In today's world, 'integrity' does not exist. Do you think people will say that you are clean because you wouldn't accept any gifts? Forget it! They would say that you don't want help, or you feel the money is not enough or the way they sent it is not appropriate. Don't you understand this, mom?"

Qi Yun said, "Let them say whatever they want."

Lu Wei said, "Mom, the guy said he wants to see you if he could not meet dad. Because you are very capable, he'll give up if he runs into a wall with you. What should I do?"

Qi Yun thought for a while, and said, "Bring him here. I'll deal with him."

Lu Wei said, "Mom, you must be cautious. Nowadays people are offended if their gifts are not accepted. If you don't leave them some face when you turn down their gifts, you are sure to make enemies. We can't afford doing that."

Qi Yun said, "Don't worry. I know what to do."

"Then I'll bring him in a while," said Lu Wei.

After hanging up, Qi Yun thought that since the man is a relative of her son's classmate, I'd better give him a warm reception. She prepared a fruit tray and some tea. After that, she sat down quietly to think about how she should deal with the matter so that the guy would not feel embarrassed.

The door bell rang. She opened the door and saw two men standing at the door, one middle aged and the other younger.

"Is this the Secretary Lu's home?" asked the middle aged.

Qi Yun mistook them as whom her son talked about, and replied, "Yes. Please come in," and ushered them to the couch. When the two sat down, Qi Yun asked, "Where is Lu Wei? He did not come?"

The middle-aged man asked, "Who is Lu Wei? We don't know him."

"Then where are you from?" asked Qi Yun. The two hesitated. "Then who are you looking for in my house?"

"You," the young guy said bluntly. Qi Yun became nervous. There had been incidents in which homes were robbed when perpetrators used various pretexts to get home owner to open the door. Are these two robbers? She thought fast and acted fast. She grabbed a chair and stood behind the back of the chair with her hands holding the chair. In case something happened, she could push the chair to block the two men and take the opportunity to escape into the kitchen and close the door behind her. She could also defend herself with a kitchen knife, and call for help from the kitchen window.

The strangers saw her standing. They also stood up, and said, "Won't you sit down?"

"I have a problem with my legs and can't sit. Please sit down." The two sat down again. "Anything I can do for you?" asked Qi Yun.

The young man replied, "Seeking justice."

Qi Yun said, "Then you should go to the court or the discipline committee."

"None of them could solve our problem, only Secretary Lu can."

Qi Yun said, "Secretary Lu is not home. Why don't you go to his office?"

The middle aged man said, "We've been there this morning. His staffer told us that he'd gone to the hospital. When we got there we didn't see any car in front of the hospital. It's obvious we were lied to. We went to his office in the afternoon and were told he was at a meeting. They then drove us out. We have no other recourses and had to come to you."

"I'm his family, not Secretary Lu himself. I only do housework. Please leave."

The middle aged man said, "You have a leg problem, we don't want to trouble you for too long. We have a letter and hope you can pass it to Secretary Lu. We won't trust anyone else with it. They will surely intercept it. But you can pass it to him. We hope you can help."

Qi Yun said, "That I can help. Please leave it with me."

The two stood up and the young man took out a letter and put it on the coffee table. The two then bowed out with apologies written all over their faces. What a scare for nothing! Qi Yun felt her behavior rather laughable, and at the same time apologetic. Had she known, she would have poured tea for them. But on the other hand social order and public security hadn't been good lately. People feared for their lives and property. Leading cadres like Lu were especially targeted by bad guys. They shouldn't blame me for this.

Then Lu Wei called to tell her that the guy had other obligations and would not come today, asking her to wait no more. When she put down the phone, Qi Yun suddenly remembered it was the weekend and her husband should have chicken for dinner. She had to go shopping. As she was putting on the overcoat, she saw the letter again. She remembered the mysterious look on the two visitor's faces. She was anxious to know who they were reporting about, but put the letter on her husband's desk. Then she rushed out.

When Lu Haoyu came home from work, four steaming dishes were already on the dinner table. Qi Yun asked, "Are there activities this evening?"

Lu Haoyu replied, "No."

Qi Yun regretted, "I wouldn't have bought cooked chicken legs had I know this. It's not bragging, these are far less tasty than what I cook."

Lu Haoyu tried it and said, "You did not exaggerate, it indeed cannot compare with what you cook."

Qi Yun said, "Since my husband hates exaggeration the most, how could I *add water in what I say*?"

Lu Haoyu said, "It looks indeed nobody knows one better than one's wife. But I wish it is

4.7 In addition to on-the-job training by position rotations, the CCP also has a large system of Party schools where cadres undergo more formal training and ideological indoctrination. Like universities, some Party schools also offer postgraduate degree programs. See Essay No. 3 for more details

true in all areas." Qi Yun felt a thud in her heart. Her husband implied something.

After dinner and watching the news on the TV, Qi Yun was about to get the letter for her husband when the door bell rang. Qi Yun opened the door and was surprised. "Ah, Mayor Huang!"

Huang Shanbai said while walking in, "Sister Qi, it feels so distant when you address me like that. At first you called me Shanbai, then Old Huang, and now Mayor Huang. You've promoted me step by step all the way."

Qi Yun said, "Isn't it fashionable to address one by his title? Please sit down."

Lu Haoyu was also a bit surprised. He rose quickly, and said, "I've learned the lesson. Please, sit down Old Huang."

"That's better," said Huang Shanbai while seating himself. "We addressed each other Old Huang and Old Lu when we were students. Besides, we are meeting at home."

The two were indeed classmates at the Central Party School 15 years ago. They were buddies together all day long, and frequently chatted past midnight. One night, they got excited with their discussion and sat up from bed. Huang said, "Old Lu, after we graduate from here I hope we two are assigned to the same county, you as the party secretary and I the county magistrate. We'll draw a five year plan to turn that county around and in ten years make it a model county. That way, we would have fulfilled our mission in life."

After graduation, the two were assigned to two neighboring counties as party secretary and county magistrate respectively. Like rivers eventually emptying to the sea, after many position in their respective prefectures, they ended up together in the city of Donghuan. Huang arrived one year earlier to be the mayor, and a year later Lu came to take over the top spot as the party secretary. Their dream came true and they were very happy about it. However, as they say, at home friends feel like relatives, but in the world of officialdom even brothers turn against each other. After only one year, the relationship between them cooled down. They rarely paid each other a visit outside official business. Later on, differences and even friction emerged between the two. That was why the Lu's were surprised with Huang's visit.

Qi Yun hurried to make tea, get cigarettes, and the fruit tray. When it was done, she said to the two men, "You two talk. I'll go see a neighbor."

After Qi Yun left, Huang said, "Today I did not come as the mayor to see the party secretary. Instead, I came as a classmate for a chat."

Lu Haoyu said, "You are welcome indeed. You know me, I'm a lazy man, not good at socializing."

Huang said, "I know. That's why I came to you. Do you feel strange that since we became colleagues we seem more distant to each other? I don't. Even pots, plates, and dishes in the kitchen bump against each other, let alone working together as colleagues. It is very common that the first and second leaders do not see eye to eye or even become enemies reporting on each other behind the back or undermining each other. It is considered as in good relationship if the two still can sit together like us now. Do you agree with me on this judgment?"

Lu Haoyu refilled Huang's cup with tea and said, "Your assessment is on target, and I appreciate your honesty.

Huang Shanbai was filled with emotions of all kinds. He sipped the tea and said, "Friendship — friction — friendship. This is probably an objective law. True friendship will eventually return."

Lu Haoyu nodded, "It'll come back to stay when we retire next year."

10.4 Here is a vivid description how the notorious practice of buying office works. Corrupt officials also sell office posts to the highest bidders.

Huang nodded also. "By then, we may even do something together. But think about it, why should we wait till retirement? Isn't it better that we do it in the final year we are in office?"

Lu Haoyu said, "That is even better. I'm the squad leader and I should control myself better and do more self-criticism."

"As a matter of fact, there's nothing serious at all, just some difference of opinion on personnel matters. It's easy to solve."

Lu Haoyu appeared to be very interested, asking, "Let it out. What's your solution?"

Huang drew a mouthful of smoke, sipped some tea, and then began, "The same article, some say it's good, and some say it's bad. The same opera draws also different opinions whether it's a success or failure. The same goes for cadres. Looking from different angles, people see different things in the same cadre. So what do we do about it? Respect each other's opinions. I have counted roughly that before we retire next year, there will be another 28 vacant positions to be filled. So, all together we will make 40 appointments in our last year in office. I respect your opinion and give you 20 to reflect your judgment. I myself am satisfied to have 15 that you also support me on. As to the remaining five, we must also take into consideration the deputy secretaries. Of course, this can't be laid on the table. It's between you and me."

Lu Haoyu was deeply shaken by these shocking statements. He looked at this classmate of his and the latter appeared relaxed and confident. This sent aftershocks throughout his body like after a major earthquake. Immediately a rhyme circulating in society at the time jumped into his mind, "To get rich through cadre appointment is to always deliberate on it but never announce it so that the highest bidder gets it." He felt how distant it had become from their late night chats at the Central Party School. He adjusted his posture and tried to calm down himself. Then he lowered his voice and whispered into Huang's ear, as if making fun, "Old classmate, you mean we two hold a big auction together?"

"You don't have to put it that way," Huang said with a smile.

8.2 The privileges enjoyed by cadres incite resentment from the people. In recent years, land grabbing, forcible demolition of people's houses, and pollution — all caused by local governments' pursuit of GDP growth — have led to widespread protests and a tense state–society relationship.

"What I mean is that we move every cadre who should be moved while we are in office. We don't want to leave the favor to others, do we? Each time you promote a cadre, s/he owes you one, no matter s/he openly acknowledges or says it or not. This is common psychology. You and I are humans also. Therefore, we shouldn't feel ashamed of such thoughts."

Lu Haoyu fell into a silence. He did not expect that Huang could have said such things and did not know how to react at the time. Then his chief of staff Wang called. Lu picked up the phone in a hurry, and Wang also sounded loud and urgent. "Secretary Lu, the peasants at the development zone are making trouble. They have surrounded the headquarters for an hour now."

"Where are the leading cadres?"

"Only the few in the headquarters. I have reported to (deputy) Mayor Liu."

Lu Haoyu said, "All right."

Huang Shanbai already heard it. He stood up and said to Lu, "I'll go deal with it. I'll keep you posted." He then left in a hurry.

Having seen off Mayor Huang, Lu began pacing up and down in his living room, then entered his study. He was not worried about the protesting peasants. Huang was capable of dealing with it. He was however still in shock from what Huang Shanbai had just said. His mind was roaring in chaos and he could not sort it out. Then he saw the letter on the desk and opened it. He first looked at the signature. It was "masses who dare not use real names." He then read it carefully.

Qi Yun returned at this time. "The neighbors had to go out to take care of some business. So I have come back earlier. Huang Shanbai has left already?"

Lu Haoyu nodded and asked, "Where did this letter come from?" Qi Yun told him about the two unexpected visitors. Lu Haoyu sighed heavily, and said, "Today I have had such an extraordinary day. In the morning, I went to see Gao Qili in the hospital. In the afternoon, I got this letter and at evening Huang Shanbai came. Everything comes together."

"Gao Qili is hospitalized?" asked Qi Yun. "How is he?

"He's fine."

"How did your talk go?"

"Very frank."

Qi Yun further asked, "Did you read the letter? Whom is it reporting on?"

"Huang Shanbai."

Qi Yun said, "I just heard from Old Li that Huang has begun lobbying in the province. He wants to be promoted to vice provincial level. But so far as I know most of those who have been lifted were prefecture party secretaries and governors — very few mayors. But again it's hard to tell. Things are done by people. It makes a great deal of difference whether you make an effort. We may well end in a situation that the mayor of Donguan city moves to the province while its party secretary goes home to take care of his grand-son. If that comes to pass you'll feel resentment, but it'll be too late. You could only blame yourself for being too passive."

Lu Haoyu leaned back on the chair with a knot in between his eyebrows. He said to his wife, "Qi Yun, I'm having a huge headache as if my head's going to split up. I cannot sustain the pressure anymore."

Qi Yun said in a hurry, "Go to bed. Take another sleeping pill."

Reading Questions:

1. What is the purpose of Mayor Huang's visit to the Lu family? What did he propose?
2. Comment on the generational differences between Lu Wei and his father. Which China would you feel more comfortable with: one filled with people like Lu Wei or one populated by people like his father? Why?

IX

It was Saturday the next day. Qi Yun went to the fair early in the morning. Lu Haoyu made himself a soy bean drink and two boiled eggs. Then he left home. He did not return the whole morning. Qi Yun waited till one in the afternoon and began to wonder. There had been cases that he had to entertain guests at the dinner table for official business, but he had always called to let her know. What happened today?

At dinner time, he still did not come back. Qi Yun could no longer stand it. She called both his chauffeur and secretary. Both said they did not see him. The two then went to search all around the city in restaurants, hotels, and other places he might be, but turned up nothing.

Qi Yun was scared. She called Lu Wei home and told him, "Your dad has disappeared. What should we do?" and told him about the whole day.

Lu Wei said, "He usually lets us know when he is attending a meeting. Why he has not told anyone this time?" He went into the study and soon called from there, "Mom, didn't you see the note he left on the desk?"

"Really? I always clean the desk for him every day. I did not do it today. Besides, he usually leaves his notes on the coffee table. Let me read it." On the note it was written,

"Qi Yun, I'll take a rest and be alone for a couple of days. Don't make a fuss looking for me. I'm not a child and will not get lost. I will be back Monday morning when the working week starts."

Qi Yun sat down on the sofa in silence. Lu Wei picked up the note and carefully read it once more. "Strange!" said he. "Where has he gone? Couldn't he rest at home over the weekend? Why does he hide out even from his family? I feel something unusual this time. I can't figure it out."

Qi Yun said, "He said he had an extraordinary day yesterday. I think it has something to do with it." She then told Lu Wei about the day before.

"He wouldn't change his mind, would he?"

"It's hard to say," said Qi Yun.

"Mom, you are very good at analysis and know dad best. In your judgment, would he change his mind?"

"Maybe, or maybe not. It's hard to say," said Qi Yun. Then she leaned back on the sofa thinking silently. After a while she suddenly remembered that she had not had dinner yet. She got up slowly and went into the kitchen.

Lu Wei did not get any comfort from his mom, and became really worried. He must now figure out a way on his own.

Reading Questions:

Why does Lu characterize the day he just had "extraordinary"?

Proverbs:

— Flowing water never goes bad; the door hubs never gather termites. (流水不腐, 户枢不蠹)
— There is no wave without wind. (无风不起浪)

Overall Questions:

1. As a result of the fundamental social transformation in China described in the story, is the Chinese society become more similar or more different from your society? What is driving social change in China? In your opinion, does life become better or worse as a result?
2. What do you think about Qi Yun's solution to the worries about retirement? Is she a corrupt person or does she have a point? Putting yourself in her shoes, what would you do?
3. Lu Haoyi in many ways typifies the model cadre the CCP want all party members, especially the leading cadres, to be. What behavioral principles and beliefs the CCP has instilled in him, judging from his thoughts and activities in the story?
4. What are the clues in the story that expose the CCP cadre corps' rural peasant roots?
5. Lu Haoyi and Huang Shanbai were classmates and shared the same ideal when they were at the Central Party School. Why did they turn out so differently? Do you think they will converge as Huang confidently assumes during their frank conversation at the end of the story?
6. How do you think Lu Haoyi will deal with the anonymous letter reporting the corruption or wrong doings of Mayor Huang, given he himself is on the verge of caving in to corruption?
7. Obviously Lu Haoyi is at a turning point in his life and is suffering from great agony over which direction to go. What do you think his

decision would be after he returns from his self-imposed seclusion? Give your reasons.

8. Is the husband–wife relationship as depicted in this story different from such a relationship in your culture? If yes, explain in what ways?
9. Is the kid–parent relationship as depicted in this story different from such a relationship in your culture? If yes, explain in what ways?
10. What do you think Lu Wei will do if he has to "figure out a way on his own"?

Exercises:

1. Go online and find out as much as possible about the Chinese notion of *guanxi*, write an analytic essay about it.
2. Form two teams to debate on whether a good public official could survive with integrity in the Chinese environment. Is Lu Haoyi a figure of author's idealization? Can a person like him really exist in the Chinese environment? Carefully sort out your respective reasons.
3. Describe the on-going and rapid social changes in China and their impact upon the lives of cadres as well as ordinary people.
4. Describe the strengths and weaknesses in the Chinese political system. Draw a reform plan to change it for the better and discuss the feasibility of your reform program with a professor of political science.
5. Enact the "knock-head" meeting of the four leading cadres.

STORY 4: ADMINISTRATIVE ACHIEVEMENT[1]

Xiang Dong[2]

This story reveals a crucial aspect in China's economic boom: local officials are intimately involved in development. They are powerful economic actors with a lot of resources in their hands that are not ordinarily available to private entrepreneurs. For example, they can tear down people's houses for development projects; they can sell land to raise capital and offer concessionary policies to attract capital from elsewhere.

When Liu De, the new township director was taking his morning jog, secretary[3] Xiao Mao greeted him on the way. He took Liu's jacket and ran after Liu. It was not long before the two were panting and dripping sweat. They then started towards the hillside, shaking their arms as a kind of relaxation exercise. At the sign post "Golf Court," Liu stopped and asked Xiao, "Care for a few swings?" Xiao Mao managed to squeeze out a bitter smile. "The sign's put up alright but we cannot play because the court is unfinished."

Liu looked at Xiao with a question mark. The latter wiped the sweat off his face. "The golf court required too much capital and the investor pulled out halfway. The township does not have that kind of money and the project is thus aborted."

---

[1] *Zhengji* (政绩) in Chinese. It refers to job performance and the results delivered by an official, especially the chief executive of a local government.
[2] From Wang Yaowen *et al.* 2011. *Being an Official (youguan zaishen)*. Nanjing, China: Jiangsu People's Press.
[3] Here the word is used in its ordinary sense of a supporting staffer, *mishu* in Chinese instead of *shuji*.

6.1 Almost every local government in China sets a growth rate target for the year and then tries everything in their power to achieve that target. One way of promoting growth is to attract foreign direct investment.

"So large a stretch of land becomes idle just like that?" asked Liu De.

"Indeed," said Xiao Mao in resignation.

Liu could only let out an "Oh."

In a low voice, Xiao said, "We have here a man nicknamed 'Big-Head Luo', a fortune teller reputed as 'semi-deity.' How about I call him here to take a look after breakfast?" Liu De looked at Xiao but said nothing.

After breakfast, Xiao Mao brought Big-Head Luo to the golf court and told him, "Do some calculation and tell Director Liu what he should do with this land as he has taken over the leadership of the town."

Big-Head Luo narrowed his eyes in a line and folded up his sleeves. He extended his right hand, using the thumb to press on the fingers on the left hand quickly. He then opened his eyes suddenly, "This land is at the foot of the hill and hence very fertile. If you plant fruit trees here, it'll be very good administrative achievement."

Liu looked at Xiao Mao, who quickly shook his head, "Not a good idea. This golf court was built by the former township Director Wei. The farmers protested for several days when their land was acquired by the government. To destroy the golf court right after Director Wei was transferred makes him look bad. Besides, here originally was the orchard of the peasants. What would they say if the land is changed back from golf court to orchard?"

Big-Head Luo smiled but said nothing.

Liu De thought for a while, and said, "As it is often said, *'Serving a term as a public official, one must bring concrete benefits to the people under his jurisdiction.'* Are there any other ways around?"

Luo stroked his goatee beard with a sigh, "The golf court is almost reduced to a pasture."

Xiao pointed at the nose of Luo, "Wasn't it your idea to build a golf course?"

Luo looked at Xiao, murmured, "That company wasn't very smart to pull out."

Xiao wanted to say something but Liu De stopped him. "Big-Head Luo's words give me an idea. Building a ranch here may not be a bad idea."

Xiao Mao nodded quickly, "Indeed, indeed!"

Big-Head Luo lined up his eyes again, "Director wants to build a ranch? I have an idea." Director Liu looked at him with great expectation. Luo cleared his throat and said, "I suggest building a hunting range. Raise deer and charge people for hunting them. It should be better than just a ranch."

Liu De waved his hand, signaling Luo to leave.

Looking at the backside of the departing Luo, Liu De told Xiao, "This Big-Head Luo plays gods and ghosts every day. You go arrange with the police to confiscate his tools and forbid him to tell fortune. If he does it again, arrest him!"

Taking charge himself, Director Liu finally convinced a company to invest three million yuan to turn the golf court into a deer park.

As the breeze gently blew, deer could be sighted from time to time amidst the grass. For a time, it became a popular place in the region. However, most of the hunters were higher level state officials, which made it very difficult for the company to collect the fees. Before long, 100 or so deer were slayed and the company sank into red. The manager confronted Liu De, who was desperate *as an ant on a hot wok*. He reported the matter to upper level leaders, who promoted him elsewhere.

The next township director was Wu Gang.

As soon as Wu settled down, he called the township secretary Xiao Mao to show him the hunting field. He scanned the grassland waving in the breeze and knelt down to dig up some soil from the grass roots. He smelt it and told Xiao that this place seemed quite suitable for planting fruit trees. Xiao Mao told him, "This place was originally an orchard. Director Wei turned it into

3.7 In an authoritarian system, officials are often promoted regardless of their public reputation. A leading cadre may be hated by the people who suffered under him but could still be promoted or transferred elsewhere to start afresh. In some cases, the people want him or her promoted (and voted for that) as long as he or she leaves.

a golf court; Director Liu built a deer park. If you, Director Wu, return it to orchard, how could you justify it as your administrative achievement?"

"Oh," but Wu said nothing.

Xiao Mao suggested sending for the fortune teller Big-Head Luo to see what he had to say. By following his ideas, the previous township directors all got promoted.

Before long, Big-Head Luo showed up in a hurry. After seeing the fresh soil under the feet of Wu Gang, he paused for a while and said, "This is land of good *fengshui*; why don't you build a cemetery on it?" Wu was surprised and turned to look at him. Luo smiled back, "Also plant fruit trees in the cemetery, both of these are money makers. It's like *killing two vultures with one arrow*."

Wu waved his hand and Xiao took out 200 yuan and gave it to Big-Head Luo, who nodded and left in a hurry.

When Luo was far away, Wu Gang turned to Xiao Mao, "Plough the grass land and plant fruit trees first. Then do some calculation to see how many tomb sites can be divided. If each sells for 30 gram, what would be to total?"

Xiao nodded, "OK, OK. I'll work on it right away."

As he was about to leave, Wu Gang said, "This Big-Head Luo; he practices superstition all the time. You go and notify the police to confiscate his tools and prohibit him from fortune telling. If he does it again, put him in jail!"

Wu Gang clapped his hand to get off the dirt, and gave out a long sigh. He took out from his pocket a pack of cigarette and lighted one. The smoke crawled up his face and circled around his head, before melting into the air.

Proverbs:

— If you have money, you can make the devil push your grind stone. (有钱能使鬼推磨)
— Serving a term as a public official, one must bring concrete benefits to the people under his jurisdiction. (为官一任, 造福一方)

Reading Questions:

1. Exaggeration is used in this story. What are the main points the author is driving at?
2. Judging from the story, who owns the land in China?
3. Why do you think every new township director wanted to put the fortune-teller away after adopting his advises?
4. Why did each new town director turn the unfinished golf court into a different development project rather than follow up the earlier project and complete it?
5. Is the communist ideology compatible with superstition? Why do the two go together in the story? What does that tell you about Chinese communists whom you are likely to run into on the streets of China?
6. Why did the deer range end up losing money?
7. What does the last phrase "melting into the air" symbolize?

Suggested Exercises and Assignments:

1. After reading this story, do you have better ideas why the entire China is like a construction site where so many new projects are started every day? In your own words, explain to a friend of yours the role played by local government officials in China's "economic miracle."
2. Ask an economist how GDP is calculated and how the projects in the story are likely to affect China's GDP figures, presuming similar stories have taken place over and over again across the country.
3. Paraphrase the story from your memory and write it down. Compare what your memory captures with the original text. What is missing and what does your memory pick up?

4. Bureaucratic Entrepreneurialism and Local State Corporatism

As described with greater details in Essay 1, China's market economy emerges without a wholesale privatization as in other former communist countries in Eastern Europe; it started as the decentralization reforms in the 1980s dissolved central planning and released state actors, such as local governments, SOEs, townships and villages, and other organizations in the party-state establishment, from rigid state control to become market players. While private entrepreneurs have emerged as a formidable force in the economy, these statist actors are still the dominant players in the marketplace because of their advantages in resources control and their regulatory power. A scene of vibrant "bureaucratic entrepreneurialism" has emerged. Local governments are the main promoters of local economic development and all sorts of state sector organizations besides SOEs, such as colleges, universities, high schools, hospitals, research institutes, government departments or agencies and so on, pursue business opportunities in the open market. Cadres heading these entities are bureaucratic entrepreneurs because they are simultaneously embedded in the party-state hierarchy and respond to incentives in both the market and the state. Competition and rivalry among them provides a crucial dynamism in the Chinese political economy that has helped to drive the three decade long economic boom. The SOEs initially suffered from the disadvantage of tight state control and rigid internal organization structure when they began competing with new enterprises. The massive loss they incurred led to their restructuring in the late 1990s in which most of the small and medium-sized enterprises were privatized. The remaining ones under the central government are eventually consolidated into 100 or so giant state-owned corporations. By 2012, China became the second largest contributor to the Fortune Global 500 firms, next only to the United States. The overwhelming majority of firms made to the list were SOEs. The top

(Continued)

(Continued)

management and the board are mostly appointed by the Organization Department of the CCP; they are CCP cadres who may return to the government some day.

Meanwhile, development-oriented local governments have organized local growth machines and invented many local development models, the most famous being the Wenzhou model, the southern Jiangsu model, and the Pearl River Delta model. Many organizational innovations were undertaken by local governments, who reorganized local businessess into a kind of diversified corporations, with the government acting like the board of directors, the departments in charge of industries like branch corporations and the enterprises they controlled like subsidiaries. Such jurisdiction-based local growth machines are dubbed by some China scholars as "local state corporatism." Compared to private corporations, it controls much more resources, not only economic but also political, regulatory, and organizational resources. Financial innovations in the first decade of the new century led to the establishment of thousands of local financial vehicles through which local governments raised capital (using land and other state-owned assets as collaterals) for infrastructure, property, as well as industrial development. Such investment-driven development presents considerable financial risks and has led to large over-capacity in almost all industries. It also created the dependence on the export markets.

STORY 5: AN ENDLESS STREET

Liu Zhengquan[1]

Only 10 meters left before the end of the street. A hint of smile finally climbed up the face of Lin Jiancheng and the smothering anger began to subside. When he reached the end of this street, this small city would be out of his sight forever. Tomorrow, he will be transferred to a bigger city.

But for now, his status is still the county party secretary of this small city. Walking through this street has been his wish for a long time.

This is a bustling street lined with stores and shops. Five years ago, however, the street was dusty in sunshine and muddy in rain. He was almost stabbed while relocating the residents living on the street. Several times, he was surrounded by people who called him all kinds of names. He finally understood the true meaning of the proverb *"It's hard to budge even an inch"* that his middle school teacher taught him.

He also learned the meaning of the phrase *"as if walking on thin ice"* when the construction of the new commercial street was completed. For many other county officials had their eyes fixed on his position, hoping he would head toward a big fall on this street project. Fortunately, his foresight has proven beneficial to all and his superiors regarded him differently now.

> 8.3 In recent years, land grabbing, forcible demolition of people's houses, and pollution — all caused by local governments' pursuit of GDP growth — have led to widespread protests and a tense state–society relationship.

---

[1] From Wang Yaowen *et al. Being an Official (youguan zaishen)* Nanjing, China: Jiangsu People's Press, 2011.

More than once, Lin wanted to take a walk on this street to hear the praises the shopkeepers and business owners would shower on him but he was stopped short by reason: *Do not show off when you are prosperous*! He suppressed the urge to walk on the business street for the time being. In a few hours, he would no longer have problems with this city. Lin sneaked away from the farewell party thrown for him. He knew that the party would be followed by a big banquet. Such welcome and farewell ceremony is an old tradition in the Chinese world of officialdom. Besides, the city he was being transferred to had jurisdiction over this county-level city. *The tea gets cold upon the departure of the guest* (人一走, 茶就凉) won't be a problem this time.

He was a bit annoyed at seeing the Urban Construction Bureau chief Song Tao when he barely walked for 10 meters on that street. Song faked the expression of being surprised and said, while shaking hands with Lin, "Secretary Lin, it's so kind of you to come out this late to inspect people's life." Lin Jiancheng smiled rather bitterly: he really did not want to run into his subordinates on this street. He came for a walk, a walk with a feeling of accomplishment and private joy. Lin was also surprised to see Song here at this late hour and asked Song about it. Song put up a dutiful expression and answered, "Recently, our bureau has received quite a few letters from citizens complaining about the rude attitude of the law enforcement. I came out to see for myself."

"*Nonsense,*" said Lin to himself, "*He must have ulterior motive.*" And he was right: Song grabbed Lin by hand and said, "It must be our fate that we meet today. Let us get together at the hotel of our urban construction department as a way to say goodbye to you."

Lin now realized that he was waiting for him here. When this street was first open for business, he joked to Song that one day when he stepped down he must come to take a walk on this street. He did not expect that Song kept that in mind.

After going through great trouble to get rid of Song, Lin merged into the stream of pedestrians. However, before the second 10 meters was finished he ran into Business Bureau chief Li Gang. Li was better than Song in persuasion. He pointed to the foreigner he was with and introduced, "This is Tom, the foreign businessman

I invited. He is here to investigate the investment environment. As the top leader of the locality you must do one more favor to our county before you leave. Tonight we are having dinner together and you must come. After all, we all are trying hard to contribute to the prosperity of our county!"

Lin Jiancheng wanted to smile but could not. For such a small commercial street there was no need for foreign investment. He was just making use of the foreigner. Besides, this guy was no Tom; he was Peter, the foreign teacher at the county's No. 1 Middle School. Li Gang probably did not know that, although Lin's own portfolio did not include education, his wife was an English teacher at that middle school. She even had a picture taken with Peter.

Lin did not want to expose his lie. "Leave the opportunity to the new party secretary instead," said he nonchalantly. "Give him a boost from the start so that his work can go smoothly. It shouldn't be only me alone to make contribution to economic prosperity, right?"

Being rebuffed, Li Gang felt awkward. Lin cast him a cold smile and walked briskly away.

> *6.3 Attracting investment is a top priority for many local governments. They often divide the target amongst their cadres, each responsible for attracting certain amount of capital inflow as a quota they must fulfill in a year. The Chinese phrase for it is* 招商引资.

Before he began another 10 meters, he felt a pat on his shoulder. When he turned he saw the smiling face of the Industrial and Commercial Bureau chief Mr. Wu.

Then he saw four or five people in uniform behind Wu. "What are you up to?"

"Secretary Lin, you are just being a little too bureaucratist today," joked Wu. "We are performing 'Everyday is March 15th'[2] activity. It is predestined that we meet today. We would like to invite you to our beat to give instructions on our work. You must lend your support."

---

[2] March 15 is the Consumers' day in China.

Lin frowned slightly, saying to himself, "Predestined? You ambushed me here."

It was after considerable trouble that Secretary Lin finally got rid of Wu. By now the joy was all but gone.

Further along were the ambushes by the directors of the Bureau of Public Health, the Bureau of Finance and several other work units. Lin thought to himself, this street is only about 200 meters long; how come it is more difficult to finish than the Long March? Several times, Lin was almost kidnapped into cars.

Lin got smarter. For the final 10 meters he took out his hand phone and pressed "110"[3] in case someone "chanced" into him again. He would without hesitation press the dial button and let the police to deal with those people. He was really too tired of dealing with them himself.

In the last 8 meters, someone grabbed his arm. There was only one person in this small city who dared to grab his arm — Chen Ming, director of the Bureau of Retired Cadres' Affairs. Chen would retire in half a year; he had nothing to worry about and no one to be afraid of. Chen Ming said, "Secretary Lin, let's have a drink together!" His mouth already smelled strong of alcohol. Lin Jiancheng pressed the dial button and told the police at the other end, "Someone is making trouble on Commercial Street, please help!"

3.4 When Chinese officials retire they do not just go home. They are also taken care of by the Bureau of Retired Cadres of the local government or government bureaucracies where they used to work. The bureau is in some way like the Department of Veteran Affairs of the United States.

Within three minutes, the police arrived, as if waiting for this trouble. The police officer first loaded Chen Ming into the police car and then saluted Lin Chengjian, "Sir, please come with us also."

Lin Chengjian asked "Why should I have to go?" The police officer said "We have to investigate the case since you called in

[3]Chinese emergency number.

the police. This is the regulation and we would greatly appreciate your cooperation!"

Lin was speechless. He then said, after thought it for a while, "Is it OK that I go with you after I finish walking this street?"

The police officer was dead serious, "No!"

Lin Chengjian had to climb into the police car. He closed his eye in smoldering anger but heard a familiar voice from the driver's seat, "Secretary Lin, you surrendered yourself! Let's go to the 'Big Tycoon' and let us give you a farewell banquet."

Lin opened his eyes and saw at the steering wheel was no other than the police chief Zheng Tong. This Zheng Tong was said so close to Chen Ming that they *may as well wear the same pair of pants*. Lin turned around to look at Chen, who was faking drunk, snoring.

With the snore, the car dashed out of the final 8 meters of the street.

Proverbs:

— Clear conscience never fears midnight knocking. (不做亏心事, 不怕鬼敲门)
— Reshape one's foot to try to fit into a new shoe. (削足适履)

Reading Questions:

1. In your political and legal system, is it OK for a mayor to forcibly relocate people in order to clear the place for commercial projects that may benefit more people? Do you think Secretary Lin was justified in his actions? (For decades, the entire China was like a construction site and therefore forced massive relocation happened all the time)
2. Why Secretary Lin subject himself to such dangers (almost getting stabbed, being called names, and ill-wished by his colleagues etc.) to embark on this project? What did he hope to get from it?
3. Why do you think those cadres tried all kinds of tricks to get secretary Lin to their places when it was the last night Lin stayed in that city?

Suggested Exercises and Assignments:

1. Find out as much as you can about "work unit" (*danwei*) as a communist institution. Write a five-page essay to explain it.
2. Find out as much as you can about the Chinese concept of *guanxi*. Write a five-page essay explaining it.
3. Enact the 200 meter street walk of Mr. Lin.
4. Paraphrase the story from your memory and write it down. Compare what your memory captures with the original text. What is missing and what does your memory pick up?

STORY 6: THE DISADVANTAGED AMONG THE PRIVILEGED

Pu Yang[1]

The first thing that I did upon returning to Jiangnan City was to get online. I found out that it was true that my videos and interviews with the Chinavoice Net and Tencent Net were all taken down. I became anxious: Had I made some top leaders in the provincial party committee unhappy? Hopefully it would not develop into a political incident. But if it came to pass, it mattered little if I lost my position but my young buddies at the China voice Net would all lose their jobs. In panic, I called the newspaper to ask them what had happened. They replied, "Nothing to worry about. The title used by the reporter is a bit too scary. The provincial propaganda department called and ordered it to be taken down, and so we took it down — simple as that."

"Did they say somebody is going to be punished?" I was still worried.

"Not at all. They did not say anything else." It did not sound as if they were in trouble and I felt relieved completely.

But still I was unhappy. I did not say anything wrong. If the title was improper then all they had to do was to change it. It was not necessary to pull down the whole thing. Many people would think I was in great trouble. As I was fuming, Zichun, a friend of mine who worked for the commentary forum of a website, called to invite me to participate in an online exchange with netizens at 2 o'clock that afternoon. I turned him down with excuses. He appeared to understand my mind perfectly and said, "I admire

---

[1] From Pu Yang's autobiography *Guanlu* (The road in officialdom). Beijing: Whysbooks 2011. The author, whose real name is Jiang Zongfu, used to be a deputy mayor of a city in Hunan province. In disillusionment, he eventually quit his job and took up teaching.

leaders like you who dare to speak their minds. I know you are under great pressure recently. In particular, the public misunderstands you on the issue of 'assets disclosure for leading cadres'. The purpose of this program is to give you a chance to clarify yourself. Our forum is a reputable one and we hope you can give our audience a chance to exchange with you face-to-face. ..."

Moved by his sincerity, I agreed reluctantly. During the real-time exchange with netizens around the country, many asked me again to disclose my assets. I complied without reserve: 2,600 yuan per month salary[2]; zero savings; a 179 m^2 apartment on which I owed 150,000 yuan and 20-year mortgage; 30,000 to 40,000 yuan of stocks, and that's it. To my big surprise, less than two minutes after finishing the program the news release from some websites went: "Assets disclosure by deputy mayor of Jiangnan: no savings but speculating on stocks." I was furious but helpless. I phoned Zichun, "Now you can see that I am right that it's not yet the time for assets disclosure. No sooner than I finished the program, people are already making up stories, and they call 30,000 to 40,000 yuan 'speculation on the stock market'? That's ridiculous! Media and business are indeed a terrifying combination!"

Zichun laughed. He was used to such things.

To ordinary people, government officials are affluent and consequently there is strong hatred toward officials. In fact, it is a misunderstanding. There are disadvantaged groups among public officials. Lives for the really clean and upright officials are hard. Take the municipal tourist bureau for example. It was an agency with little power and resources. I often joked that even if you embezzled the entire budget of the bureau you would only get less than 20 years prison sentence. The bureau had a 20 or so staff and per capita annual income of slightly more than 30,000 yuan. However, half of them had family members who were laid off. Check up my resume online and you would find that I had never served in a powerful *danwei* with lots of money. My wife was laid

---

[2]This story is set in 2000s and hence the salary is much higher than that of Lu Haoyu in Story 3, which is set in the 1990s.

off also and my family could barely make ends meet. One thing going for me was that I could earn some extra from writing every year. When the organization department made it official of my appointment as the deputy mayor of Jiangnan, many friends and relatives said that it was my turn to make a fortune. I said to my wife: "My dear, who doesn't want to drive a BMW and live in a mansion? I also want to make a fortune but this is a fortune that I cannot seek. If I do I will expect to spend the latter half of my life in prison. In one word, if you want to be an official, forget about making money; if you want to make money, don't become an official. Therefore, do not expect me to get rich in this life time."

I often quipped, "To be a decent person you must be able to endure obscurity and to be a good official you must be content with a simple life." You may be able to endure obscurity if you make an effort but it is extremely difficult to live a simple life. For a really clean and upright official will go through endless troubles.

The greatest trouble is donation. You must donate to poverty relief, to helping the disabled, to charities, to earthquake relief, to flood victims and so on. If your portfolio includes education, you will have to donate to education funds, relief for students from poor families etc. Faced with major disaster reliefs, charities and public causes, the leading cadres must serve as exemplars. If others donate 100 yuan, a leading cadre must donate at least 200. It adds up to a major expense in a year. I ran into several such donation campaigns when I first arrived at Jiangnan in 2005; I was almost crushed under the burden. One day I went to the cafeteria of the municipal Agricultural Commission to have lunch after making a donation, I found the municipal Party Secretary was there also. I was puzzled: he must take the lead at each donation campaign but his salary was not high; how could he manage it? Maybe the *danwei* that ran the campaign provided him with the money so that he was just making a show of it. Or the general office of the municipal government may be actually footing the bill. I am a person who can never hide anything and I always speak my mind unfiltered. I raised my doubt directly to the Party Secretary. He did not get angry; instead he laughed and replied with humor, "Look, even Comrade Zhiyuan has such ideas; no wonder, the masses could not understand. As leaders we are having a hard time explaining ourselves. If you donate more, they would curse us: look how generous they are — these corrupt officials who have embezzled a great deal. If you donate less, then too you get the blame: look how miserly they are, these son-of-a-bitch corrupt officials who embezzled so much public fund! …"

This reminded me of assets disclosure for leading cadres: wouldn't the masses think the same way? It is inevitable before the trust is established between the masses and the leading cadres.

The second biggest trouble is the high debts cumulated in maintaining human relations. The masses only see the grey side of leading cadres collecting money from hosting events. They do not know that they also have to spend a great deal in maintaining *guanxi*. An ordinary citizen who goes to a wedding banquet or funeral only has to pay 100 — or 200 yuan maximum. This amount is considered insufficient for leading cadres. The targets of gift-giving for leading cadres are either colleagues or, more likely, municipal leaders. Each time it would be between 500 and 5000 yuan. It is a big expense in a year. A leading cadre of my rank usually does not have to spend anything on meals or cigarettes but still no money is saved in a year. Where does the money go? It is not enough for gift-giving. I am not someone who likes to kiss up to superiors and therefore do not have to spend on big gifts. However, there are numerous small gifts that must be paid. There are so many colleagues plus the members of the leading squads of the *danwei* that fall under my jurisdiction. You will have to go when any of them have family events such as weddings and funerals. Otherwise, they will say that you are cold and do not know how to behave properly. Of course, I do not have to worry so much if I were just a little "unclean." Didn't many leaders get reimbursed for the gifts they send under some seemingly legitimate claims? How many of them paid with their own money?

The third biggest headache comes from the family. Despite being on the same ranking as other public officials, others lead a life of opulence but your wife is laid off and you have to struggle to make ends meet. Such sharp contrast is difficult for family members to swallow. My wife is mild in temperament and generally above materialism. Nevertheless, she has complained from time to time. She would babble when I come home, "As deputy mayor I do not expect you to get rich but it isn't asking for too much to find a job for me, is it? That husband (of someone I know) is only a township party secretary and yet he managed to transfer his wife to the financial bureau. Is it really true that you are less capable than a township party secretary?" I eventually became impatient with her on this issue, "Don't blame me that you lost your job. Blame yourself for your incompetence." My wife was resentful and called me useless. A family war inevitably broke out.

Of course, there are understanding people too. At the end of 2009, school teachers were planning a collective petition at the city of Yunmeng for unpaid subsidies that the government had promised. In order to stop them, the municipal party committee assigned every municipal leader a few schools to placate the teachers. I was assigned to No. 5 Middle School. I met with the representatives of the teachers in the principal's office. During our exchange we began to talk about our salaries. I asked them, "Do you believe my monthly salary is less than yours?" All teachers shook their heads and nobody believed it. I then gave them a detailed account of my monthly income. They were all surprised and felt pitiful for me. I said to the teachers, "I have no other intentions in sharing with you the information about my income than to make two points. First, the status of teachers is higher now and, second, we all face difficulties. Therefore, we must understand each other. Jiangnan is facing budgetary difficulties but no matter how difficult it is we will try to find a way out — we cannot short-change the engineers of human souls. Municipal party secretary Liu has said that no matter how difficult it is he will find a way to solve the problem. Teachers first, cadres second, and leaders the last; we'll do our best to solve the problem before the end of the year!"

The sincere talk moved the teachers to tears and an incident of collective petition was thus prevented.

Since I expressed online my view against family assets disclosure for leading cadres, I was questioned by many netizens: "Is it a case of officials watching each other's back or is it cowardice?" In fact, it was neither. I am not against property disclosure but believe it is not the time yet. Labeling me as an "opponent to property disclosure" is a common way for websites to increase their traffic volume. They took my word out of the context. They said, "Why did he make the comment that 'assets disclosure for officials will cause social unrest'?" It was based entirely on my understanding of the real conditions of China and the real conditions of the grassroots society.

I believed that premature implementation of assets disclosure will first of all intensify the resentment among the masses against the widening income gap and hence the hatred against the officialdom. Because our national economy has gone through the central planning period, the commodity economy period, the planned commodity period and now the market economy period, the asset structure of officials has become extremely complicated; even courts would not be able to draw the lines between legal, illegal and grey incomes. The most damaging is the very large income gap. Even if we suppose all the incomes are legitimate, the masses will feel seriously deprived if the assets of cadres are disclosed. For example, the CEO of an SOE would have family assets worth more than ten million yuan. We are all tax payers but why he should earn so much more than us? How can the masses not feel angry and resentful? The purpose of property disclosure is to maintain social tranquility by punishing corruption; disclosure causing social unrest would defeat the purpose. Therefore, it is better to disclose gradually. First, set up the mechanisms and then institutionalize them; finally, such practices of disclosure would become a habit. Only then, everything will fall in place. Disclosure done in a haphazard way will result in the masses further losing confidence in the officialdom. Disclosure will also expose the extent of nepotism. The officialdom is filled with people with blood ties — husband and wife, father and son/daughter, brothers, sister-in-laws, brother-in-laws etc. In many localities, tribal forces have taken over the government. Can the masses really accept this?

In China, it is very possible that I am the first official who has disclosed personal assets. As soon as I disclosed them, various problems emerged. First of all, many people did not believe that I was that "poor." Even without embezzlement, a deputy mayor would

have collected enough by only attending a few ribbon-cutting ceremonies and accepting a few "red envelopes" a year. Secondly, my
daughter has lost face, being teased by her schoolmates, "Isn't your
dad a deputy mayor? How come your family still owes so much in
mortgage loans?" Thirdly, my wife is even more embarrassed.
Despite being laid off, she is still presented as the wife of the deputy
mayor. But now everybody knows how "poor" we are. In a world
overflowing with materialistic desires, how many people still take
pride in having few possessions? Finally, it goes without saying that
all this puts great pressure on me. My superiors and colleagues have
kept silent but I am positive about the resentment they feel toward
me: "So many leaders haven't yet disclosed their assets; why should
you do it ahead of them? Isn't it clear that you are forcing the leaders to follow your footsteps?"

Honestly I had not thought of it that way. I just wanted to figure
out a way to safely and steadily implement a good system.
I have two suggestions on this. First, notarize the properties before
a leading cadre is appointed to a post; notarize them again at the
time he or she is considered for promotion. If the increase of assets
is too large without proper cause, then this cadre is not fit for promotion. In this way, corruption can be prevented. When leading
cadres get used to such procedure, resistance to property disclosure
will be minimized. The second suggestion is to push for public
disclosure of the expenditures by leading cadres. This can be implemented immediately. This is an area where corruption is more likely
to occur and public disclosure can effectively prevent it.

5. Political Participation

Generally speaking, political participation refers to activities by
private citizens designed to influence government's decision-
making. Different political systems grant different levels of freedom and different forms of political participation by citizens. In
a democracy, election of political figures into public offices is the
primary channel of political participation. Such option is very

(Continued)

(Continued)

limited in China. Legal channels are also very limited and other institutional channels are often ineffective — such as the "letters and visits department."

On the other hand, the demand for political participation is on the rise. In general, the demand comes less from some ideological or philosophic ideals than from people's practical need to address personal grievances. These include forcible demolition of homes and businesses by local governments for development projects, land grabbing or inadequate compensation for land acquisition by the state or developers, corruption and power abuse by local cadres, pollution and environmental degradation, wage disputes, "not-in-my backyard" investment projects and so on. As the formal and legal channels of participation are limited or ineffective, common forms of political participation are street protests, strikes, online campaigns, seizure of government offices or officials, blockage of traffic, incessant petitioning, sit-ins in front of government buildings, riots and so on. Official figures put the number of "mass incidents" (*qunti shijian*) that involve 10 or more people in the hundreds of thousands per year in recent years. At any given day, there is a large population of petitioners from around the country surrounding various party and government office compounds in Beijing. The government so far has been successful containing these as isolated and localized incidents and is fairly responsive to the demands raised. As a result, China is relatively stable despite the mounting problems and conflicts inevitably associated with rapid socioeconomic transformation.

The role of the People's Congress and People's Political Consultative Conference has been elevated somewhat in the reform era and seeking membership in these bodies has become an important channel of political participation by private entrepreneurs and other social notables. The government has tried to expand grassroots elections of petty officials such as village

(Continued)

(Continued)

heads and community leaders. The deputies of the township and county level people's congresses are by law popularly elected. However, the ubiquitous presence of the organizations of the ruling party in society has effectively neutralized such elections since only the CCP has the wherewithal to put its own candidates on the ballot while shutting off other candidates it deems undesirable or threatening. This trend was particularly evident during the Hu–Wen regime (2003–2013) which made maintaining social stability a top priority. The recently installed Xi–Li leadership has indicated some willingness to allow the development of non-politically sensitive "social organizations" such as charities, environmental groups, trade associations etc. that can help the government to maintain order and deliver services. The impact of these organizations in mobilizing political participation is yet to be seen.

Proverbs:

— It is easy to dodge a spear that comes in front of you but hard to keep harm away from an arrow shot from behind. (明枪易躲，暗箭难防)
— Water can float a boat; it can sink it also. (水可载舟, 也可覆舟。)

Reading Questions:

1. Why does the narrator — the deputy mayor — call cadres like him "the disadvantaged" in the Chinese officialdom?
2. Should public officials disclose their income and family assets? Are they required to do so in your country?
3. The deputy mayor has disclosed his family assets; why is he against a general disclosure for all leading cadres?
4. What are the overall priorities of the Chinese state revealed from the story?
5. When the deputy mayor says, "Media and business are indeed a terrifying combination!" Do you agree with him? Compare with the media in your country — is China unique?

Suggested Exercises and Assignments:

1. Find out the propaganda department on the organization chart of the CCP and the main role this department plays.
2. In general, do you think the deep mistrust of the public in the official-dom is justified? Give your reasons.
3. Describe the pressure from the new media on public officials in China.
4. Debate: Is low salary the reason for corruption?

STORY 7: THE TAO OF CAREERISM
IN THE WORLD OF OFFICIALDOM

Zhong Daoxin[1]

I

Another working day ended, people poured out from the office buildings of the Downtown District Government of Beijing, and rushed impatiently for their sweet homes. Once back home, they would relax, recover, recharge their batteries, open their mails, make love, and live a life that truly is their own.

Deputy District Magistrate Kim Yet approached the window of his office. He stretched his neck and spinal cord as far as he could to look at the newly finished 30 story building — Kimghan Hotel — situated right across the street from the District Government. The name said it all: it was a joint venture between firms of China and South Korea. Somehow, Kim Yet was stubborn of the opinion that it was a fake joint venture. In numerous cases of Sino–foreign joint ventures, the foreign part of the investment was either absent all together or withdrawn soon after its initial appearance. Even worse: some of the so-called "foreign capital" was in fact the money of Chinese firms. They found a way to move their capital off-shore and then re-invest back into China as "foreign capital."

> *7.2 Privileges derived from political power are creating an elite class that is becoming a major source of frictions and popular resentment in the Chinese society. The politics developed around this class may well determine China's future.*

[1] From Guan Shanyue *et al. Shitu* (Careers with the Government). Beijing: Zhongguo Xiju chubanshe, 2002 (Vol. 1)

117

The incentive for them to do so was the preferential treatment the Chinese government granted to foreign inventors. This way, large quantities of state-owned assets dissipated during this detour abroad. Such policy was in essence a form of discrimination against domestic firms. Kim talked about this at several conferences, but was ignored. However, he believed such policy would eventually be scrapped, just like the FEC (Foreign Exchange Certificate).

Apparently, Kingham Hotel was hosting a large banquet. In a span of just ten minutes the number of sedans at the gate in increased dramatically. Guests were being ushered in by several pretty girls in traditional Chinese costumes. It was obvious that this was an up-scale event, as Kim Yet studied the rows of luxury cars glittering under the sun. In addition to such status symbols as car phones, another unmistakable indicator of VIP was found on the license plates — almost all of them started with the letter "A." The really powerful just decide on a letter for the license plates of their cars. The cars headed under this letter would never need to pay at any toll booths or parking lots. They would make left turns at any street where such turns are prohibited or make U-turns in places where such turns are banned.

Kim Yet cut short his train of thoughts and returned to his desk. He was 43, in good health and had a wholesome family. His late father started as a leader of student movements and became the deputy party secretary of a university after Liberation.[2] His career ended as a bureau chief in the Ministry of Education. In other words, he was a middle-level cadre. However, a middle level cadre in Beijing is "middle-level" in its classic sense, for there are too many middle-level cadres in Beijing. Many of those who would be considered "high ranking cadres" in the provinces do not even have a government supplied car in Beijing.

Kim Yet joined the Communist Youth League early, before the Cultural Revolution, when he was at middle school and was soon promoted to secretary of the Youth League branch at the middle

---

[2] "Liberation" is commonly used in mainland China to refer to 1949, the year the PRC was founded.

school. The school he attended was a key middle school, where the only thing people valued was a good grade. Not many students wanted to become a cadre because student cadres were involved in many chores that took time and energy away from study. However, Kim Yet believed such extra work would enhance one's leadership capability and therefore enjoyed doing them. As a result, he was naturally categorized as a "loyalist"[3] when the Cultural Revolution began, and participated in it reluctantly.

Later on, he was the first of the school to volunteer for resettlement in the countryside and requested to be sent places where living conditions were the hardest. As a result he was sent to Yan'an County, Shaanxi Province.[4] There his organizational skills and leadership ability found a free realm to be fully utilized, and soon he became a model youth and represented the 80,000 "sent down" youth from Beijing to visit and study Mao's model production brigade — Dazai Brigade in Shanxi province. He was later on recommended by the commune to attend Beijing Industrial College as a "worker-peasant-soldier student."[5]

The county government held a pompous "seeing off" ceremony for his group of "workers-peasants-soldiers students." At the ceremony, he vowed with tears that he would come back to continue to serve the peasants after graduation.

However, he was retained by his *Alma Mater* as a lecturer — nobody by then still remembered his pledge to return anymore — none

---

[3] The Cultural Revolution generally divided people into two broad coalitions — the loyalists who supported the *status quo* and the rebels who wanted to turn the establishment upside down. However, often each side accused the other "loyalists."

[4] Yan'an was the capital of the communists during the Second World War in a remote region on the borders of three of China's poorest provinces in the northwest. It was during the Yanan decade (1935–1945) that the CCP matured and found its Chinese identity.

[5] The whole higher education ground to a halt as soon as the Cultural Revolution broke out in 1966. Later on, as part of Mao's education reforms new college students were selected from among the working masses without the usual entrance exams and other academic qualifications. They were called "worker–peasant–soldier students."

is more forgetful as the masses. In a sense, the masses have no memory; all they have is mood.

He stayed at the college for only a year before he requested to be sent down again to base-level units to gain first-hand experiences. The college leaders first praised him and then approved his request. He was sent to a military factory in southern China. The leader of that factory wanted to assign him to the technology department but he insisted to be assigned to the shop floor, where he served as a technician in the production team for three years.

During these three years, he worked conscientiously. He drew the blueprint, even a draft print, with uttermost seriousness. Every day after the shift when everyone had left, he would clean the machines and sweep the shop floor. At first, co-workers laughed at him, believing that he was trying to make a name for himself. Gradually people got used to it, so much so that they missed him dearly as the workshop got dirtier everyday during the few days of his honeymoon leave.

5.3 "Only Mao knew what the Chinese people were thinking and how to run the country"? With the country being ruined by the Cultural Revolution, Mao obviously would not be considered a great manager in the West. But this is beside the point; what people like Kim Yet admired was his ability to sway the entire nation at will. Notice what is valued in the Chinese political culture about a politician. Mao's ability to connect with the masses and speak their language underlies his continued popularity among segments of the population even today.

He was now fully conscious of what he wanted to accomplish — he was playing strategically. His guiding thought was that China was way too chaotic now but chaos would inevitably lead to new order; when order returned there would be a great demand for people with good education and practical experiences. College educated people may not be hard to find, but those with a combination of education and experiences would, and he would be one among the few.

Such thinking, still profound even now, came from two sources. One was his extensive reading — even before he went to the countryside he had read "The Khrushchev Era" and "The New Clan," and of course Mao's works. Unlike others who read Mao simply because it was trendy, he took it seriously. He gained a deeply appreciation of the greatness of Mao from the readings. Only Mao knew what the Chinese people were thinking and how to run the country. The reading during his years in the countryside became more diverse: literature history and philosophy, etc. He was the one who read for practical purposes. He did a great deal of thinking and was also able to tie it to real-life situations. That was why he did not turn into those intellectuals who Mao described as "the more they read, the more stupid they get." The second source was the teachings of his father. Being an intellectual within the party, his father could read many internal confidential documents and also experienced many political movements. After he obtained the doctor's diagnosis of liver cancer, he hid away the lab report and began a series of lectures to his only son about politics and political skills. The latter was rarely heard before 1976.

Because of his conscientiousness, organization skills, and fairness, he was promoted to the director of technical department of the factory in 1977, and a year later deputy factory manager, then director of the municipal office of science and engineering for national defense, then director of the professional affairs office of the municipal economic commission, almost one step up per year. As director of the professional affairs office, he served as member of a Chinese delegation negotiating with a multinational group organized by the World Bank. The Japanese members of the delegation expressed their strong desire to invest in China. However, because of historical reasons,[6] the Chinese side lacked enthusiasm. Such thought was in the back of everybody's mind: Japan is capitalist and we are socialist. Capitalism is always the enemy of

---

[6] Referring to the Japanese invasion of China during WWII.

socialism, not to mention the hatred developed between the two nations from as early as the Jin Dynasty. These ideas and emotions subtly dominated the whole negotiation process. Just before the end of the negotiation, Kim Yet went to the hotel room of the head of the Chinese delegation — deputy commissioner of the State Economic Commission. Commissioner Ding's secretary was a middle age man with an air of "having seen it all." He tried to turn Kim away with "the commissioner is about to retire for the night." Kim waved the heavy document folders, claiming important matters to report to Ding. The secretary put up a poker face and with a "matter of business" voice, said, "No matter how important is the matter, you will have to wait till tomorrow."

"Isn't he leaving tomorrow?"

"You can come to see him in his office."

But Kim persisted. He knew once Ding returned to State Economic Commission, it would be impossible for a cadre of his rank to see him.

The noise at the door drew Commissioner Ding from inside. Ding allowed Kim Yet to come in. The commissioner was indeed about to go to bed. He just came out from shower and was in pajamas and slippers, reading a newspaper.

"What's up, young man?" said Commissioner Ding kindly, nodding for Kim Yet to sit down.

Ding was known as an "industrialist" among China's high-ranking officials. He was a college student in Shanghai when the war with Japan broke out. With youthful zeal, he went to Yan'an. After graduating from the Political and Military Academy of the CCP, he was assigned to work for the industrial department of the government. At the time, the border region had nearly nothing of industry except textiles, grain processing and machine repairs. It was this pitiful little industry that determined his whole career. Before the entire country was liberated, he was sent to the Northeast to take charge of the hydroelectric power industry.

Manchuria was the largest heavy industrial base of China and the CCP, even though it was still based in Yan'an, understood its importance. Whoever had Manchuria was in a position to take over the whole China. This ran contrary to the ancient Chinese wisdom that whoever controlled central China was in a position to control "all under heaven," but it was true then. He became truly a manager of heavy industries during his years in Manchuria. Later on, he was assigned again to Shanghai to be in charge of the textile industry there. He was just over 30 at the time and in his prime. Soon he was put in charge of the whole industrial sector of Shanghai. At the time, the industry at Shanghai was almost synonymous to modern industry of China. But unfortunately before long he ran into conflict with the Soviet advisors on policy issues.

It was the honeymoon period in Sino–Soviet relation and whoever got in the way of this relationship — no matter for what reason and in whatever manner — would meet with sure misfortune. For in comparison to political interests vested in the overall relationship between the two countries, any other interests were minor and local. Ding was about to be stripped of almost all his positions when one of his former superiors lent a helping hand by transferring him to the State Economic Commission to become an inspector. Later on, when Sino–Soviet relation dropped below zero, he was assigned to Daqin Oil Field.

Industry is different from politics; it requires certain scientific method in its management. Ding thus again found his stage, one on which his talent and experiences were fully utilized. He was soon restored to his previous rank and even promoted a bit. But when the Cultural Revolution began, he was dragged away by the workers of Daqin Oil Field from Beijing (where he was in his new position) back to Daqin to be subjected to the "dictatorship at the proletariat." He lost one eye when he returned to Beijing.

After 1976, he was back at State Economic Commission in charge of planning. There was little a planner could do because the then top leaders were enormously ambitious, hoping to rebuild the country

4.6 Documents' flows are the main channels of power network in the system. The intention of the authorities and public opinions are all channeled through them. They were his daily must read.

with another "great leap forward." They produced an ambitious plan for national development accordingly. However, there were many problems with this plan: it far exceeded the national resource base and had a skewed distribution of industrial investment. This time he did not oppose it head on. Instead, he resisted passively by staying away under the excuse of illness. He re-emerged when the "whatever faction"[7] lost in the political struggle.

Kim Yet had heard a lot of stories about the deputy commissioner, and that was why he dared to come to his room in such manner. When seated, he began at once: "I know your time is precious, I'll make my report brief." The central idea of his report was that Japan was a pragmatic country and underlining their thinking and behavior was an intense nationalism. Therefore, their first concern here was not about capitalism versus socialism. It was instead national interests; political ideology was irrelevant to them.

Commissioner Ding was a bit amused when he looked at the young man with the one eye left from torture. He paused for about one minute before he asked, "So the Japanese are sort of like us: it doesn't matter what the color of a cat is, as long as it catches mice?"

Kim Yet nodded.

"Anything else?"

Kim Yet shook his head.

"We have chatted for so long, but I still don't know your name, nor your work unit," the commissioner asked as Kim Yet stood up ready to say goodbye. Kim told him, but did not believe the commissioner could remember it."

The next day, the meeting was over. Although there was no substantive progress made during the conference, the participants' minds were liberated to varying degrees. As well put by Commissioner Ding in his concluding remarks: "Liberation, to liberate a city,

---

[7] Huag Guofeng, Mao's hand-picked successor, declared in 1976, in an attempt to claim legitimacy on Mao's endorsement that whatever Mao said, he would follow and whatever Mao had decided he would obey. His faction was thus dubbed "whatever faction."

this or that. The most difficult is to liberate one's mind." Commissioner Ding did not forget Kim Yet though. He transferred Kim to State Economic Commission to become the section chief in the Bureau of Non-productive Business Management. This was a section chief at the central government — a half step higher in rank than a section chief at the local government as Kim had been till then.

In 1985, Shenzhen needed cadres badly and requested Beijing to send them some. The Personnel Department at SEC recommended Kim. However, Commissioner Ding wouldn't let him go. He told Kim, "Work with me for another couple of years till I retire. Then you can leave." Naturally, Kim agreed. In the eyes of ordinary people, Shenzhen was a land laid with gold, but Kim did not think himself as a gold rusher and therefore did not have to go there. Commissioner Ding did not eat his word. Before he retired, he sought the opinion of Kim and recommended him to become the deputy magistrate of Beijing's downtown district.

Kim Yet opened the files on his desk and began reading attentively. His days would be fully occupied by meetings, receptions and inspections. He could only read these official documents in the afterhours. Documents flows are the main channels of power network in the system. The intention of the authorities and public opinions are all channeled through them. They were his daily must read.

It had been three years since he came to the Downtown District; as his wife put it, "three years of toil." At the beginning, the district party secretary assigned him to be in charge of public health and family planning. To an ordinary person, these are trivial and yet difficult jobs with little to gain from them. However, he believed that to be an official was to manage public affairs and it made no difference what kind of public affairs. As long as you did it well, you'd be promoted just the same. Therefore, he performed every job perfectly and earned several medals of achievement from the government. All the while he followed the motto "there's no small matter in Downtown District," which is the crystallization of the experiences of many predecessors for many decades. The reason is simple: many top cadres of the party-state lived here.

For instance, these high ranking cadres or a central government organ would issue an order to clean up the street; you could get into serious trouble if you did not comply or comply to their satisfaction. His predecessor was forced into early retirement because of something like this. To be sure, his early retirement was only two months earlier, but if you had the backing of some powerful figure above — not the kind derived from kinship or other blood ties, for these are predetermined — but the kind growing out of appreciation of your work, and nobody raised the question of your age at the succession, you then could have another term.

This graduate of Beida[8] (class 1953) would ordinarily not even touch alcohol, but got drunk at the farewell party thrown by the District Government for him and other retirees. He raised his cup to Kim and said: "There was a saying in the late Qing Dynasty," and after citing the proverb, which was rendered in archaic classic Chinese, he continued, "You are not a graduate of Beida and you majored in engineering. You probably don't understand it. But I'll bet after 3 or 5 years in my position you'll know it very well."

Kim wasn't indeed a Beida graduate, but he understood the saying. Roughly, it meant that it was bad luck for a county magistrate if he happened to be headquartered in the same city as the provincial governor; and much worse if he was stationed in the capital city. For he would not enjoy the power and pomp of a "parental official" in the shadow of more powerful figures. However, Kim looked at this matter from a dialectic perspective: from a different angle a bad thing was also a good thing. For instance, if you are diligent enough to do a superb job in public hygiene, in greening the city and maintaining good public security, the return to your effort would be much higher in Beijing than if you are stationed elsewhere.

Nevertheless, doing a good job is not synonymous to single-minded shoe shining or sycophancy. For example, the year before, a cadre under his jurisdiction sought his instruction regarding a proposal made by a local business executive to build a statue of the God of Longevity in a park at the company's expense. At first, he wasn't

[8] Peking University.

paying much attention and asked casually, "how much would it cost?" The answer was fuzzy "in the 300,000–500,000 yuan range." Kim got angry: Some people treat 300,000–500,000 yuan as if it was 3–5 yuan. But he kept his cool, reminding himself of the motto "No affairs in the Downtown District are small affairs." The department that the cadre was in charge of had been in existence for a very long time and must have accumulated broad and deep connections in the locality. He asked, "A statue costs so much? Does it include the land use fee?"

The reply was that the park management would not dream of charging a land-use fee on such a hard-to-come-by opportunity. Kim knew that this was a national park. Although it was located in his district, he had no real authority over the leading cadres of that park. "Strange, why are they so generous this time?" Kim asked, pretending to be perplexed. The cadre was eager to show to his boss his background and connections, and soon poured everything out.

9.2 Senior Chinese officials are often supported by a personal staff office made of secretaries specialized in various areas, including taking care of the senior officials' daily life such as food, clothing, entertainment, health care etc. These secretaries are an important source of cadres because their current boss usually makes sure they rise steadily in the system. They are the source of influence of the senior officials after they retire and they themselves often form a fraternity helping each other in their careers even after their boss passed away.

His Venerable Old Zhang, a retired high-ranking official of the Party, a revered and influential figure, came to the park everyday to take a stroll. It would be his 80th birthday at the end of this year. How pleased he would be if a statue of the God of Longevity appeared in the park at this time? Of course one could not just build an ordinary statue out of concrete. It must use real materials, a gilded copper statue.

Kim once again played dumb, asking, "Isn't he already retired?" That cadre obviously enjoyed the role of a teacher, and began elaborating on the secret of successfully navigating the labyrinthine of the world of officialdom: Some people occupy high offices but do not have real power. Others however remain powerful even after they retire, or become more powerful sometimes. Power does not originate from formal positions. Power is influence. That's why to please his Venerable Zhang was a good investment. He further elaborated his idea, this time from the perspective of human nature. When people get old, they return to childhood. Like children, they are easily pleased by small vanities. But unlike kids, what they give in return to their pleasers are not candies but political power.

Kim Yet quickly learned everything about the matter. The idea of building a statue of the God of Longevity came from Old Zhang's former office director[9] and the CEO of the company that offered to foot the bill used to be Zhang's personal secretary in charge of Zhang's living matters.

However, Kim decided that he could not give the go ahead. No doubt, Zhang would be pleased if he approved the project, but ordinary citizens would not be happy. Nowadays, the most precious thing is a piece of greenery amidst the high rises. The park in question was located right in the heart of the city and hence the favorite of everybody. He often saw families relaxing there with kids chasing each other on the lawn. Nobody with a conscience would ever forget such a "happy family" scene.

But he did not directly veto it. Instead he brought it to the district party committee meeting, because he knew nothing could be kept secret nowadays. The more secretive it was, the faster the news leaked. To use the metaphor of the market: news is like a commodity; the scarcer it is, the higher it is in demand. Instead of discussing the issue at the committee meeting, he proposed to send the matter to the District People's Congress. The district party secretary agreed immediately, understanding his intent perfectly.

---

[9] Equivalent to chief of staff in the American political system.

As expected, the "matter of God of Longevity Statue" was swiftly voted down. The People's Congress meeting is neither the mayor's business meeting nor the district party committee meeting. At People's Congress meetings, everybody has one vote. The vote of an ordinary deputy is legally equal to that of the chairman of People's Congress. That is why people would continue bickering about the mayor or the party secretary after their requests were turned down at government or party committee meetings; but it is unheard that someone would continue to appeal to the PC chairman after his proposal was voted down by People's Congress. That's also why Kim Yet thought that People's Congress was a great invention. But, of course, the main agenda of PC meetings is screened by the district party committee, or at least discussed informally among the main leaders of the district beforehand.

The successful disposal of the issue of "the Statue of the God of Longevity" increased Kim Yet's weight on the scale of the District Party Secretary, who promoted Kim to replace the managing deputy district magistrate when the latter was promoted to a position elsewhere.

When Kim Yet finished all the documents on his desk, the banquet across the street at the Kimghan Hotel was also winding down.

Discussion Questions and Exercises:

1. Draw a time line of the PRC history and try to fit Kim Yet's personal history into it (and the histories of other figures in the story as you go along). How did the larger history shape the life of the protagonist?
2. Why did Kim insist to be "sent down" repeatedly? In your opinion, did he benefit from his long experiences working at the bottom level of society?
3. Discuss the role of *guanxi* (personal connections) in Chinese politics: how does it shape careers, power, and influence?
4. Compare the life and career trajectories of Xi Jinping and Kim Yet and find out the main parallels and differences.

II

As soon as Kim Yet turned on his Compaq, planning to jot down some information and thoughts, someone knocked on the door.

"Come in please," Kim Yet showed no sign of irritation. Good human relations is a must for his job.

Two men and a woman came in. Judging from their clothing, Kim decided that they are either community cadres or teachers of primary or middle schools. And as soon as they began to talk, Kim knew it was the latter.

"We want to see the District Magistrate or Party Secretary to discuss matters of our school," the middle-aged woman began.

"Please sit down, teachers." Kim Yet poured tea for them. If the visitors were community cadres he would save this part because they are all cadres and played by the same rules. Furthermore, if he is too nice to his underlings, they may lose the sense of distance and propriety. Without either, the government would not be able to function properly. But school teachers are different; they are intellectuals or, in ancient terms, they are the "literati."

And there should be clear distinction between "literati" and "officials." He still remembered a story: once, a not-so-famous architect went on a business trip to a Central American country. A few days after he arrived he suffered from a heart attack. That was an "underdeveloped country" with poor medical facilities. The doctor at the Chinese embassy there suggested that he return to China for treatment. However, there was only one flight to China a week. Fortunately for him, one of his former students was the deputy director of the CAAC's local liaison's office.[10]

1.2 Since Wudi Emporer of the Han Dynasty (reigning between 140 and 86 B.C.), intellectuals as public opinion leaders were known as the "uncrowned kings." Teachers in the Confucian tradition also serve as role models for their pupils.

---

[10] CAAC stands for Civil Aviation Administration of China.

"You are in luck," said his student. "So-and-so has been on an official visit to Central America and here is his last stop. He'll return to China tomorrow. I'll arrange for you to travel home in his plane."

The architect was of course overjoyed. Early next morning he went aboard the plane. About one hour later, the staff members of so-and-so came in. They saw the architect but none said anything. It is quite normal for official airplanes to offer rides to people, just like the trains offer ride to the friends or relatives of those associated with the railway — the captain, the director of the railway station, or a crew member, etc. People usually are discrete enough not to ask questions. So-and-so was the last coming on board, still waving his arms to those farewell sayers at the airport. Just as the crew was about to close the door, he saw the face of a stranger, and asked, "Which *danwei* are you from?" The architect told him. So-and-so thought for a moment and asked, "How did you get on the plane?"

The architect had been a teacher and role model all his life; so he told him the truth. But so-and-so flew into a rage, pointing to the gate, "Get out!" The architect got out with hand covering both his chest and face. Those farewell people were puzzled as well. The poor architect's condition got worse and he almost died in that country. It took several months for him to recover after he got back.

> 4.5 "Which danwei are you from?" This used to be the most terrifying question and the most effective way Chinese officials exercised power, because almost everyone used to belong to (many still are) a danwei, which is an integral part of the party-state hierarchy. It could bring down on you with the full weight of the entire political system.

Later on, the architect happened to be a deputy of the municipal delegation to the annual National People Congress session. Kim Yet also attended that session, representing the Downtown District Government. Together with a few other deputies the architect summoned so-and-so for a hearing. At first, so-and-so was confident — he'd been through thick and thin throughout in his political career. However, soon he felt the heat and apologized, but the architect would not let him go, and more and more deputies joined the hearing. In the end, it took a senior official whose rank was higher than so-and-so to make the peace. A few months later, so-and-so's retirement was announced.

When Kim Yet told his wife the story, she couldn't believe that an NP deputy had so much power. Kim explained to her, "The architect probably did not indeed have such powers. The real reasons for any high-ranking official's downfall are politics. The architect provided an opportunity for the political opponents of so-and-so. It may amount to nothing that a man tripped and fell; it is also nothing that a car drove by on that road. But if you fell at the same time the car drove by, then you are in trouble." His wife still could not understand it fully, but Kim Yet learned a lesson from the incident: you can exert pressure on cadres under you but you must give intellectuals some leeway even if such freedom is only superficial.

The female teacher claimed to be the principal at Guanghua Elementary School.

"I'm the executive deputy magistrate of the Downtown District. You can speak to me." Although education was not in his portfolio, but the word "executive" in his title meant he could take over any business.

One of the male teachers handed him a report. Kim Yet quickly finished reading it. "Please go ahead," said Kim to the male teacher, who had taken out a pack of cigarettes but was putting it back in his pocket when he saw the "No Smoking" sign on the desk.

"I know about the merger of Guanghua Elementary with Hui Elementary. The District People's Congress okayed it." Kim Yet indeed knew it very well. Guanghua Elementary was demolished together with the street blocks around it in an urban renewal project, the same one that brought in Kingham Hotel. The merger was intended to solve the employment problems of the former Guanghua Elementary staff. However, at the time when the bulldozers flattened the area, the majority of Guanghua students were re-assigned to other schools. As a result, the student body of Guanghua at least halved — only eight classes were added to the

Hui Elementary whereas the former Guanghua Elementary had 24 classes. The result was that there were too many teachers. Schools now were generally on a fixed budget contract; accepting unneeded teachers would incur financial loses.

"I graduated from a secondary teacher's college and since then have worked in education all the way till now. I was the principal for six years and according to the document of District Education Commission I am of full section chief rank. However, the Hui Elementary refused to treat me as such!"

Kim Yet knew that a section rank would not accord her much additional benefit. Judging from her age, her salary should far exceed that of a section chief, perhaps even higher than a department chief. But still he promised, "I'll check the matter out with Hui Elementary."

"They would not make arrangements for me, a former principal, let alone the curriculum director and the director of supplies of our Guanghua Elementary." The woman raised her voice even higher, "They wouldn't accept even a single one of us."

"I'm afraid the last comment was not a complete assessment of the situation," Kim Yet said, pulling himself back to increase the distance from the visitors.

"They only picked a few good teachers." The director of supplies spoke in a Shandong accent, but the woman principal cast him a stern look — she still possessed some authority over him.

"I'm a distinguished teacher of high school, but they only treat me as an ordinary teacher," the curriculum director showed Kim Yet his old job contract. "Don't you think they are so unreasonable?" He then handed Kim Yet his certificates and repeated. "Don't you think that they are unreasonable?"

"Let's analyze the concrete situation," Kim Yet opened the certificate and went on, "The board only certifies your qualification." He began to read. "The Municipal Board of Professional Assessment, after careful evaluation, hereby certify that so-and-so is qualified as an advanced teaching professional." Kim turned a page and continues, "In accordance with the regulations on the procedures of hiring, so-and-so is hired as advanced teacher." Kim returned the certificate to the curriculum director. "If nobody hired you, you won't be able to take the position despite your certificates, just like me. If I was not passed by 50% votes by the District People's Congress, I wouldn't be able to become a deputy District Magistrate."[11] He was very familiar with the procedure.

"In the 1970s, I invented the "Combination Method of Teaching" and my paper was carried by many newspapers and journals." The director of curriculum took out some old newspapers from a brown envelope, "look" he said.

Kim Yet browsed through them and found these were all published in 1977 and 1978; the so-called "Combination Method of Teaching" is nothing but a version of Mao's "education combined with workers and peasants."[12] There's absolutely no value at all today. He returned them to the director, who opened his mouth as if saying something but stopped.

Kim Yet stood up, using his body language to indicate to his guests that it was time for them to leave. All the three were sensitive enough to stand up. "Teachers are the engineers of the human soul. Comrade Xiaoping also told us that his biggest mistake was in education," said Kim Yet while walking toward the door to see the teachers off. "I'll deal with the problems you raise as soon as possible."

The three put on expressions of gratitude.

Returning to the office, Kim Yet jotted down the concerns of the three teachers and wrote his instructions: "The Bureau of Education should work on this matter and report to me within one week." He made a photocopy of it from the fax machine.

This was his way of doing things. The government bureaucracies were stiff with inertia. Nothing moves if nobody pushes it. Despite that they used to be principal and directors, these teachers must have mastered enough courage to come here. It is a deeply embedded habit of the Chinese people to avoid seeing a government

[11] Increasingly, candidates for public office nominated by the party must pass a vote by the People's Congress; those who fail to draw a certain percentage of approval votes (in Kim's case it was 50%) would be automatically disqualified.
[12] Mao's populist education philosophy holds that education not only has to serve the ordinary people but the ordinary people — the workers and peasants — should serve as teachers.

official wherever and whenever possible. But on the other hand, he also believed that these were not top-notch teachers. They had long resumes and many professional certificates but not good teaching skills. "If they indeed possessed such skills, they would have been grabbed by employers long ago," Kim Yet said to himself. Nowadays, it is easy to find a good bureau chief but extremely difficult to find a good doctor, a good teacher or a good chauffeur.

Discussion Questions and Exercises:

1. Comment on the way Magistrate Kim treated the petitioning teachers. What cultural tradition and what real-life issues does it reflect?
2. Find out what are the Chinese "literati" and the role this class of people played in the society and politics of traditional China.
3. Obviously, the official visiting Central America did not cultivate good human relations and suffered fatally from it as a result. Here we find another function of the People's Congress (PC). Considering it together with the previous instance of the Statue, what role does the PC play in the Chinese political system and what role it has the potential to play? Follow or search for the news report on the annual proceedings of the National People's Congress (usually in March) for evidence.
4. Describe a typical traditional Chinese intellectual. For example, why did the professor cover both his chest and his face when ordered to get out of the airplane?
5. China adopts an authoritatian political system. However, as Kim demonstrates, to do well in this system depends heavily on good human relations. Why do you think this is the case? In your opinion, does the need to cultivate good human relations dilute the rigidity of the power hierarchy? Find someone from China to discuss this issue with.

III

Shortly after 12 o'clock, Kim Yet entered the Kingham Hotel. It was his first visit, despite the fact that the District Government was right across the street.

"The place is really stylish," he thought while walking, "Even those brass nails holding the carpet are sparkling. Indeed, there are indeed lots to learn from foreign management. However, business administration is just part of the super structure that must be supported by the cultural and economic foundations."

When he stepped into the English Hall, he found Zen Kofan and the deputy director of the Organization Bureau,[13] Mr. Su, already ordered the dishes. Kim Yet made a hand gesture to apologize for his tardiness.

"It is fully understandable for a high ranking official to be late." Zen pulled for him a chair at the head of the table, and introduced to him the deputy chief.

4.8 Notice Kofan's father's design for his youngest son's career was almost exactly the same as Kim Yet designed for himself early on. Why do you think this is the case? What does it tell you about the Chinese communists?

"I have heard about you for a long time." Kim Yet shook hands with Director Su. He knew that Su used to be the chief of staff of Zen's father, and now the deputy director of the Personnel and Organization Bureau of the Municipal Government.

Zen Kofan asked a waitress to read back the order to Kim Yet, who made a gesture to the waitress that it was not necessary. Zen was his high school classmate and their last meeting was at the school's anniversary four years ago. Zen looked distinctively older, but Kim Yet still paid him the compliment "You seem to be able to resist the corrosion by the flow of time."

Zen was delighted, stroking his well-dyed hair. His father was already a high ranking senior official at the time of Liberation and had since worked in the Planning Bureau. The old man was successful throughout his career, and even the Cultural Revolution did

---

[13] Organization Department is a communist party organ in charge of personnel. It is an integral part of all major party committees and considered one of the most important organs of the party. It is also usually merged with the human resources department/bureau of the government. In this case, Mr. Su is apparently from the municipal organization bureau that has direct jurisdiction over Kim's career.

not do much harm to him. He had three sons named Zen Problem, Zen Decision, and Zen Solution, till one day a classmate of Zen Kofan, whose father was the chief presecutor told him, "Following your father's logic of naming the children, the kids in our family should be called "investigation," "establishing a case" and "arrest warrant." After that he changed his named into "Kofan."

His brother Problem is now an official of the IMF, with an annual salary of a hundred thousand US dollars. He was not assigned by the Chinese government but a private employee at IMF. The other brother "Decision" is currently the secretary of a high ranking official — a rising star.

Among the three, the old man is most fond of Zen Kofan. Ten years ago, he wanted to send him to a county to gain practical experiences, then to the party school, and finally make him a government official. However, Kofan refused. He told his father: "You are a high ranking official, but it's just an empty shell. In other words, there are no concrete economic benefits from it."

The old man disagreed. "I ride in the best Mercedes, live in the renovated house of the Defense Minister of the former Qing Dynasty, and in addition, have the best medical service in the country. Translating all this into monetary terms, it would be at least a couple of million *yuan* per year. Forget about other places, in Beijing, how many people have assets worth two millions?"

Zen Kofan laughed. "I won't speak about how many people in Beijing have two millions. You won't believe it anyway. Let's talk about this: when you retire, you will probably get to keep your car and chauffeur, but it would not be as convenient. You probably will be able to live in the same house as you do now, but the pre-condition is that after you and mother pass away the house must be returned. More importantly, your medical care will not be as good."

The old man immediately countered, "Medical care is not going to change, I'll still be able to use Beijing Hospital's special wards for senior cadres."

Kofan laughed again. "Now you are deceiving yourself. You know Beijing Hospital better. Last time when your lung showed a little shade on X-ray, even I knew it's nothing serious. Nevertheless, a medical team consisting of the best doctors of China was assembled. They drew a detailed treatment plan and proposed three principles," Zen Kofan mimicked the Southern accent of the doctor, "First, must ensure his Excellency's safety. Second, root out the disease. Third, reduce the pain of his Excellency to the minimum."

He paused for a moment and went on, "All these are derivatives of power, not something that inherently belong to you. The characteristic of public ownership is that, when you are in control, everything is yours. Once you no longer control it, nothing is yours. In addition, it is short-lived." His words apparently shook the foundation of the old man. He thought for a long, long time, and asked, "What do you have in mind?"

"To turn those empty things of yours into solid benefits."

The old man asked how to do it, and it was only then when Zen Kofan told him his plan: "by going into business." Next day, the old man approved his son's plan. Zen Kofan was brilliant in executing the plan. Not long after he became a billionaire.

6.2 The "political multiplier effect" of the party-state hierarchy: because cadres at each of the five levels are primarily responsible to their superiors, they are motivated to impress the latter with better than required results. The hierarchy hence works like a magnifying glass to expand the targets set by the central government, an incremental each level down. If the task is too big, they would often resort to doctored statistics.

Soon the dishes were brought to the table. Kim Yet slowly and carefully tasted the food while guessing why Zen invited him to dinner.

"I heard there will be a reshuffle of bureau level cadres soon," deputy director Su said with an even tone. Kim Yet looked at Su attentively, but did not reply. He had learned from many sources about Su. When Zen's father was in power, Su was his chief of staff, and known as a wheeler-dealer. In other words, a considerable part of the old man's power was exercised by Su.

The Zen senior was no fool of course, nor was he incompetent for his job. However, his job portfolio was simply too broad to be handled by anybody alone. Under such conditions even a great man like Mao Zedong is easily deceived. At a conference after the Great Leap Forward, Mao said to the leaders of the provinces and regional branches of the Central Committee, "I knew you were exaggerating the output figures and hence divided the figures you reported to me by two. I didn't know the result was still eight times greater than the actual output." No one can say that Mao was negligent in investigation. He frequently took inspection tours. But local officials had their counter-strategies. You want to find out grain input? OK, before you arrive I'll move the crops of several acres into one acre of land to show you. If you want to know steel output, I'll doctor the books so that the output of several months would appear as that of one month. If that still looks inadequate, I'll buy some more from somewhere else.

We couldn't say that Mao was completely ignorant of such practices. He later on wouldn't even read the reports and often asked his bodyguards to do some reality check for him when they took leave to see their families in the countryside. However, all this precautionary measures mattered little since policy decisions had to be based on some numbers and state plan was made according to the numbers reported by lower-level governments.

Breadth is however only one side of the story. The other is too high a level of centralization. At a certain level, power is specific. Take for example, the allocation of housing. The head of the housing section knows it like the back of his hand who in his *danwei* do not have housing and who have already been allocated an apartment, as well as who live in houses of poor quality. As the issue comes to the desk of the director of administration, such specificity no longer exists. He only knows the general situation. That is, he knows only how many apartments are allocated to work unit **A** and how many to work unit **B**. When the matter reaches the bureau chief, the concern turns from allocation into how to raise funds to build new housing. To the provincial governor, the issue becomes how to balance the budget; he will not normally concern himself with matters such as whether the money is used for building new houses or purchasing new equipment. Suppose this governor is a devoted public servant and a super-energetic workaholic who does not trust the bureaucrats to use budget money all on its intended areas and begins to investigate by himself. The average province has, at a minimum, two to three dozen bureaucratic organs at the city, prefectural and bureau levels each. Suppose he spent only two days on each of them, then he'll spend the whole year doing nothing else.

Therefore, when power is too centralized, it'll exceed the capability of any individual. Decentralization of power is hence a must. The first beneficiaries of decentralization were people like Su who worked at the side of senior officials. These people, together with senior leaders they worked for constituted the nerve center of the entire system. Someone might say: it won't become a problem if appropriate people are selected. However, there's still a question of "too broad" and "too centralized." Evaluating a cadre's performance is like auditing an accounting book. An unusually diligent provincial governor who travels frequently to the cities and countries of the province could at best come to know, when his term ends, all the county magistrates and party secretaries, let alone their deputies.

Therefore, Su knew his worth and made full use of the power delegated to him. The essence of power lies in it being used. Power is like farmland, if you allow whoever is willing to till it without your permission and paying you the rent, then your ownership amounts to nothing. If you are naïve enough to believe in the motto "serve the people," and work diligently to answer every request from the people, then you'll truly become "public servant (slave)."

As soon as Zen Kofan went into business, he formed a partnership with Su. As a result, he could easily obtain various scarce supplies and rationed goods and produce. In return, Su was greatly emboldened by Zen Kofan's business dealings that provided him with the convenience and legitimacy. He was a very shrewd man, and managed, right before the Old Zen's retirement, to be transferred to the Personnel Department of Beijing,[14] switching from one in charge of finance to one in charge of people.

"There's no free lunch, as the saying goes. Can you tell me how could I be of service to you two?" Kim Yet knew that it's better to clarify the situation as early as possible.

Director Su did not respond, focusing on the crabs in his plate.

"A friend of ours wants to lease the basement of this hotel to open an entertainment business," Zen Kofan replied instead. Kim Yet looked puzzled, staring at Zen: business deals like this do not need the approval of the government.

"The problem is that this is a joint venture with a Korean company, and joint ventures must have your approval. This is the first step; without it nothing can happen."

Kim Yet had his own opinion on joint ventures like this, but still he indicated his willingness to give the go ahead. But Zen went on, "Here is the second issue, and equally important: the type of entertainment is somewhat unique." This time Kim Yet did not ask, although he knew immediately what it might be. It was better to let Zen himself say it.

"The friend of mine wants to operate tiger machines, and…" Zen's word was no longer as smooth due to Kim's lack of response.

"In other words, a casino?" Kim knew he must nail down the essence of the matter.

"Not entirely. We would only use the plastic token at the hotel. In other words, the money won could only be spent in the hotel."

"You probably know better than me what really is 'internal consumption'. The plastic tokens of the so-called internal consumption can be exchanged, with a little percentage off its surface value, into hard cash. Even if the hotel forbids it, people will still do it under the table."

---

[14] Government's personnel department is usually the same as the organization department of the party committee at the same level. This is "the-party-controls-cadres" principle in practice.

"It doesn't matter what it really is, it's not against the law." Zen Kofan had done many similar things before and knew it very well.

"More importantly," he went on, "this club opens to foreigners only. Only those who have foreign passports are allowed in."

Kim Yet regarded it as self-deception and said, "This matter is very complicated. If I remember correctly, businesses like this will need the approval of the Bureau of Public Security." He knew the regulation very well, but intentionally sounded as if he was not.

"We'll deal with the Public Security Bureau," Zen said. "The key is that the process must be initiated by you."

"It should be you who must initiate it," Kim said with a smile. "I'm just a screener."

"Of course, we are the initiators," Zen admitted his error. "The first hurdle is the District Government. Nothing can be done if you don't approve."

"I can't give you an answer right away. Let me do some consultation first."

"Better be fast." Zen looked a little displeased. He had always been quite successful in other places.

"You can't be hasty doing anything," Director Su intervened. "Let's toast," he raised his cup.

Kim knocked his cup with the two, but only symbolically drank a bit. Su and Zen emptied their cups in one sip. Zen also showed Kim the bottom of his cup.

"I have a meeting this afternoon," said Kim.

"Who hasn't a meeting?" Zen Kofan teased. "It's not like that. I know very well how much you can drink in a meal."

"I heard that the former Foreign Minister Qiao Guanhua and the deputy Foreign Minister were both heavy drinkers. Once the two invited the Albanian ambassador to a banquet and plotted to get him drunk. However, the ambassador would not even touch alcohol; so the two began to work on the counselor. The counselor could not resist the two and by the time the banquet was over, was drunk from head to toe. On his way home, his car ran over a pedestrian and killed him instantly. The counselor had diplomatic immunity but still the incident caused a quite some negative publicity, for Albania was then the only socialist country in Europe that was friendly to China. Later on, Premier Zhou Enlai learned about it and severely reprimanded the two. He then made a rule: at banquets entertaining foreign guests, nobody was allowed to drink one-third of his capacity for alcohol." Kim Yet turned the cup in his hand and went on. "From the day I heard this story, I adopted that rule."

"Rules are meant to be broken," Zen still insisted on Kim Yet finishing his cup.

"Well, a rule is a rule. It makes no sense breaking one's own rule." Kim Yet was not swayed easily.

Director Su felt obligated to intervene, *"The host should follow the guest's wishes."* Zen Kofan no longer insisted, "You may turn down my toast, but you must take care of my business as soon as possible."

"This matter is somewhat sensitive and I'll have to study it and seek instructions from my superior. As soon as these are done I'll let you know the result." Kim Yet was a superb administrator and would not allow others to dictate his action.

"You are the executive Deputy Magistrate and you should be able to decide things like this." Zen Kofan had drunk too much by now and could not get his thinking straight.

"The meaning of the so-called executive Deputy Magistrate is to frequently report to the District Magistrate, who happens to be a man not easily persuaded." Kim Yet used the Magistrate in as his shield. "Come on," he raised his cup and said. "However this matter ends, let's finish this last cup."

When they went out of the door of the hotel and Zen Kofan left to get his car. Deputy Director Su said, as if casually, "Say hello to Old Leo when you go back."

"Sure thing." Kim Yet knew the "Old Leo" referred to the District Party Secretary.

"I heard he's going to be moved."

"This is the first time I heard this," Kim Yet knew that the info was meant as a valuable present to him. However, he did not want such a gift and therefore he did not follow up on it.

Kim Yet attended meetings the whole afternoon. When he returned to his office after the meetings he found his wife, a doctor of internal medicine at the municipal hospital, waiting for him.

"How did you get in?" he smiled.

"After all I am your wife, so the secretary[15] let me in."

Kim Yet asked where she came from.

"This time our routine workshop was held in the hospital of your district, so I came conveniently," said the wife, while touching up her hair.

"Did you find a valuable case?" asked Kim.

The medical community of Beijing had a very good tradition: every month they would hold a professional workshop to discuss the various difficult-to-treat or hard-to-diagnose cases encountered by the participating hospitals during the month, and the hospitals hosted the meetings in turns.

The wife, the head doctor of internal medicine, loved her profession and began telling him the cases discussed in the workshop that day. Kim Yet was a layman to medicine, but listened attentively. When she finished, he asked, "I find that your discussions are all based on autopsy. What would you do if the relatives of the deceased would not allow an autopsy?"

"The hospital will pay big bucks to get it."

"What if they still refuse to sell it?"

The wife helped the husband put on his overcoat, and said, "I'll tell you if you promise not to tell anyone."

Kim Yet hooked his little finger with his wife's (a rather childish ritual of pledging), who then told him. "Normally, there would be someone to encourage the relatives to sue the hospital for medical malpractice — you have to have an autopsy to bring a law suit."

"What a rogue idea!" Kim closed the door behind them.

---

[15] Mishu (office assistant). Although in English it is one word, in Chinese "secretary" can be rendered into two words with vastly different meanings: *shuji* and *mishu*. The former is much more powerful.

"Hurting one family to benefit the public, in the jargon of your officialdom, this is 'local interests subordinating to the overall interests'." When they walked out of the building, the wife asked, "Why don't you have a car today?"

"I never ride a car home unless it is on the way from a meeting somewhere else." Kim took his wife's arm and said, "Let's walk home."

"I thought I could get a ride today."

"Didn't you tell me that the essence of life is movement?"

"I also told you 'the essence of promotion is to go for it,' how come I never see you 'go for it'?"

"I wouldn't let you know even if I did."

As the two trading words, a Nissan pulled over and stopped in front of them. "Magistrate Kim, let me drive you both home." The driver lowered the power window.

"We just go cross the street," said Kim Yet. The driver stepped on the gas pedal and sped away. When the car disappeared from sight, the wife spoke, "it looks you really want to walk home."

"I might have accepted the offer had it been someone else's car." Kim smiled, and went on, "The key issue here is that the car is the District Magistrate's official transport; others should not ride in it. In other words, that's not a car; it's a symbol of power."

"It looks your world of officialdom is very much like our medical profession — both are strictly hierarchical."

"If nobody heeds your words as the head doctor and prescribes drugs at will, then all patients are going to die."

What Kim Yet said about not taking the offer for a ride was not the real reason. The real reason was that he did not like the driver. Once he rode with the District Magistrate in the latter's car to attend a meeting at Beidaihe seaside resort. On the way, the two were discussing personnel matters. The driver suddenly turned around and began commenting on the candidates, disparaging this one and that one. Kim Yet frowned but did not say anything because the District Magistrate had not reacted. Later on, when chauffeuring for Kim that driver did the same. Kim did not stop him but instead lectured him afterwards, "All drivers under heaven are the same. The most valuable commodity they have is the news they heard from their passengers. Of course, there is something unique about the 'Driver of the District Magistrate.' However, in this phrase the noun 'driver' is used as the object of 'District Magistrate'. If some day these two words are gone, then there is only a plain 'driver' left." Since then that driver was very meek whenever he met Kim Yet.

Discussion Questions and Exercises:

1. According to Zen, what is the main characteristic of public ownership? Are you convinced by him? Can you find similar examples in your own country?
2. Why do you think Zen brought Mr. Su to dinner with Kim Yet? What kind of psychological game he was playing? Comment on the way Kim responded.
3. Can you imagine what disaster can distorted information flow in a political system bring about? Do a research project on the Great Leap Forward and its aftermath (1958-62) to find out the magnitude of the man-made disaster — by far the deadliest in known human history, and analyze the information flow in the system and how it was systematically distorted. What changes must be made to the system in order to prevent it from happening again?
4. Role play: select someone from the class to be the supreme leader who decides the lives and careers of all other people in the class while also depending on them to achieve his or her objectives (a target quota of steel output for example). Interact with each other to see if you could create a situation in which everyone behaves rationally to maximize his or her interests but the entire group end up behaving irrationally to create disasters similar to the Great Leap Forward and Cultural Revolution. Seek help from faculty members with expertise in social psychology or group behavior.
5. Discuss the formidability of business partnership between Zen Jr. and director Su (a partnership between money and power). Can you think of ways to constrain it and stem corruption from it? If this is absent from or muted in your country's political system, what are the key conditions that have prevented it from emerging? Can these conditions emerge in China as well?

IV

The annual conference of the district People's Congress was drawing near, and the district government was due for re-election during that conference. Kim Yet was entrusted by the District Magistrate with drafting the district government's work report. In comparison to the seriousness of the Magistrate, Secretary Leo did not seem particularly enthusiastic about it. He could not help remembering Director Su's words that "Secretary Leo was going to be moved." Kim Yet, however, did not mention this to anybody. In his eye, gossiping about others, no matter whom — superior, subordinates, colleagues etc., was a bad habit. Nobody was going to change because of your gossiping.

He arrived at Newstar Hotel on time. There were altogether eight stories in this hotel; it was simple but sturdy and practical. He would bet that this was not a star-ranked hotel. It was built with funds provided by the District Government. Whenever he was assigned to take charge of drafting a major government report, he would gather his writing team to this hotel.

When he first started working at the Downtown District, he used to prefer to stay at a suburban resort to cook government reports. Another deputy magistrate asked about it once, and he replied: "First, Newstar is too expensive; second, it is not clean."

The other deputy magistrate laughed, "There is no such a thing as 'too expensive'. Newstar is our own hotel. The money you spend is taken from the government's administrative budget and put into account of that reception house. It's like the central government giving funds to this or that province — it's still inside China. But if you go to a resort, the money spent is really spent. As to poor service, that's for ordinary guests. From now on, whenever you need to use the hotel I'll notify the management beforehand. It will turn into a star-ranked quality at once. As to how clean it will be, you'll have to judge for yourself."

At the time, Kim Yet did not accept the advice. For, being an official, it is not advisable to accept other's ideas immediately — especially from some of the same rank. You should always accept only tacit suggestions but not open advises because the latter is an indication of your incompetence. However, after continuing to go to the suburban resort a few more times, Kim Yet understood what the deputy magistrate was driving at. Resorts like this, especially those located in the distant suburbs, were still operating on a model of the planned economy. There was no commercial spirit at all. For example, when everybody worked overtime and wanted to get something to eat: no way. No matter how much you are willing to pay. More importantly, if the district Secretary or Magistrate needed you for some reason, or the leaders from the Municipality came to inspect the district, you would have to rush back immediately. Back and forth, a couple of days would be wasted on the way. That greatly affected Kim Yet's job performance. He then gave Newstar a try. A few days later, he understood the saying *'the best hideout is in the thick of the city'*.

When he saw that the members of his writing team were all here, Kim Yet announced the meeting to begin.

He never used the term "writing team" in public, because only top leaders of the central, provincial, and cabinet levels are entitled to have their own writing teams. Although the term "writing team" was not to be used openly, what they were doing was essentially the same. It is also the same thing that platoon, company, or battalion commanders do not formally have their own security guards or personal secretaries; but they enjoy similar services provided by the soldiers in the communications or the logistic services.

Kim Yet had already told them his basic ideas. So he immediately asked everybody to air their ideas. This was Kim Yet's way of writing a report. Once a major piece of writing was assigned to him, he would gather together those who he knew as capable writers and told them the central themes and objectives, assigned each person a part to write on their own. After a few days or a week, he would call them back again to discuss the progress made. After a few rounds the basic shape of the report.

The discussion he chaired that day was the government report of the fiscal year 1998. Government business is unlike those of the military, agriculture, or industry that are concrete. Government affairs are abstract and not easy to get a grip of. The annual work report is the primary vehicle to demonstrate the government's achievements in the year.

The meeting was held in a spacious room. An oval table in the middle was surrounded by a dozen or so large chairs with soft cushions. Sitting at the head of the table, Kim Yet looked tidy and neat. His hair was smooth, shirt all buttoned up, and his tie also done nicely. The impression he emitted was one of seriousness and energetic. He read Part One of the "work report" and asked others to comment on it. The tone, phonetic and speed were all perfectly

3.9 By Chinese Constitution, top government officials should be elected by the People's Congress. Because the nomination of candidates are controlled by the communist party and the deputies of the People's Congress are practically appointed by the party (most are CCP members as well), the "election" is just a formality. Nevertheless, the government must submit a work report every year to the People's Congress. The Constitution provides that any citizen can run for the deputy of the lowest level of the People's Congress (township, urban district etc.) and increasingly people take advantage of this provision to run as independent candidates despite CCP's fairly successful effort to stamp down on it and to persecute them as "dissidents." With increasing voter participation that is also becoming more genuine, PC elections may prove to be the breakthrough point in China's democratization.

appropriate like those of a news anchor. Part of this came from natural gift, and part he learned from a professional. Once he had a surgery and met a radio announcer at the same hospital ward. From the latter, he learned some valuable techniques of controlling voice. The radio announcer soon died. Whenever Kim used his techniques he could not help feeling that the radio announcer was still alive through his voice. Voice is an important external marker of one's personality. Rarely one is able to see the inside of another person. Therefore, external appearance is more important than the innate qualities in dealing with people.

When Kim finished reading the *Introduction*, the discussion took off gradually. Soon it began losing cohesion. Everyone pushed for his own ideas and wordings. This did not bother Kim Yet a bit. In fact it was what he intentionally created. A government report is almost boundless in its coverage, and no one could possibly do it alone. It has to be a collective project. The chaos of group discussion is the ideal situation to discover new ideas and perspectives.

"I disagree with the conclusion on industry." The speaker was the office director of Bureau of Industries. "On the surface, the industrial output value did not increase substantially during the period; in reality, it did increase substantially. It only does not look like a substantial increase."

Upon hearing this, the two new college graduates burst out laughing.

"What are you laughing at?" asked the General Office Director of the District government.

"What he said was illogical," replied Lee Hong, who graduated from Beida with a master degree in Chinese. He requested to be assigned to a grassroots unit when he first joined the district government. However, Kim Yet insisted that he stayed in the government.

"Hey, young man," said the GO director. "There are many kinds of logics: the government has a governmental logic, a work report has the logic of a report; your college has its own logic. These are all different."

"But fundamentally there is only one logic". Lee Hong was not easily put down. "The small logic must obey the big logic."

"OK, let's talk about small and big logics." The GO director might tolerate the opposing opinion if it came from the senior members of the writing team, but he would not allow a green lad who joined just a few days ago to go against him. He did not have much formal education, but he wrote very well, and because of this he looked down on those with a college degree.

"Some expressions are indeed illogical," Kim Yet gestured with his hand. "For example, Professor John King Fairbank, who once taught at your Beida, described in one of his articles two girls this way: each is prettier than the other. Would you say this is illogical?"

Lee Hong shook his head.

"Of course, it is not consistent with the logic as in philosophy, but it is perfectly logical in aesthetics because it conveys the idea very effectively." For some reason, Kim Yet believed that Lee Hong's previous name must be "Lee Hongwei" (Red Guard Lee), for he was born in 1967. Nobody at that time would name his child "hong," a word smelt strongly of Buddhism.

Lee Hong nodded.

Kim Yet gestured for Director Q to continue. The role of the chair of a meeting is to engineer smooth transitions so that the flow of discussion is not disrupted. Director Q then slowly but steadily elaborated his ideas. In a nutshell, in order to pursue real efficiency, the district government and its industrial bureau did drastic restructuring of the SOEs of the District. Some closed down, some merged, some switched to other lines of production etc. The statistics indicated a decline in the output value, but in reality a major improvement in efficiency was achieved. He quoted various numbers, both current and projected to substantiate his argument. He had an amazing memory for numbers, citing seven- or eight-digit numbers like his own birthday.

Kim Yet trusted him on these numbers — at least Director Q himself would not fabricate these. He was busy thinking how to translate the numbers into languages that the deputies of the People's Congress could understand — these people are not extremely fond of numbers. In most cases, concrete examples are more effective than abstractions. This is the reason why literature cannot compete with movies and television.

"In other words, we achieved real progress while the output value increased steadily," said Old Q, the senior researcher from the government's Policy Research Office. Kim Yet could not help saying 'bravo' in his heart. Old Q had a special talent of turning the most mundane things into beautifully written prose. The writing was flawless and artistic; the argumentation was logical, succinct, comprehensive and systematic, reminding the readers of Hegelian dialectics.

"When Old Q makes a point, he is like a lady of high class putting on her makeup, picking from her jewelry collection the best and most appropriate for the occasion," once Kim Yet told his wife.

"In contrast, your writing is like me selecting from my jewelry box: there are only very few to choose from," teased his wife.

The meeting went on smoothly.

"We must emphasize the leadership role of the Party in the work of the government," said the deputy director of the propaganda department of the District Party Committee when the meeting was drawing close to the end.

"We have emphasized this point in Part One, Part Three, and the concluding part," said the GO director of the District Government.

"I did not say that you did not emphasize it. You did not emphasize enough" replied the deputy director, with his eyes scanning across the room with the air of an important leader. The GO director wanted to say something but stopped. Normally, a deputy director of the Propaganda Department would not speak to a GO director of the Government like this because both his ranking and importance of his position were lower. However, deputy director Li was a special case. He used to be a secretary to a senior leader responsible for the latter's daily life. When this leader was about to retire and was making arrangements for the people working for him, he asked Li where did he want to go. Li replied that he wanted to come to the Downtown District. The senior leader asked further what kind of position he wanted and he replied that he wanted to work in the Organizational Department of the District Party Committee. Some people control money, some control assets, but neither compares with those who control personnel. The Organization Department of the District Party Committee, unlike that personnel department of the government or the human resources office of an enterprise, controls cadres ranked at the section level and above. Li had long experiences living inside the center of politics and understood this. The senior leader then made a phone call to the District Party Secretary Leo, who immediately agreed to take Li. However, he did not at the time carefully think through Li's assignment, and ran into strong resistance at the Party

Committee meeting. He tried three times before Li's appointment was decided, but it was in the Propaganda Department instead of the Organizational Department.

Li was very angry about this, and the senior leader also called to demand an explanation. The story goes that the secretary replied that he himself had no problem with it but he could not push it through the party committee meeting. The senior leader said,

"In my long work experience, every item on the agenda of a meeting should have been agreed upon beforehand through informal consultations."

"I did, but there was difference of opinion even then, and I also told Li about it before the committee meeting."

The senior leader did not press further. "I'll entrust him to you for the time being. I'll move him when opportunity comes, but you must take good care of him."

Secretary Leo promised him.

Before deputy director Li took office, the senior leader retired and soon after that passed away. For some time Li was very depressed, till one of the senior leader's many secretaries, the one in charge of theoretical matters, was chosen by a main leader of the Municipal Party Committee and promoted to head the municipal organizational department. As a member of the senior leader's fraternity, deputy director Li also came alive.

"Will you please take the issue raised by deputy director Li into consideration, and go over the draft once more?" Kim Yet said to the GO director, who then began collecting his documents from the table without looking at Kim Yet.

However, deputy director Li, disregarding the body languages of others to end the meeting, went on with his speech as if he were a great theoretician. Kim Yet pretended to be listening but a train of thoughts ran through his mind —"*others may not know how you've got your current position, but I know it. Not only that, I know how you leap-frogged several steps of ranking but I also know you are a mediocre. I am not denying that you have some social skills, but don't act as if you were a great theoretician too. It's like a comedian trying to play the role of a master artist. In the government it won't work if you insist on being*

Drawing by one of my former students.

*rational in doing everything, because there are many things in policy and
decision making and implementation that are irrational but nevertheless
necessary. Even more so if all you rely on is your social skill. It is true that
you can accomplish many things with it, just as what PR can do for a
business firm. However, no business relies on PR alone; its products must
be accepted by consumers too. There are at least three sources of authority:
delegation by higher authorities, trust by people below, and one's own
competence. This guy lacks at least two of these."*

As these thoughts ran on, deputy director Li was talking
eloquently.

Discussion Questions and Exercises:

1. Find someone from China around you and ask him or her to see how
   much they know about PC elections, for example, what kind of people
   usually get "elected" into the People's Congress.
2. Explain the decision making procedure (formal and informal) in
   China's one-party rule.
3. Would you describe what Old Q, and indeed Kim and the entire writing team, was doing as spin-doctoring? Does it serve any substantive
   purpose at all? How does what they were doing compare with PR?
4. Discuss the "secretary gang" phenomenon in the Chinese political
   system and elite politics.

V

When Kim Yet returned to his own office his secretary told him, "Mr. Zen called three times asking for you." Kim Yet then dialed Zen's mobile phone number.

"How is the thing we talked about going?" Zen went directly for it.

"The planning bureau checked it out. Because you want to purchase the entire basement level of the Kingham Hotel, the matter has to go through the approval procedures of a new joint venture." Deep down, Kim Yet was not in favor of Zen's business proposal. Gambling has never been a good thing since ancient times.

"I know how things work. Everything is going to be fine if you yourself approve it."

"Leadership is not just one person, but a whole team. Everything must follow the rules which are the result of years of valuable experiences of many people."

"I am a businessman and time is money," Zen still insisted.

"Government is different from business. It's a bit like farming. You must keep appropriate timing. Otherwise, you'll be punished by nature."

But Zen persisted.

"My friend," Kim Yet tried to ease the situation. "You've read many books and must know the words of the Xu Jie of the Ming Dynasty: 'Power and prestige go to the monarch; government administration belongs to the bureaucracies, crime and punishment must be dealt in accordance with justice.'"

"When will you approve?" Zen could care less about ancient wisdoms.

"As soon as you pass the capital auditing and have the approval of the planning authorities." Kim Yet was a bit annoyed. *Although you are the son of an important cadre and have many connections in many important government organs, I am also, after all, representing a level of government.*

Zen did not say any more and turned off the mobile phone.

Kim Yet strolled along in the misty evening light. Beijing is indeed very large, he thought, so large that not a single person could really see it through. However, fundamentally it was created unintentionally. Since Ming Dynasty moved its capital here, later generations built it up over the centuries into today's shape. In other words, even the highest officials lack a clear sense of participation in its daily bustling. *Although I myself could by no means develop an overall comprehension of it, but I am one participant. As long as this is the case, I'll do my best to clean the area that my broom can reach, just the way I used to work on the workshop floor many years ago.*

After dinner, he played for while a kind of one-person card game on the table of his study. He seldom took part in entertainment activities because normally any form of entertainment involved at least two persons. This spelled trouble given his status. He used to collect postal stamps. When he was at middle school, his 'special theme' collection won an award. Naturally, when the Downtown District's Association of Stamp Collectors was founded, he joined. As a result, many people tried to develop *guanxi* with him though this channel. Among them a manager of a joint venture offered him a complete set of the memorial stamps since the founding of the People's Republic of China — at face value.

"Do you realize that the current value of it is many times its face value?" He asked the man, who replied, "No." He returned

Drawing by one of my former students.

the stamps and said, "You'd better find it out at the stamps market before you do so."

He also loved chess. Once at a conference on industrial development he used the strategy of chess as an example to discuss industrial allocation. After the meeting he was surrounded by chess lovers. Once he was invited to participate in a tournament and found himself winning all the way to the top. Many amateur fifth level players and even a second level professional were among those he defeated. He knew that level five amateurs were very skilled players and a level two professional could beat him easily even if allowing him 30 points advantage. After the tournament the organizer awarded him a special prize: a set of Yunzi chess. The so-called Yunzi is made of the famous colored marble of Yunnan Province. The white pieces appear yellowish and black ones greenish, very pleasing to the eye. It costs a minimum a few thousand *yuan*. As soon as he accepted the award, the chairman of the Downtown District Chess Association came up and asked him to allocate some government fund for the activities of the Association, and said to him, "The Chairman of the Sports Commission already approved it; you only need to sign it for the good of our Association." He specially emphasized the word 'our'."

Without a word, Kim Yet approved it. He would have approved it more comfortably if those first class players did not intentionally lose to him and he did not accept the expensive award. Under the current situation, he almost felt being fooled. From then on he never participated in any chess game again.

Things in China are indeed this strange. He reshuffled the deck of cards on the table and redistributed it. Work is pleasure; meetings turn into sightseeing; formal

7.1 Despite continued domination of politicians, ordinary people like Sir Niu, who used to be the laughing stock of everybody and considered a good-for-nothing, can prosper in a market economy if they can find a market niche. This is bound to change the incentive structure of society in a profound way.

banquet becomes a drinking contest. On the flip side, play is actually work. Playing Mahjong is in fact a form of bribery through intentionally losing money in order to nail down a business contract. No form of entertainment could escape this.

He remembered his encounter, a few days earlier, with a middle school classmate whose surname was Niu. This guy is a Manchu, claiming to be the descendent of the Pure Yellow Banner Tribe.[16] However, his family lived in the Blue Banner Camp in Haidian District. His dad was a notorious playboy who raised a large flock of doves and a dozen tanks of fish. He was extremely good at bird trapping. The songbirds he trained for luring wild birds were simply master imitators — they could imitate any birds that they happened to see. Like father, like son. The only difference is that the son is a bit more refined than the father. He could play a traditional music instrument used in Beijing Opera, and could also paint a little.

The day when he ran into this former classmate of his, the latter was driving a "Blue Bird," clad in name brands. He asked, "Sir Niu, in what business are you now prospering?" said he mockingly, using archaic Chinese expressions.

"Jobless", "Sir Niu" replied cheerfully.

"Then it must be that you've dug up some more treasure from your backyard," joked Kim Yet. This guy was a well-known bragger at the middle school. Whenever he saw somebody had something, he would claim that his family also had it. When the classmates could not find any in his home, he would say that it was buried in the backyard.

Sir Niu went on describing his success as "both depending and not depending on the ancestors," and then began telling the story of his success.

"I have little physical strength, and therefore I have utilized my superior brain power." He quickly stopped Kim Yet who was about to challenge his claim, saying, "I don't mean things like

---

[16] The Manchus organized their society into eight color-coded "banners" for military purposes: yellow, sub-yellow, white, sub-white, red, sub-red, blue and sub-blue. The blue banner was the lowest ranked.

Drawing by one of my former students.

computer or atomic energy — these are small brainers. I mean really big scholarship."

By "big scholarship" he referred to fishing. He started from fishing on the ponds in the near suburbs, but gradually the fish in these places became smaller and scarcer, and later on the ponds were filled and high-rises were built upon them. He had to ride his bike to the distant suburbs. In addition, he also worked on the fish ponds in the parks. One must pay a fee to fish in the ponds of Beijing's parks. At first be made a folding rod and tried to sneak in without paying. But this was not really a long term solution. He hence turned to work on the bait so as to be able to catch more fish in the limited time paid for. Gradually, the quantity of fish he caught each time increased substantially, so much so that he was known to all the parks that had a fishing pond, and was denied entrance no matter how much he would pay. For a while even his livelihood was up in the air.

But once again, his fortune turned when fishing became a popular pastime, and went on to become the favored setting in which people develop *guanxi* and making under-the-table business deals — the same way the chess game turned out for Kim Yet. People would invite the VIPs to go fishing in these parks. The more fish they caught usually the better mood they would be in and the easier to get business done. In this environment, the fish bait of Sir Niu became a valuable commodity.

"I thought people normally go to the pond of fish farms when they entertain an important guest." Kim Yet was constantly looking for holes in his story.

"Yes, at first. But gradually they would feel bored — what's the difference from buy it from the fish market? People want real fishing experience. But fishing is not like Mahjong that you can play any way you choose. Fish only go after bait, and the bait I make is pure magic. It was based on the formula passed down from my ancestors combined with modern hi-tech processing method. I make a handsome income selling baits alone."

Kim Yet did not trust his word, and said "Don't you think other people would come up with similar products by simply analyzing the ingredients of your bait?"

"It won't be my family secret if it can be copied. Take Beijing roast duck for example, no matter what scientific methods they use the Japanese will never be able to get the same flavor. Another example is Maotai.[17] It is no use to know the formula. Contrary to what people believe, the key is not the water used but liquor molecules floating in the air over the Maotai Brewery. The same goes for the beef soup of Beijing's Full-moon Restaurant." Sir Niu sounded like a scholar giving a lecture.

Normally, Kim Yet would not take his words seriously. However, after that encounter whenever he mentioned Sir Niu to others, many did hear about him. They did not call him "Sir Niu" but "Fishing Bird" instead. They also told Kim Yet that it would cost a minimum of two thousand *yuan* to get him to give onsite lessons.

After all these experiences Kim Yet had to cut back on his entertainment involvement till he had to play solo in the game of cards to refresh him. However, he did not feel refreshed when he finished the solitary card game.

---

[17] The most famous brand of liquor in China used in State Banquet.

Discussion Questions and Exercises:

1. This chapter contains vivid depictions of the Chinese society. How do you characterize the society? Can you find people like Sir Niu in your country?
2. Reflect on the Chinese way: work is play and play is work.

VI

The phone rang suddenly at midnight. Usually calls in these hours were for his wife for medical emergencies. Gradually, Kim Yet learned to ignore them and continued his sleep.

"It's for you," his wife whispered in his ear when she returned from the living room.

"From whom?" he was still half asleep.

"Secretary Leo"

Kim Yet immediately got up and hurried into the living room. Once before Secretary Leo had called but was told by his wife that Kim Yet had already retired for the night. When he learned about this the next day he solemnly told his wife that whenever Secretary Leo or the District Magistrate called she must wake him up immediately. At the time his wife was in residency at Beijing Hospital; she retorted, "they are but middle level cadres. I've seen leaders ten times higher in rank than them."[18] He knew his wife misunderstood him and tried to explain to her.

"Those high-ranking officials in your hospital are your patients, but Secretary Leo and the Magistrate are my bosses. These are totally different relations. I must play by rules."

Secretary Leo was direct, "Zen Kofan came to me. Is it possible to process his case faster"?

Kim Yet explained to Secretary Leo about the nature of the project and difficulties involved. Somehow he felt that Leo was not listening.

---

[18] Beijing Hospital is one of the main healthcare providers for the most senior leaders of China.

"Zen Kofan had someone talking to me. It's hard for me to turn him down. Will you please deal with this matter as fast as possible"?

This person whom Leo found "difficult to turn down" must be a powerful figure. Kim Yet wanted to further test the water.

"The Center is very serious about capital frauds in joint ventures. If something goes wrong, we could be made an example for others."

"Zen told me that the foreign partner is now in Beijing. You should go to see him." Leo hung up abruptly.

"What should I do after seeing the foreigner?" thought Kim Yet while putting down the phone. *Since Secretary Leo did not make it clear, I'll have to improvise according to the situation.*

The businesses handed down by Secretary Leo had the top priority. As soon as Kim Yet got to his office the next morning he called Zen Kofan. Zen was certain that the CEO of BC Corporation of the UK, Mr. Hamilton, was currently in Beijing.

"Please arrange a meeting with him" said Kim Yet.

"You can do it now," Zen knew Secretary Leo was effective.

"I may not have time today." Kim Yet's morning schedule was still open but he did not want to go immediately lest sending a wrong signal and raising the expectation too high.

"But he'll return to London tomorrow," Zen sounded desperate. Kim Yet let him waited for a while and then said, "I may be able to spare an hour this afternoon."

"Then we'll see him at Kelly Hotel at three."

But Kim Yet would not go to Kelly. He considered it inappropriate for an official of the host government to pay a visit to a businessman. After some wrangling, Zen proposed to meet at a neutral territory: the Commerce Hotel. Kim Yet agreed.

When they left the Commerce Hotel at 5, Zen insisted to give Kim Yet a ride in his car. Kim understood that some compromise in non-essential matters were necessary at times, and hence instructed his driver to follow Zen's car.

"Send your car home, please. Are you afraid that I won't take you home?"

Kim Yet did not reply. As long as he had his own transportation he would have the initiative.

"Is that your own car?" asked Zen when they got on the Third Ring Road.

"A cadre of my rank is more than satisfied if business use of a car is guaranteed."

"What's your impression of Hamilton?"

"I can't tell yet." Kim Yet patted on the thick envelope of document in his hand. "I'll have to wait till my men finish studying these." Inside the envelope was a whole set of the BC Corporation's credentials.

1.5 In the world of Chinese officialdom, ranking is an all important and extremely sensitive matter. There has been a long methodological tradition among China watchers and scholars of elite politics of deciphering Chinese politics through analyzing the official media report on the activities of Chinese leaders: the frequency of media appearance of various leaders, their seating sequence, the size of their photos etc. These give cues to what is happening behind the bamboo curtain.

"Officials like you," Zen sped up to 120/km, "of course my old man included, tend to take a small matter too seriously."

Kim Yet did not respond.

"A few days ago at the mid-Autumn Festival celebration a high official asked him, 'Elder Zen, do you still drink? Guess what happened?"

Kim Yet shook his head.

"The old man was in a cheerful mood for many days." Zen sped up further. "He wasn't like this before. He met Chairman Mao and Premier Zhou but even did not mention it to us."

Kim Yet looked into the rearview mirror to see if his driver was still following.

"Some time ago, the General Office notified us that so-and-so would pay a visit to old comrades, and the old man did not sleep the whole night. He got up very early and jogged in the yard. I said to him, is this necessary? He stared at me without saying anything. However, when he heard the car he immediately went back inside.

7.3 "The era of dad contest. "You probably already know the Chinese word "guanxi"(connections). The ultimate guanxi consists of blood ties. As you can see, children whose fathers are or used to be in high places — the so-called "princelings," enjoy tremendous advantages over others. While this is true in all societies, it is more prevalent in China because of its authoritarian system. Hard working is no match for having a well-placed dad; this reality leads to the term "the era of dad contest." The implication is that upward social mobility is declining.

Do you know why?" Kim Yet indicated that he did not. "My family live in the same compound with the Trade Minister Wang. The two's rank and background are very much alike. Therefore, the old man wanted to see whose house so-and-so would go to first."

"Which one did he go first?" Kim Yet became interested.

"He went to Minister Wang's and then left" Zen slowed down. "The old man was very angry but had no one to talk to. For the whole day he would yell at anyone he saw, from our cook to my mother."

Kim Yet also felt that this so-and-so was not careful enough.

"However, the next afternoon so-and-so came again. He apologized immediately and said that "yesterday I did not know you Elder Zen also live here. Otherwise, I would have visited both of you and save me another trip."

Kim Yet already understood the shrewdness of so-and-so.

Zen continued, "Do you honestly believe that he didn't know? Even if he really did not, his many secretaries world have reminded him."

Kim Yet also understood what Zen Kofan was driving at. He wanted to him to know that his old man was still a force to be reckoned.

"Shall we have lunch together?"

"We are like brothers and you should not treat me like a guest. Besides I have an appointment."

"Since you refuse to dine with me, I'll give you the money for the meal." Zen handed him an envelope. Kim Yet felt it with his hand. The envelope was thin. He asked,

"How much money is in here?"

"As much as you want."

Kim Yet felt that he had to take a look. Inside the envelope was an American Express card. He had heard about it. One must have at least 10,000 US dollars to open an account of this card.

"I was going to give you something like a Great Wall card, but those cards are too conspicuous because they deal with domestic currency. For the sake of your safety, I decided to give you this instead. You may call it 'actualized profit abroad'."

"How much money then is in this card's account?"

Zen Kofan took this as Kim Yet had accepted the gift, and spoke more frankly, "As long as you don't use it to start a business, you'll never spend it. Do you know the profit margin of a casino?"

Kim Yet said "no." When he visited Hong Kong on official business, his host proposed to take him to the casino after the evening banquet but he turned it down immediately. It's a matter of principle.

"Let me put it this way. We spent two million in another province to set up a casino, and another million to smooth out the relations in the local government. We also told them that it was a foreigners-only operation. However, two months after we started operation it was shut down by the local public security. Still, the money we made during that two short months was almost enough to recover our investment."

These two months' earning almost equals the profit of a medium-sized enterprise, thought Kim Yet.

"Therefore you just go ahead spending as much as you can."

"My father-in-law, like you, was also a business man. He was fairly well-known in Shanghai before Liberation. Once he told me, it does not matter whether in business or government, one must strike a balance between 'eat well' and 'sleep well'."

Zen asked "what does that mean?" Kim Yet felt that he over-estimated Zen's intelligence, and had to explain to him that the so-called 'eat well' knows no boundary because life's goodies were countless. The so-called 'sleep well' refers to relaxation or tranquility of the heart. If a man has nothing to eat but plenty of time to sleep, this it is not good. If he eats well but could not go to sleep, it's even worse. He signaled Zen to stop the car. Zen mechanically pulled over to the road side.

"In order to let me sleep well, you've have to keep this for yourself." He put the envelope on the dashboard and got out. "Of course, your business has nothing to do with this. I'll continue to work on it as usual."

Zen Kofan was stunned, watching Kim Yet getting into his Santana from his rearview mirror.

Discussion Questions and Exercises:

1. Examine more closely the cultural rituals described in this chapter. Can you discern the underpinning value system? How is it different from the value system in your society?
2. Is Kim Yet biased against the business of Mr. Zen from the beginning? If so, do you find it fair? Is this a case of government intervention in businesses and should such intervention happen?

VII

Around 5.50 p.m., Kim Yet made a call to Pan Xing: "May I treat you to dinner this evening?"

"That's the most beautiful sentence in the world. I don't care where and with whom."

Pan was a high school classmate of his. When the "Sent-down Movement" came for urban youth to go to live in the countryside for "re-education," he did not follow the crowd to Shaanxi province. Instead, he and a few others who shared the same interests in philosophy and history went together to Shanxi province, where they founded a 'collective household of thinkers'. When colleges re-opened, he only managed to get into a teachers' college because of his poor showing in the foreign language exam. Upon graduation he was retained by the college as a lecturer. Soon after that he published a few articles on the economy, which paved his way into the Institute of Economics. Kim Yet adored the breadth and depth of his thought and loved to chat with him whenever he could.

"Tell me which restaurant are we going? My gastric juice is like the candidate right before the election — already active."

"What and where to eat, it's all yours to decide." Kim Yet sounded very generous.

"I can bankrupt you with just one meal," laughed Pan.

"It should not be too big a problem if we keep focused on the food rather than the setting of a restaurant."

"I've dined all over Beijing and know that there are only two things that fit your criteria: roast duck and hotpot mutton. I just had roast duck yesterday evening; therefore, let's go for the hotpot."

"That stuff seems to be meant for snowy days', said Kim Yet.

8.1 The Cultural Revolution was a national as well as personal disaster for millions. However, throughout this story, you can detect certain nostalgia about the far-gone years of hardships and trials. This is perhaps natural but another part of the reason is that the turbulent years were also an era of idealism and passion, which poses a sharp contrast with today's rampant corruption and materialism.

"Custom is meant to be broken. Besides, there are hardly any real snowy days these years. You just follow me and I guarantee that you won't regret it." Pan Xing hung up.

"Think about the scale measuring wind speed. If we use it to measure the traffic of Beijing, this hour would be rated at 10." Pan Xing skillfully navigated his car in the traffic.

"It's like the saying, '*after a gentleman is away for three days, you must treat him as a new person when he returns*'." Kim Yet admired

Pan's driving skill. He himself wanted very much to learn to drive but had neither the time nor a car.

"Before I went to college, I was already a truck driver for the transportation company of Yanbei Prefecture, Shanxi province. Do you know anything about Yanbei at all?"

"Very well. As an ancient poem put it, 'Beyond the Yanmen Pass there is but wilderness, where the locals know nothing of the ways of civilization.' There are many coal mines and the famous Yungang Cave Sculptures."

"At the time I drove a Liberation truck with trailer. The most glorious moment of my life then was driving at a snowy night through the Yanmen Pass on a zigzagging mountain road. When I arrived at the foot of the mountain, the highway had been sealed by snowstorm for three days. The inns and hotels alongside the road were jam-packed with drivers who did not dare to venture into the mountain. However, I bought some straw-made ropes to put on the wheels and successfully went through."

"My uncle," said Kim Yet, "was a professor at Qinghua University. He once told me that when he was sent down to do manual labor at a 'May 7th Cadre School'[19] in Liyuzhou of Jiangxi province, he used to carry on his back a 180 lb bag and climbed a 45 degree mountain path. I did not believe him. Later on, however, I found it was true all right. The only caveat is that he put two things in one sentence: he did carry 180 lb load on his back and he did climb a 45 degree mountain path made of stone steps, but he never did both at the same time. Are you also playing the same trick?"

"I must express my enormous, heart-felt indignation for your downgrading of my credit rating." Pan made a shallow turn and drove into a small back alley.

---

[19] Essentially labor camps where cadres were sent to farm, raise chicken or pigs, and do other manual labor during the Cultural Revolution. They were created in accordance with Mao's directives issued on May 7th, 1968 and hence the name. Mao's intention was to re-educate cadres and intellectuals about the lives of the working masses so that they would not become "bourgeoisized." But the camps were also used as punishment for people on the wrong side of politics.

"I could care less about your indignation." Kim Yet half-way lied down on the back seat, relaxing both his body and mind. "A truck driver must be damn proud in those days." Kim Yet skipped f-word, a habit he learned at college.

"Prouder than driving a Rolls-Royce these days." Pan pointed to the white car in front of him. Kim Yet carefully examined it and asked, "This is Rolls-Royce? It looks no different than any other cars." Kim Yet gently touched the small stature of an angel on the tip of the hood with his hand.

"Don't touch it!" shouted the driver sternly.

Kim Yet was annoyed — nobody had yelled at him like that for many years.

"What's the fuss about touching it?"

"Once I parked this car in front of Wangfu Hotel. A window cleaner stepped on it to reach the upper part of the window. Do you know how much money did it cost to remove the foot print?" the chauffeur looked at these two in plain clothes and the small Sally next to them, and went on, "one foot print for 10,000 *yuan!*"

"Only 10,000? I was thinking of a much bigger figure." said Pan contemptuously.

The chauffeur did not bother to respond. He took out a piece of deer hide from a black box and said, "This car uses eight types of cleaners. It has to be waxed every fortnight. Even a fly could not land on it, let alone dust. However, handprint can do great deal of damage to it. Three towels may not be enough to clean it, especially if the hand is dirty. Look, even the towels are made especially for the purpose." He flagged the towel in his hand, "Which towel is used for which part of the car is all specified. This thing is 100% cotton, much better than the towel you use to wash face."

Pan Xing and Kim Yet would have left if not for this last remark.

"I'll have to see what kind of superior towel this is." Pan launched the attack first. "Go and get your boss."

"Our boss is not someone whom everybody can see." The chauffeur was well dressed and looked handsome. "Once a traffic police wanted to take a look at my car. He flashed the red light and shouted with a loudspeaker, 'The Rolls, pull over'. I did not dare to get into trouble with a traffic police but somebody did. My boss slowly stepped out of the car and said to the guy, 'young comrade, I am on my way to the Angler's State Guesthouse for a meeting. Could you please inspect it after I am back from the meeting?' But, he would not listen. He insisted I went with him to the station. My boss made a call with the car phone — which had the priority of line use — to the chief of the police department. Within ten minutes the deputy chief arrived. He severely reprimanded the patrolman, saying "Is such a car something you can take a look at as you wish?"

Pan Xing became angrier, shouting, "go get your boss!"

"What if I don't?" The chauffeur swung the gilded car key in his hand.

"If you don't go," Kim Yet also got angry, "I'll use this to cut the paint of your car!"

The chauffeur was immediately subdued. He ran in a hurry toward the door of the building, but suddenly stopped half way and took out his hand phone instead. "Boss, I ran into two hard nuts. Could you please come out?"

In less than a minute, a middle-aged man in casual dress came. When he saw Kim Yet, he closed his hands in front of his chest to make a traditional salute, and said, "I did not know it was your Excellency and our parental official. Please forgive me for not having come to meet and welcome you in the first place. How are you recently?"

"Far from well. Boss Ji." Kim Yet pointed to the chauffeur, "your chauffeur almost ate me alive."

"What's wrong with you?" Boss Ji yelled at his chauffeur, "Don't you recognize our district magistrate?"

The chauffeur opened his mouth but failed to say anything.

"I just touched this car and this guy wanted 10,000 *yuan* compensation." said Kim Yet.

"I'll have absolutely no objection even if you drove the car into a telephone pole, let alone touching it!" Obviously Boss Ji was a very slippery individual who knew how to please with words. "You are our parental official, and I am sure you will forgive the ignorance of commoners like us."

Kim Yet lost interest in this meaningless battle of words. He said to Pan, "Let's go get something to eat." Pan nodded. Boss Ji eagerly offered to foot the bill for their meal.

"We don't have a Rolls-Royce, but I think we can afford a meal." said Pan Xing. They started towards the restaurant without looking at chauffeur.

1.1 In traditional China, the class pecking order was: scholar-officials first, farmers second, handicraftsmen third, and merchants at the bottom (of course, above all these was the imperial household). As far as the relationship between state officials and business owners goes, the order hasn't changed much.

When Pan and Kim Yet entered a plain-looking courtyard, Pan asked, "What kind of business does this Boss Ji do?" Kim Yet told Pan a simplified version of Boss Ji's history. He started as a machine dealer but was now in the pharmaceutical business.

"I thought he must be a big tycoon like Lee Kaisheng or Shao Yifu." Pan pushed aside the branches of a willow tree that were blocking their way, and went on, "Nevertheless, selling drugs is very lucrative. As they say, it's second only to highway robbery."

"I think he probably is not as rich as people believe."

"Then how could he afford such a car?"

"It's all the more important to be showy if you are not that rich."

While chatting, they reached the middle of the courtyard. It was plain-looking from outside but the inside was spacious. There were a few fish tanks and pomegranate trees, as well as a framed shade above.

"It must have been the mansion of a high-ranking official." Although he had been working in the downtown district for several years, Kim Yet was not familiar with the streets and houses here because his job portfolio did not involve him in this aspect of the government's work.

It was Pan Xing's moment. "It was just the residence of the ordinary employees working for the six imperial ministries of the late Qing Dynasty."

"What six ministries?" Kim Yet was always interested in oral or unofficial histories. He showered Pan with compliments to entice him to go on. "You are the most learned person I've ever known. There is no book you haven't read, and I'd appreciate it very much if you won't mind taking the trouble to further elaborate for me."

Pan Xing also loved to take the opportunity to show off his scholarship. "The six Ministries were the Treasury, Civil Engineering, Defense, Personnel, Justice and the Ministry of Rites. The *liubukou* (meaning "gateway to the six ministries") of Beijing got its name because that's where the six ministries used to be. The term *xuli* in today's language would be "ordinary cadres.""

"Even ordinary cadres lived in such luxurious housing?" Kim Yet tempted him to go further.

"Listen to me," Pan looked like a master scholar testing his pupil. "Most of these people came from Shaoxing, Zhejiang Province and had been professional bureaucrats for generations. There was a saying in the late Qing Dynasty: you cannot build an army without the Hunanese; you cannot run a government without Shaoxingers. These people were extremely talented in argumentative tactics; their pens were as deadly as knives, and they made a living out of their literary skills. The Treasury was the most lucrative among the six because it handled budget and state revenues. When the provinces applied for reimbursing their expenditures they often had to give kickbacks to the bureaucrats at the Treasury, often as high as 10%, or they would have to wait two or three years to get their money. The Personnel and Defense Ministries were also very powerful. Officials of the provinces must pay tribute or briberies to them if they wanted to get promoted or reappointed. The Ministry of Civil Engineering was also rich. There was lots of money in big projects. Don't you remember in the novel *A Dream of the Red Chambers* a small project of building a family garden attracted so many contractors? Then, there was the Ministry of Justice.

"When a country is corrupt in general, its judicial system is necessarily shrouded in darkness, under the cover of which corruption runs rampant. The poorest of all was the Ministry of Rites. Bureaucrats there had to wait for major events, such as the wedding or burial of the emperor etc., to have their chance of a run for the money. Otherwise thsey had little to do. However, they could also create opportunities for themselves. For example, when the mother of an official died, according to rules he must stay at home close to his mother's tomb for two to three years to show his *filial piety* and fulfill his obligations as a son." Pan lighted a cigarette, drew a long puff and went on, "Well, the length of this period was decided by the Personnel Ministry and co-signed by the Ministry of Rites. One had to pull some strings to buy off the Ministry of Personnel to shorten this period, one year instead two, for example. For if he actually left his position for three years, his career was finished, and there was nothing he could do to save it. However, even if he had bought off the Ministry of Personnel, he still had to pass the hurdle of the Ministry of Rites, and this was the opportunity bureaucrats there were waiting for."

"Even if there was money to be made, the minister and assistant ministers would be the first, if not the only ones, to wet their beaks." But Kim Yet disagreed.

"You don't know much about the late Qing bureaucracy. It was a pyramid structure and the decisions made by each level of the hierarchy had to be based on the recommendations of the lower level bureaucrats." As Pan was explaining, the owner of the restaurant, Mr. Shue, came to welcome them and showed them in.

The inside was a completely different scene. It was brand new and luxurious. The air conditioners were manufacturing an indoor winter. The windows on the street side

9.4 In the bureaucratic world the source of power is position, but not necessarily higher position.

were all sealed; the air inside was maintained by exhaust fans and air purifiers.

"I am working on a book now. For it I have to mix up with business people quite often. I also analyze the bureaucratic structure." Pan lighted another cigarette. "For instance, you and I compete for a business deal. You bribed the departmental director but I bought off the section chief and the clerk. You'll lose the deal to me even if your product is cheaper. Here is why: in the report to the director of the department, the section chief and the clerk could write something like this: 'the product of Boss Kim's company is cheaper, but the quality is not up to standard. In addition, it does not meet the requirements of the end users.' As such, even if the director wants to help you, he could not dare to write on the report: despite this, we will still buy from Boss Kim."

Kim Yet was speechless, thinking.

6.5 Decentralization reforms in the 1980s and 1990s have created complicated central–local relations; so much so that it is hard to conceptualize China's as a unitary, authoritarian communist state. On the economic side at least it is more fragmented than people expect from such a regime.

"What I try to say is this: Yes indeed the decision power is in the hand of the top leader, but he could only do so within the boundary set by his underlings, who can manipulate the information to sway the decision of their superiors."

A young but plain looking waitress came in and asked what do they wanted for drink.

"This place used to be owned by a Shaoxing scholar-official, therefore we will of course have Shaoxing rice wine."

Soon a vase of filled with wine was brought in. It looked like an antique art object. Kim Yet heard about Shaoxing rice wine but never tasted it. He carefully studied the vase.

"I've already checked it up. It's fake, but if it were the real thing it would worth as much as Louis XIII." Pan poured the wine into two cups and lighted the hotpot. It was choice lamb, from sheep raised on the grassland north of the Zhangjiakou Pass. There was also liver, kidney and other stuff.

"Quality food is only one side. The other side is the setting of this restaurant, very relaxing and enjoyable. Don't you feel so?"

When they finished the rice wine, Kim Yet took from his pocket the business card of Mr. Hamilton and passed it to Pan.

"Your English is better than mine. Help me out with it," said Kim Yet.

"Your English worth mentioning?" Pan put on his glasses and studied the card for a while. "This fellow is the vice president of BC Corporation. He is also an aristocrat."

Kim Yet asked about his title.

"A Baron." Pan returned the card to Kim Yet. "He probably could get away with it if he claimed himself a Bachelor. There is no Baron in the West Indies."

Kim Yet asked why. If he wanted to turn down Zen Kofan's application, especially if he was to face Secretary Leo for its decision he must have adequate reasons like this, the more, the better.

Here was Pan's reasoning: there are all together 1,000 or so aristocrats in Great Britain, among which 300 are not hereditary. Of course, these do not include the Knight titles conferred by the Queen to accomplished people. These aristocrats are concentrated in England; some are in Ireland, but usually not in a colony.

Pan Xing took Hamilton's business card to put it into his pocket, and remarked "You've got your money's worth for this meal."

"I have another request."

"I guess it makes no difference being ripped off once or twice. Fire away."

Kim Yet handed to him the files of Zen Kofan and said, "I wonder why a billionaire like him wants to involve himself in this matter."

"By nature money is always circulating. Today it is here and tomorrow it may be in your place. Some people spend their whole lives accumulating money, which they bury with them when they die. However, a few years later their treasure would be dug up by tomb robbers who would sell it on the market." Pan refused to finish the last cup of wine, despite Kim Yet's urging.

Discussion Questions and Exercises:

1. What does the episode of the Rolls-Royce tell you about Chinese political culture and power relations?
2. The story about the Six Ministries traces the deep cultural and historical roots of the rampant corruption we see in China. Can the same thing happen in your own country? If so, will it happen in the same way? Taking advantage of your comparative perspectives as an outsider, what China can do to cure corruption?
3. Information is an increasing important source of power. What does the fact that in background check Kim Yet did not seek the help from the police or state intelligence agencies but from his friend instead tell you the power shift brought about by the information revolution? How do you think it will continue to impact Chinese politics?
4. Go to a Chinese restaurant and order a hotpot, also called steamboat in some places.

VIII

When Kim Yet entered his office, the first thing he saw was the fax sent by Pan Xing. Pan's handwriting was exceedingly difficult to read: "The internet tells us that Hamilton of yours and his BC Corporation have as their mainline of business in hotels, restaurants and casinos. Of the three, the hotel line holds the bulk of their investment assets but the casino line generates the most profit." Kim Yet easily made out this line: "In fact the main business of BC Corporation is gambling. The revenue generated by his hotels came from two sources: room bookings by gamblers and incorporating casino revenues into the hotel accounts." This was followed by statistics and the BC Corporation's worldwide subsidiaries. It was a long list, at the bottom of which was St. Petersburg of Russia.

Pan Xing's handwriting continued. "This Hamilton had monopolized the casino business of Leningrad and now is salivating at our city. My advice is that you have already had enough problems and could live without this one."

In comparison, Pan provided very little information about Zen and his company. They had suffered some losses in their attempt to sell coal to Taiwan via an intermediary in Southeast Asia, and were also burnt by the bankruptcy of the International Commercial Bank. In the end, Pan regretted that the internet did not yield more information on Zen and his company. The limited information obtained came from other channels and may or may not be accurate, and therefore, could only be used as a reference.

The Chinese government had a ban in effect on exporting coal to Taiwan. However, it was commercially viable if the coal landed first at a third country's port. There was considerable risk involved. The mainland authority may find out about it, the intermediary could also rip him off. Kim Yet knew more about the case of International Commercial Bank. It was involved in trafficking drugs, weapons and so on. Its global assets were frozen a few years ago.

Zen Kofan had so much money, why did he run the risk to involve in the gambling business? Kim Yet tore the paper from the fax machine. As people say, money is forever restless, flowing to wherever there is a profit to be made. It could put people's lives in danger if the profit is enough to entice risky behavior.

Kim Yet picked up the phone and summoned Deputy Director Ma into his office. Ma was in charge of non-productive management in the Planning Bureau.

"Have you reached a conclusion on Zen Kofan's proposal?"

"The project should not be approved." Ma was 58 and had been on that position for ten years. Many of his former colleagues and subordinates had become his superiors. In his words he woke up early, got up late and walked too slow.

"Apart from the project itself, did you find anything else?" Kim Yet looked at Mr. Ma directly into his eyes. The deputy director knew intimately all the skeletons in the closet of the District Government. He looked back at Kim Yet but did not tell him anything. He knew every detail about this matter. Zen

7.5 There seems to be a general agreement that today people are richer but morally degraded. Director Xiang is rich but less respected. "Hatred for the rich" is a widely reported phenomenon.

Kofan had paid him a visit at his home. He raised the banner[20] (of Secretary Leo) and at the same time brought Ma some very expensive presents. Ma took the message but returned the presents. He was very shrewd and experienced. Doing a favor for one's boss itself is reward enough. If he accepted the gift but could not deliver, he would put himself in a difficult position.

"If you did not find anything else, write a report on this." Kim Yet knew he could not get anything more out of Ma, and he did not really want to know any more either. On his part, Ma also knew that Secretary Leo had a role in it, but it was between the leaders themselves. It is better to let them sort things out. *A clay pot should stay away from iron woks.*

Kim Yet closed the office door behind deputy director Ma, and wanted to carefully consider Zen Kofan's case. Whenever he encountered problems, he always acted only after carefully weighing the various factors. Many people tend to substituting action with thinking; this is in fact a serious tragic flaw. He thinks before acting. However, as he barely started, Pan Xing broke in with a bearded man.

Pan introduced the man to Kim Yet, "This is the general producer of the large-scale dancing and music show 'We are the Sons and Daughters of the Republic."

Kim Yet stood up and shook hands with the director, apparently with some reluctance, and asked him about the purpose of his visit. The director briefly explained that the show was produced in memory of the "sent-down movement" during the Cultural Revolution. They had raised some money but still fell short, and hoped Kim Yet could lend him a hand.

Kim Yet looked at Pan, who avoided eye contact. He had more than once discussed with Pan about the "Sent-down Movement." He believed it was a disaster for his generation. From a legal perspective, it was also unconstitutional — it robbed a whole generation of young people of their rights to receive higher education, which he considered a heaven-given right, just like a patient has

---

[20] Meaning he used the name of Leo.

the right to see a doctor. Of course, some would say 'nobody forced you to go."

Indeed, they were not forced at gun point like prisoners. Ostensibly you were persuaded to go. The teachers of your school encouraged you to go, the military propaganda team urged you to go, and the old ladies of the neighborhood committee came to congratulate you on your decision to go — a decision not made yet — beating drums and gongs. If you still refused to go after all these, they would go to the work unit of your parents and tell them that to send or not to send down your kids was the watershed between a revolutionary and a counter-revolutionary. In those days, nobody could resist such pressure.

Because of this, Kim Yet turned down all the requests from those who were relatively successful among his "sent-down" generation to contribute to books of reminiscence they were compiling. Being too busy was his usual excuse, but in reality he did not want to have anything to do with it. For had he done it, it would have helped to create the impression that suffering were the stepping stone to success. He believed that poverty and hardships were beneficial to nobody. As to the few successes among his generation, their accomplishments came at the cost of the fall of millions. In his district, 10% of the janitorial workers were the returned "sent-down" youths. In other words, the successful ones were the exceptions, and exceptions existed because of the norm. More in-depth examination would reveal that the so-called "success stories" among his generation were mostly in sports and the literary fields. There were perhaps none in science. And this is precisely the point: formal education is irreplaceable.

The General Director seated himself comfortably facing Kim Yet, lit up a cigarette and said, "We'll all be happy if you give us 30,000 yuan."

"The District Government's funds all run through the planning channels."

"There has to be some extra-budgetary money somewhere."

"In financial matters there is only one pen. Even if there were some, only the District Magistrate has the power to decide how to spend it."

"The money does not necessarily have to come out of the district government coffer. A phone call of yours to a company in your district may as well yield the money."

Director Xiang tapped on the cigarette in his hand with his index finger; the ash fell to the clean floor. He was an old hand at fund raising, having had successes for sports events and TV series before. "We will follow the common practice to give you 10% kickbacks." He played his ace card that had never failed before.

The original meaning of rebate in commerce was quite different. For example, a certain merchandize is priced at $10; the merchant can't simply lower the price because someone is his old customer; he still has to sell it for ten dollars; Well, what makes the difference is that afterwards he will give the customer one dollar rebate. Nowadays, the word "rebate" has become the euphemism for bribery.

Kim Yet opened the window to let out the heavy smoke. No doubt there were people in his generation who had managed to read a few books amidst poverty and hardships. However, the more valuable thing they learned was the skill to survive in the most inhospitable environment. This survival instinct cultivated in those years in the countryside had now become a skill in which they were far superior to those of the previous generation and the generation to follow.

10.2 Fund raising is a booming business in China. Kickbacks and other forms of corruption are part of the reason. Another part is state ownership and extensive role of the government in the economy. The state can order the SOEs to contribute while state officials get the kickback. The state can also pressurize private businesses to contribute because the latter are under the mercy of the state in so many ways (except of course the special private firms owned by princelings such as Zen Kofan). Targeting state officials is the key to prosper in the fundraising business.

"I really can't help you on this right now." Kim Yet wanted to say that he wouldn't throw money away for this kind of thing even if he had it, but he felt it was unnecessary. After all, they belong to the same fraternity of the "sent-down" youths. "Please allow me to give you a ride back in my car." The director left with a "thank you all the same" and did not appear too upset.

"You offer him a ride in your car?" said Pan Xing, "His car is way better than yours!"

"He got it all from fund-raising?"

"I've no idea where he gets his money from; we were like piss and shit going separate ways."

Kim Yet then asked Pan how he got to know the General Director. Pan told him nonchalantly, "He is the spiritual leader of our collective household whom I have often talked about to you, the one I admired the most."

It was Kim Yet's turn to be stunned. He could not imagine the hero of Pan Xing, a person so witty and intelligent, one who could recite *Three Hundred Poems of the Tang Dynasty* and *A Collection of Ancient Classics*, and who could give lectures on 'History of the French Revolution' and Hegel's philosophy, could have been reduced to such a worldly man.

"What's wrong with being a worldly man?" Pan was suddenly overtaken by an anonymous anger, "Someone even did a dissertation on the life of 'sent-down' youths and got a ridiculous degree for it."

"Don't be mad, my dearest thinker." Kim Yet was good at reading people's mind. He knew it was painful for Pan to see the degradation of his idol.

"Don't give me 'thinker this and thinker that'. Let me tell you this: all great Chinese thinkers have lived a short life. They have original ideas when they are young but the burden of life would in the end crash them all. And who is to blame? You bureaucrats!"

Kim Yet smiled. He understood Pan completely and liked him for his scholarly courage. "Not all have crashed. One of them is standing right in front of me."

Pan Xing also laughed, then switching the topic, "Are you wearing a branded suit?"

"The world of the officialdom is very different from the world of artists and scholars. Few here wear exotic outfits." Kim Yet straightened his suit and answered, "I got it on sale."

Pan Xing did not believe him. He turned over Kim Yet's collar to take a look; it was indeed an unknown brand. "Nevertheless," said Pan, "you look smart in it."

As soon as Pan Xing stepped out of the door, the phone rang. It was Deputy Chief Su. After brief formalities of greeting, Su said, "I have news for you: Secretary Leo will be reassigned." He paused, apparently waiting for Kim Yet to ask where to and the successor etc. but Kim Yet did not. "Thank you very much for telling me."

Su had to hang up.

The objective of telling me this news is obvious: if I helped Zen Kofan then he would help me to secure the position as District Magistrate when the current one is promoted to be the new party secretary. Kim Yet quickly analyzed the situation.

There is not a single government official who does not want to be promoted. The higher an official goes, the bigger the things he can accomplish. A wooden barrow could only hold so much water. If you want to put more water in it, you must expand the container. *But I have a choice.* For the first time Kim Yet lit up a cigarette. *My cost is not being able to become the District Magistrate, but the benefit is maintaining my integrity.* He summoned Deputy Bureau Chief Ma. He wrote on the report Ma presented to him: "Approval not recommended, but let Secretary Leo make the final decision."

Discussion Questions and Exercises:

1. Zen Kofan had so much money; why then he still ran the risk to get involved in the gambling business?
2. Mao's popularity among at least certain segments of the population has surged time and again since 1993 (Mao's centennial anniversary). Recent years, have seen the rise of the new left. From the story, do you see the rationale of Mao in launching the Cultural Revolution? If you were Mao, what would you do to deal with the rising inequality and the privileged class amongst your own comrades?

3. Identify a few sources of corruption in the Chinese system from this chapter.
4. Please comment on the authority relationships in the political system.

IX

After a whole day's mediation between Water Bureau and Power Bureau, Kim Yet felt exhausted when he came home.

"Any result?" Normally his wife seldom inquired about his official business. She did today because one of her colleagues was affected by the dispute.

Kim Yet shook his head, "Both sides insisted that the other side make concessions."

"Nowadays, there are too many bureaucratic frictions like this. Sometimes you need to stand out as government authority to exert some pressure when necessary."

Kim Yet poured himself a cup of tea, but did not respond. If pressure worked, it would have been resolved long ago. He felt it was not necessary to explain official business to his family.

"Isn't it true that for either side, the additional revenue collected would go to government coffer anyway?" His wife replenished his cup with hot water and passed to him.

"Yours is an old idea of the planned economy era. Nowadays the revenue collected by each department is mostly spent by that department. Sometimes even the central government is unable to collect tax from them. They vie to construct highways and toll-booths along them because the revenue collected is at their disposal. The loss of revenues this way is the ultimate reason that the central and local governments operate under tight budgets."

"Can't the state coerce them to pay what they owe?"

"Good question," Kim Yet put down his cup. "This is exactly the question I've pondered on for a long time. State capacity is the ability of the central government to realize its own goals and enforce its own will. It consists of four parts: the ability to enforce its policies, the ability at macro-economic regulation, the ability to gain legitimacy, and the ability to extract revenue. Among these the most important is the ability to extract revenue. Without this all the others are up in the air. And it is precisely this ability of the state that is alarmingly weak."

"To make a little thing sound like a major issue is the main ability of you bureaucrats." His wife could only understand his elaboration a little.

> *1.6 As most state officials, Kim Yet has a bias toward more centralization of power. Market-based economic decision making is by nature decentralized. Without such decentralization there will not be competition. Coming from the era of the planned economy, many Chinese officials still harbor the same centralization mentality.*

"You always hit the nail on the head." Kim Yet finished his dinner in a sweep and sat down in front of the computer to write: China is a single-party rule by the CCP and a highly centralized country. However, the state is not monolithic and decision making in the economic arena is extremely dispersed. The ability of the central state to rein in the local governments is limited and the same is true for local governments' ability to control enterprises. This inability leads to the ballooning of self-interests, self-consciousness and autonomy of local governments at each level and enterprises in all sectors. This explosion of self-interests in turn acts as catalyst to speed up the dispersion and multi-polarization of economic decision power. This is a potential threat to future economic development if they are allowed to go on unchecked.

As he finished writing and was about to turn off the computer, he remembered an old story. When Zhang Zhidong of the late Qing Dynasty, a famous reformer of the time, was still a *"hanlin"* (equivalent to a PhD candidate of today) he made many reform plans for his future career in the government. Before presenting them to the emperor he asked his elder brother Zhang Zhiwan for comments and suggestions. After reading them, Zhang Zhiwan said to him, "These are good ideas, however, keep them to yourself before you are appointed as a chief executive of a local government." Later on, Zhang Zhidong indeed became the governor of Shanxi Province, and he was able to put many of his ideas to practice.

"Will I be able to put my ideas to practice someday?" he asked himself.

The next day, deputy chief Ma brought him the document signed off by Secretary Leo. As expected, Leo only circled his name on Kim Yet's recommendation: "Approval not recommended but let Secretary Leo make the final decision."

"Please notify Zen Kofan." Although he knew it was unnecessary, Kim Yet still added, "Circle read[21] means no objections."

Chief Ma put on a mysterious smile.

"What's so funny?"

"I remembered a story."

Kim Yet looked at Ma in surprise. They had worked together for three years but never really chatted.

"Once upon a time, there was such a deputy prefecture commissioner in such a province. One day he received a note from a leading cadre of the provincial party committee, asking him to find a project for a certain contractor. This cadre then wrote an instruction on the same note: County Magistrate Hu: will you please arrange this in your county's drainage project?" The county magistrate also wrote on the note: "Please let the drainage project manager Sen attend to this matter.

Seeing the note, Sen felt that he was obligated and approved a 300,000 *yuan* contract to that contractor.

That drainage project was designed to improve the county's farmland with very high Ph values. It was a major undertaking of the county as well as the dream of the people of that county for generations. That contractor, however, did not take it seriously and soon

---

[21] In the system of document flows, the senior cadres usually circle their names on the document indicating they have read it. Sometimes, they make many comments and suggestions for revisions. If they only circle their names without any comments (*quanyue*), that indicates they have no disagreement with the document in question.

6. Central–Local Relations

China is an authoritarian unitary state under one-party rule. The legacies of Imperial China, including the Confucian political culture and a civilization-based nationalism etc., generally reinforce such polity. However, China is also a vast country with diverse local conditions. China's provinces are equivalent to major European nations in terms of population and, in some cases, size of the economy. Central control has never been easy. Since the Mao era, China has gone through many cycles of decentralization and recentralization. However, in Mao's time the cycle was premised on a planned economy and hence consisted of redistribution of power and responsibilities between state actors in the central state and in local governments. It was relatively easy for the central government to retract the power and resources delegated to the localities when the latter deviated from central policy. In the post-Mao reform era, however, the cycle occurs in the context of marketization and globalization, which substantially strengthen the position of the provinces. Local states have the primary role of promoting economic development in their respective jurisdictions and three decades of rapid growth has cumulated enormous amount of wealth and resources in the local economies. A *de facto* federalism in the economic area has emerged (see Essay 1). However, through the communist party the central state has kept tight control over the appointments of provincial leaders. In other words, politically China is very much a unitary state but economically it exhibits strong federalist features.

The competition and rivalry among local states for higher growth rate form a basic dynamism driving the Chinese economy. State actors turned into market players under the condition of decentralization, which also generated a dynamic process of policy initiation, formulation and implementation between the center and the localities. The downside includes pervasive state

(*Continued*)

(Continued)

intervention in the marketplace and distortion of market prices. Local states often set up trade barriers against other provinces and use administrative fiat to raise capital and mobilize resources to undertake grand investment projects. Their zealous pursuit of growth is to a great extent responsible for the periodic overheating of the economy and a pattern of investment-driven growth. Localism also makes it difficult for the central government to implement macro-economic policies. The competition between the central and local states for resources and power in politically non-sensitive areas has also been a constant theme in central–local relations.

A further complication arises from the ethnic minorities. China has five "autonomous regions" of ethnic minorities at the province level. Separatist movement exists in Tibet, Xinjiang and, to a lesser extent, Inner Mongolia. Ethnic strife, riots and terrorism are on the rise in recent years.

squandered the money. Later on, a Xinhua News Agency's reporter learned about it and wrote an internal report. One senior official in Beijing read it and ordered a thorough investigation to be carried out and the findings reported to him. A large team of investigators were dispatched, who easily got hold of the note. As a result, the deputy commissioner was reprimanded in public, the county magistrate was demoted and the project manager Sen lost his job.

"Did you make up the story yourself?" laughed Kim Yet.

"I was a member of the investigation team." Ma stood up and went on, "That was many years ago. Nowadays nobody is that foolish any more. In matters considered sensitive and risky, nobody would put anything in writing. Instead, they make phone calls. As soon as they hang up all traces are 'gone with the wind'."

Kim Yet suspected that someone must have worked on Ma too, but he knew that Ma would not tell him even if he asked.

Discussion Questions and Exercises:

1. Kim's wife suggested that Kim needed to assert the authority of the government over its bureaucracies when necessary. In the case of Water and Power dispute, why Kim stayed as a neutral mediator for so long? If he asserted his authority from the beginning, what do you think would happen?
2. More generally, China is an authoritarian regime. Why then authority does not seem to always work?
3. Is China a strong, a weak or a failed state? Give your reasons.
4. In your opinion, is there accountability at all in the Chinese political system? If no, how do you then explain the success of the CCP overseeing China's extraordinary development in the last three decades? If yes, what are the sources of the accountability?

CODA

Before the Lunar New Year, Secretary Leo was re-assigned to be the director of the political department of the Ministry of Nuclear Industries, becoming a cadre of the vice ministerial rank. Following the norm, the district magistrate became the district party secretary.

Kim Yet was not promoted.

When Pan Xing called, Kim Yet told him, "Nobody has ever promised me anything. In other words, I have no opportunity. In your theory, there is no choice without opportunities. Naturally there is no cost to me either."

Proverbs:

— Paper cannot wrap up fire. (纸是包不住火的)
— Prime ministers must arise from the provinces; capable generals should arise from soldiers. (宰相必起于州部，猛将必发于卒伍)
— Flies never visit an egg that has no crack. (苍蝇不叮无缝的蛋)

Discussion Questions and Exercises:

1. Kim Yet was not promoted, at least this time. Did he expect so? Kim had meticulously planned a career of climbing the bureaucratic ladder.

In the end he seemed to have given up his career dream. Or has he? Is this another of his strategic move?

2. That raises the question about Kim Yet's future. As the deputy mayor of Beijing said, "Who can keep the sun from rising?" After this setback (not being promoted to District Magistrate), will Kim Yet rise again? Divide the class into groups with different opinions and debate the question. The purpose is to find out the political logic of the Chinese system for yourself.

Overall Reading Questions and Suggested Exercises:

1. What does Chinese politics has in common with the politics in your country?
2. In what ways Kim Yet's life trajectory as well as aspiration is similar and different from that of Xi Jinping's (see "Son of the Yellow Earth" in this book)? Why do you think Kim Yet and Xi Jinping have completely opposite assessment of the "sent-down" movement that similarly affected their lives? Yet, why do they share the same admiration for Mao?
3. How does informal power work in the Chinese political system?
4. Secretary Leo's behavior in this story is worth pondering carefully. His career success culminated in his promotion to a vice ministerial level position. However, he was successful in a way quite different from the way Kim Yet obtained his success. Can you characterize their respective approach to success? Obviously, there is more than one strategy to career success even in the Chinese system. Which strategy is more robust in the Chinese environment? Kim's or Leo's?
5. Without democratic elections, where does the Chinese regime derive its legitimacy?
6. Discuss the differences and similarities, if any, between Kim and the politicians in your own country.
7. Find out all references to the People's Congress in the story and piece them together: what impressions or remarks you can draw from them about the PC?
8. Describe and explain the decision making procedures (formal and informal) in China's one-party rule.
9. The friendship between Kim and Pan forged through trying experiences during the Mao era is quite typical of the generation of Chinese

elite grown up in the 1960s and 1970s. People like Xi Jinping and Li Keqiang among this generation took the reins over in November of 2012 as the fifth generation leadership of the PRC. Although elite of this generation are dominant in politics, businesses, academics and other professions, they share the same formative experience and probably similar ideological outlook as Kim Yet. How do they impress you? Do you think you could get along with them? Based on your understanding of their character, what direction Chinese politics is likely to move under their watch?

10. Can you survive in this system as a cadre? If not, why? If you can, draw a strategy of your survival and ask someone from China to comment on it.

11. Apart from individual cadres such as Kim Yet, where do you see hopes for progress in the Chinese society?

12. There is a pervasive "rank mentality" in the Chinese society. That is, people tend to rank every individual and organizations on the same scale of the state hierarchy and use the ranking to determine how to relate to each other. Parallel to this is also the informal ranking based mainly on seniority and some long-standing cultural traditions. Find some incidents in the story that illustrate this "rank mentality" and ponder on them: do you have the same thing in your own society? Are there in the Chinese culture any implications for such things as equality, democracy, civil rights and civil liberty, individualism etc. that are the foundation of western democracies?

13. What does Chinese politics have in common with the politics in your country?

14. Discuss the differences and similarities, if any, between Kim and the politicians of your own country whom you know of.

15. Kim did not love money; he avoided bribery of any kind; he did not, according to his wife, do enough to seek promotion (Bribery is most commonly used for that purpose since ancient time); in fact several times he requested to "go down" to work at the grossroots level; in the case of Zen Kofan he seemed deliberate in ruining his career chances because he not only did not get promotion but also offended some powerful figures in the process. What is then the ultimate motivation that drove him throughout his career?

PART II

THE STUDY UNITS

As suggested in the Introduction, these eleven Study Units can be used to furnish the basic structure of the course. Each unit consists of four parts: reading material, key issues (and concepts), exercises and suggested further readings. The key issues outline the objectives of a Study Unit. In other words, the students should become familiar with these issues, including the associated concepts, theories, debates, historical figures and facts. Instead of finding ready answers and explanations in this textbooks, the students, are expected to engage in active learning, finding for themselves the answers (most if not all of them can be easily found online), formulating their own opinions, drawing their own conclusions, filling the gaps in the subject area and pursuing their own lines of inquiry — hopefully, such active learning will stimulate new interest, new ideas, and new questions. The students should be given the freedom as well as guidance to pursue these because they usually thrive when taking ownership of a line of inquiry.

Apart from those included in each unit (some have none), the readings are drawn from the various parts of the book. They are necessarily fragmented, with many gaps in them and rarely providing ready answers or complete narrative of a historical event or a historical figure. The students are expected to fill in the gaps, make the connections and develop a coherent understanding of the subject matter addressed in each unit. Such a study model may be unfamiliar to some students and hence is challenging. But hopefully it is also more rewarding because of the freedom of critical and creative thinking it enables. The main objective is to gain scholarly aptitude, not static knowledge.

STUDY UNIT 1

THE CULTURAL AND HISTORICAL CONTEXT

China is the most populous country in the world and third largest in geographic area. It is currently the second largest economy and is set to overtake the United States as the largest economy in the middle of this century if not earlier. Between 1978 and 2012, the Chinese economy sustained a near double-digit growth rate for more than 30 years. This is unprecedented in world history for a continental-sized country. China became the "factory of the world", flooding the world with cheap consumer products, driving up the price of commodities, putting great pressure on the environment while lifting 400 million people out of extreme poverty. The repercussions of the rise of China have been felt in almost every corner of the world.

China's remarkable achievements are the culmination of more than a century's agonizing struggle to transform itself and bring it into the modern industrial age. The transformation is long, torturous and exceedingly bloody because China has to overcome the inertia of the historical legacies of more than 2,000 years and highly developed cultural traditions that are often at odd with modernity. Traditional China was a highly developed agrarian civilization. It was earth-bound, stable, stationary, and stagnant. The modern Chinese history is a history of a dynamic, industrial capitalism raking havoc in such a civilization. China has struggled for nearly two centuries searching for ways to accommodate modernity while preserving its cultural identity.

The pre-modern Chinese history consisted of the rise and fall of dynasties in a cyclical pattern. The imperial system of government was established as early as 221 B.C. with the unification of the China by the Qin Dynasty. It survived the rise and fall of many dynasties for two millennia and many times the rule of foreign invaders, mainly the nomad tribes from the northern steppes such as the Mongols during the Yuan Dynasty (1279–1368) and the Manchus during the Qing Dynasty (1644–1911). The highly developed Chinese agrarian civilization was able to assimilate or Sinicize these foreign rulers until it came to a head-on collision with the modern Western industrialism backed by imperialism in the middle of the 19th century.

The conflict between the nomads and settled farmers is a recurrent narrative of the Chinese history. The agrarian civilization of traditional China is land-bound and non-expansionary, if for no other reasons than that the country is isolated from the rest of the world by seas, desserts, steppes and high mountain ranges. Its impressive cultural achievements in isolation in turn made China inward-looking and self-centered. The culturally crude nomads that China encountered throughout its history enforced a belief that China was the center of the civilized world — "the middle kingdom" (the literal translation of *zhongguo* or China), and all peoples of non-Chinese culture were barbarians up to the late 19th century. Even the repeated defeats in the hands of these militarily superior horsemen from the north did not shake this belief.

Tribal and feudal dynasties of Xia (around 21st–16th centuries B.C.), Shang (around 16th–11th centuries B.C.), and Zhou (around 11th century–221 B.C.)[1] preceded the imperial dynasties that began with the Qin (221–207 B.C.). The Chinese form of writing, developed by 2000 B.C. and still in use today, is a complex system of picture writing using forms of ideograms, pictograms, and phonograms (see Figure 1). Although scanty for the Xia and Shang dynasties, written records became abundant for the Zhou Dynasty. These early dynasties were divided into numerous warring principalities or kingdoms. By late Zhou Dynasty they consolidated into seven kingdoms and one of them, Qin, eventually conquered all others to establish the first imperial dynasty in 221 B.C.

---

[1]Further periodization would include West Zhou (11th Century–771 B.C.), Spring and Autumn (770–476 B.C.) and the Warring States (475–221 B.C.; the Zhou Court ended around 256 B.C.).

Portrait of Confucius

Ideogram

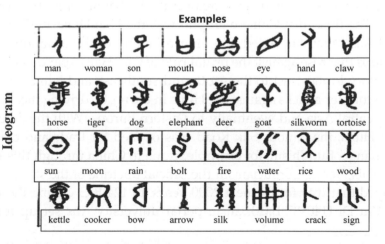

Figure 1 Ideogramic Chinese Characters

The relatively decentralized feudal dynasties produced many cultural achievements. The major philosophical schools that have had enduring influence on imperial China were all from that era: Confucianism, Taoism, Legalism and so on. Feudal China also saw the rise of a particular social class — the scholars (*shi*), who were the forerunners of the scholar-officials of the Chinese empires. In the later period of Zhou dynasty, however, they were a relatively small group of learned people. Often wandering from state to state in search of employment by the royal courts, the *shi* worked as tutors to the children of feudal princes and as advisers to various kings and dukes. The most famous of these was Confucius.

After nearly 900 years, Zhou Dynasty came to an end when the state of Qin unified China and established the first empire. The Qin Empire did not last long, but it left two enduring legacies: the name China and the idea and structure of the empire. This heritage outlasted the Qin Dynasty itself by more than 2,000 years. A centralized bureaucracy replaced the old feudal system. The empire was divided into provinces and counties, which were governed by centrally appointed governors and magistrates. Other centralizing policies included census taking and standardization of the writing system and weights and measures. The Great Wall of China was first established by the Qin Dynasty when the First Emperor connected the walls built by the other states in defense against the barbarians from the north.[2]

The first great Chinese empire was the Han Dynasty (206 B.C.– 220 A.D.) that succeeded Qin after a bloody civil war among rebel groups that rose against the brutal rule of Qin. Han expanded China's territory to the coast to the south and southeast, and launched massive counter-attacks against the Huns in the north, driving them away to Central Asia and eventually to Eastern Europe. With the defeat of the Huns, the famous Silk Road was opened for trade and cultural exchange. Buddhism, for example, came to China through this road. Han also made Confucianism the official doctrine of the state, which stayed that way for the next 2000 years. In 124 B.C. during the reign of Wu Di (140–87 B.C.), an imperial university was set up for the

---

[2]The Great Wall we see today was mostly rebuilt during the Ming Dynasty (1368–1644).

study of Confucian classics. The number of government-supported students in the university reached 30,000 by the end of the Han Dynasty. Paper making was invented during the Han Dynasty. The Chinese show their pride in Han accomplishments by calling themselves the "Han people" (Hanren) and the Chinese writing "Han characters" (Hanzi).

7. Confucianism

Confucianism is an ethical and sociopolitical system developed from the teachings of the great Chinese sage Confucius (551–479 B.C.). It is based on the ethical philosophy meant to be practiced by all the members of a society. The Confucian ethics is characterized by the promotion of virtues and the derivative code of conduct. Detailed role specifications and the code of conduct associated with each role would, if everybody behaves according to his or her prescribed roles, add up to a stable hierarchy of social and political order that governs almost every aspect of the life of an individual. Filial piety provides a stable foundation of society — the family. And loyalty ensures the stability of a hierarchically organized state.

The core of Confucianism is humanism. The focus of spiritual concern is this world and the family, not the gods nor the afterlife. This stance rests on the belief that human beings are teachable, improvable and perfectible through personal and communal endeavor. Confucian thought focuses on the cultivation of virtue and maintenance of ethics. Top Confucian virtues include *ren*, which is an obligation of altruism and humaneness for other individuals; *yi*, which is the upholding of righteousness and the moral disposition to do good; *li*, which is a system of norms and propriety that determines how a person should properly act in everyday life; *zhi*, which accentuates knowledge and wisdom; *xin*, which emphasizes personal integrity. Confucianism holds that one should give up one's life, if necessary, for the sake of upholding the cardinal moral values of *ren* and *yi*. The Confucian scholar-officials

(Continued)

(Continued)

enjoyed high prestige not only because of their learnedness but because of their high level of moral self-cultivation.

Confucianism was first adopted as the state ideology during the reign of Wudi Emperor of Han Dynasty (140–87 B.C.). The disintegration of the Han in the second century A.D. opened the way for the spiritual and other worldly doctrines of Buddhism and Daoism to dominate intellectual life at that time. A Confucian revival began during the Tang dynasty (619–907). During the later years of the Tang dynasty, Confucianism absorbed some aspects of Buddhism and Daoism and was reformulated as neo-Confucianism. This reinvigorated form was adopted as the basis of the imperial exams and the core philosophy of the scholar official class in the Song dynasty (960–1279). The New Culture intellectuals of the early 20th century blamed Confucianism for China's weaknesses against the West. They searched for imported doctrines to replace it, such as the "Three Principles of the People" with the establishment of the Republic of China in 1911, and then communism under the People's Republic of China founded in 1949. In the late 20th century, some people credited Confucianism with the rise of the East Asian economies. It is partially revived in China and to some extent promoted by the communist party as antidote to moral deterioration amidst rampant materialism and the decline of the Marxist ideology. Confucianism also forms the core of China's soft power. Hundreds of Confucius Institutes have been established around the world under the sponsorship of Chinese government.

The Han Dynasty rose against the brutality of Qin, which lost popular support and hence the "mandate of heaven." In the Confucian ideology, rebellion against the ruler is justified when the latter is believed to have lost the "mandate of heaven." This conviction is so deeply seated in the Chinese cultural psyche that even today losing the hearts and minds of the people is so dreaded that the communist regime tries hard to be responsive to popular sentiment and demand. Heeding the lessons of the fall of Qin, the early Han emperors adopted a Taoist *laissez-faire* ruling philosophy to allow the people to recoup and recover from the brutal rule of the Qin and the war ravages that brought it down. However, later on, the emperors and the ruling class became increasingly repressive. High taxations, incessant demands for labor and military services, the increasing number of landless peasants, and the frequent natural disasters and famines drove people to arms. Massive peasant rebellions towards the end of the Han Dynasty were clear indicators that the imperial court lost the "mandate of heaven", which in turn motivated regional governors and local war lords to compete for the imperial mantle. The Han Empire was split into three warring kingdoms (220–265), which were eventually united into another empire — the Jin Dynasty. This pattern of the rise and fall of Han was to be repeated many times to become known as the "dynastic cycle", the dominant historical narrative of China.

After a brief period of unification under the Jin Dynasty (265–316), China again broke up into kingdoms or smaller, localized dynasties constantly at war with each other for the next 280 years (317–589). Many of these were founded and ruled by invading tribes from the northern steps. The Sui Dynasty unified China again in 581. But like Qin, the Sui Empire was short lived (581–618), soon replaced by the second great empire of China — the Tang Dynasty (618–907). Successive major dynasties after Tang were Song (960–1279), Yuan (1271–1368), Ming (1368–1644), and Qing (1644–1911), punctured by another short period of disintegration (907–979) following the fall of the Tang Dynasty. The revolution of 1911 finally ended the dynastic cycle with the establishment of the first republic in China.

The Sui built the 1,794 km long Grand Canal, which linked up the Huang, Huai, and Yangtze rivers and connected north and south China. It also revived the Han system of recruiting government officials through examinations based on Confucian classics. The imperial examination system, called *keju* in Chinese, was further developed during the Tang Dynasty and perfected in the Song and Ming dynasties. It was the forerunner of modern civil service adopted in many countries around the world.

The Tang capital of Chang'an was one of the greatest commercial and cosmopolitan cities in the world at that time. The period was characterized by high cultural achievements, especially in poetry. Buddhism became widespread to influence art (sculpture in particular), philosophy, and lifestyle. The Buddhist Shaolin Temple became a center of martial art (kung fu) during the Tang. The invention of printing and improvements in papermaking led to the printing of a whole set of Buddhist sutras (discourses of the Buddha) by 868 and by the beginning of the 11th century all of the Confucian classics and the Taoist canon had been printed. The Tang period also marked the beginnings of China's early technological advancement over other civilizations in the fields of shipbuilding and firearms development. Both reached new heights in the succeeding dynasty of Song.

The Song period was noted for landscape painting, which in time came to be considered the highest form of classical art. In philosophy, the trend away from Buddhism and back to Confucianism that had begun in late Tang continued. In late Tang and early Song, several strands of Confucianism emerged. The great scholar Zhu Xi synthesized elements of Confucianism, Buddhism, and Taoism. This reconstituted philosophy became known as Neo-Confucianism, and it was the orthodox state doctrine until the end of the imperial system. Zhu Xi's philosophy was one that stressed dualism, the goodness of human nature, and self-cultivation by education. The ideal life of a scholar-gentleman should consist, in causal sequence, of moral self-cultivation, raising a virtuous family, contributing to good governance of the state, and bringing peace and harmony to the world.

The Mongols were the first of the northern barbarian tribes to rule all of China. Kublai Khan, the fifth "great khan" and grandson of Genghis Khan, moved the Mongol capital from Karakorum to Peking in 1267. In 1271 he declared himself emperor of China and named the dynasty Yuan, meaning "beginning", to signify that this was the beginning of a long era of Mongol rule. The great Mongol empires, stretching across Eurasia, parts of the India subcontinent and what is the Arab world today, facilitated trade and cultural exchange between East and West. Marco Polo is the best known agent of cultural exchange from this period.

Chinese scholars studying hard to pass the imperial civil service exam

Coming out of almost a century of Mongol domination (1271–1368), the Ming Dynasty (1368–1644) followed a typical dynastic cycle: initial rehabilitation of the economy and restoration of efficient government, followed by a time of stability and then a gradual decline and fall. Emperor Hong Wu modeled his government on the Tang system, restored the doctrine and practices of Confucianism and continued the trend toward concentration of power in the imperial government.

The Ming is known in today's China for its great maritime expeditions. Between 1405 and 1433, seven major maritime expeditions were launched under the leadership of a Muslim eunuch, Zheng He. Each expedition was provided with up to several hundreds of seagoing vessels. Some were 416 feet (127 meters) long, 170 feet (52 meters) high, weighed 700 tons (635 metric tons), had multiple decks and 50 or 60 cabins, and carried several hundred people. During these expeditions, the Chinese sailed the South China Sea, the Indian Ocean, the Red Sea, and the Persian Gulf. They traveled as far west as eastern Africa. During the second

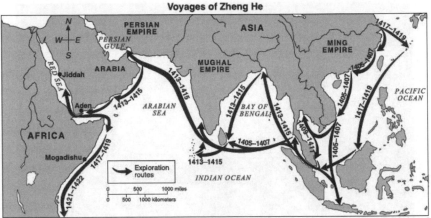

Source: Elisabeth Ellis and Anthony Esler, *World History: Connections to Today*, Prentice Hall (adapted)

half of the Ming Dynasty, European expansion began. Early in the 16th century, Portuguese traders arrived and leased the island of Macao as their trading post. In 1582, Matteo Ricci, an Italian Jesuit missionary, arrived in Macao. Because of his knowledge of science, mathematics, and astronomy and his willingness to learn the Chinese language and adapt to Chinese life, he was accepted by the Chinese and became the first westerner allowed to live in Peking permanently. More Jesuits followed him and served the Ming emperors as mapmakers, calendar reformers, and astronomers. Unlike the later Western incursions into China, the 16th-century Sino-Western relationship was culturally oriented and mutually respectful. Both the Chinese and the Jesuits tried to find common ground in their thoughts.

The turmoil of peasant rebellions towards the end of the Ming provided the opportunity for the Manchus, a tribal nation from the Amur region in the northeast of today's China, to deal the final blow to a collapsing empire and impose the second alien rule over the entire China — the Qing Dynasty (1644–1911). Unlike the 13th century Mongol conquerors, the Sinicized Manchus made their rule more acceptable to the Chinese. As a result, the Qing rule lasted 267 years, compared with 89 years for the Yuan. The Manchu conquests greatly expanded the Chinese territory to include Mongolia in the north, Xinjiang in the northwest, and Tibet in the southwest.

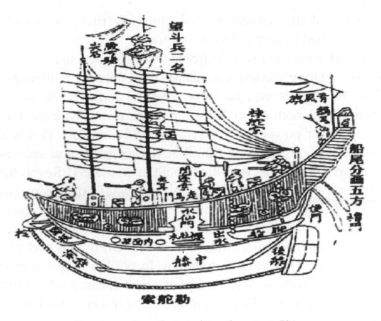

Structure of sea-faring ship of ancient China

The first of many Sino–Western conflicts in the 19th century was the Opium War, fought with the Great Britain from 1839 to 1842. The war was more than a dispute over the opium trade; it was a contest between China as the representative of an ancient eastern civilization and Britain as the forerunner of the modern West, between a stationary, inward-looking, and self-sufficient agrarian civilization and a dynamic, trade-driven industrial civilization. The Treaty of Nanking, which ended the first Opium War with a British victory, opened five ports to the British — the first of the "treaty ports" where Westerners were granted various privileges. A second Opium War, also known as the Arrow War, fought from 1856 to 1860, pitted China against Great Britain and France.

Other Western colonial powers joined the feeding frenzy. China became embroiled in a series of conflicts: the Tianjin Massacre with France in 1870, the Ili crisis with Russia in 1879, the Sino–French War from 1884 to 1885, and the Sino–Japanese War from 1894 to 1895. Each brought further humiliation to and greater impairment of the sovereignty of China. Territory was lost and indemnities had to be paid to the victors.

Unlike the nomad invaders from the land borders in the north and west, the sea-faring Western colonialists were not only militarily superior but also represented a far more powerful and dynamic industrial civilization that nothing in the Chinese agrarian civilization could match up with in power and in no way it could assimilate. This instilled a deep sense of crisis among the Chinese ruling elite and spawned a reformist movement that eventually built up to the 1911 Revolution.

The spiritual leader of that revolution was Sun Yat-sen, who is now revered as the father of modern China by Nationalists and Communists alike. Born into a peasant family near Canton, Sun was educated in Hawaii, converted to Christianity, and had a short-lived medical career before switching to politics. After forming a secret revolutionary society and plotting an unsuccessful uprising in Canton in 1894, Sun began a long period of exile outside China.

Chinese peasant couple

In 1905, in Japan, he brought together several revolutionary groups and formed the Revolutionary Alliance Society, which later became the Nationalist Party or Kuomingtang (KMT) that still rules Taiwan today. Its program consisted of the Three People's Principles: nationalism, democracy, and people's livelihood. Although Sun could not live in China, members of the Alliance infiltrated many social organizations there. The revolutionary spirit that had been developed by Sun became especially high among students' and soldiers' groups. A soldiers' mutiny on October 10, 1911 triggered the fall of the dominos that led to the collapse of the Qing Dynasty and the establishment of the first republic in Chinese history.

The three pillars of the imperial system of government founded on an agrarian society are the emperor, the bureaucratic state, and the scholar-officials upholding a Confucian ideal of government. The emperor ruled by the "mandate of heaven", a divine right that also implies popular consent as the moral precondition of a ruler's

Capitalism battering down China's Great Wall

right to rule. The Confucian ideology is fundamentally conservative; its entire objective was to maintain an ethically prescribed order that governed individual behavior, the relative and yet fixed roles between parents and children, men and women, husband and wife, elder and younger brothers, the emperor and the scholar-officials, the people and the imperial court. Peace and harmony are attained when everybody abides by his or her prescribed role.

These detailed role specifications and the code of conduct associated with each role would add up to a stable hierarchy of social and political order that governs almost every aspect of the life of an individual. It is authoritarian and yet tacitly reciprocal, entrusting power with responsibilities. The Confucian system of governance is based on primarily ethic ideals and rituals, rather than laws and rationality. The system was maintained by religion-like preaching and indoctrination, in particular, of the emperor from a very young age with the hope of turning him into a morally exemplary ruler. But with absolute and unchecked power,[3] those in authoritative positions routinely failed to live up to their moral expectations and official corruption was endemic throughout Chinese history. More importantly, the Confucian ethic system of government grants primacy to people in the political order but deprives them of effective means of holding the ruler accountable other than violence. This is an important cause of the immensely destructive dynastic cycle.

Despite the massive revolutionary changes in China's modern and contemporary history, the imperial China has left some enduring legacies that continue to shape Chinese politics of today. First and foremost is a moralist political culture. Moral self-cultivation is the foundation of the Confucian order; filial piety is the foundation of personal morality and hence the number one virtue. Such a culture holds public figures in high moral standards that few of them are able to measure up to; it also injects a familial quality into interpersonal relations as well as the relationship between state and society. The ruler (the emperor in particular), while enjoying almost

---

[3] As a Confucian saying puts it, "A minister has to die if the emperor told him to; a son has to die if his father told him to."

unlimited power, is nevertheless expected to take care of his family. The political history of China is one of unfulfilled expectations.

County magistrates are called "parental officials" (*fumuguan*) while public office holders regard the local people their "food and clothing parents" (*yishi fumu*). State and society are parents to each other but in different ways. Public officials should care for the people as if their own children and the people should reciprocate the paternalist care of the state with obedience to and respect for state authority. The familial analogy is everywhere in the Chinese society. For example, university students (graduate students in particular) under the same advisor automatically form a social hierarchy in which the teacher/advisor is the parental figure at the top (the Chinese term *shifu* can literally be translated as teacher-parent) while the students call each other elder or younger brothers and sisters (*shixiongdi* and *shijiemei* respectively in Chinese) in accordance with the year they entered school and regardless of actual age. The Chinese language has much more extensive and elaborate terms denoting familial and relative relations than English. Individuals find their identities as well as roles in such matrix of social relations. When wronged or abused by corrupt officials, people hope for the emergence of virtuous and righteous officials who can stand up for them as parents protecting kids.

The official ranking in state bureaucracies has become the gold standard to rank-order almost everything else in society. Enterprises, universities, hospitals, research institutes and sometimes even churches and Buddhist temples are accorded with official-rank equivalents; they are treated by the state and relate to one another accordingly. The imperial hierarchy is reproduced by its cultural influence.

In the agrarian subsistence economy, dubbed by Mao Zedong as "self-sufficient natural economy", the peasants produced for themselves food, shelters and most of the handicraft articles they needed. Whatever surplus exacted from them by the landed gentry class as well as by the imperial court in the form of land rent was also chiefly for private enjoyment and not for exchange. Even in the 1970s, this author personally encountered people in rural villages who were totally self-sufficient and had never set foot outside a five-kilometer parameter from their homes in their entire lives. The stationary

8. The Official-Rank "Gold Standard"

Consistent with the Confucian ethical-political order, the hierarchically organized party-state provides the "gold standard" of rank-ordering of almost all individuals and organizations in society. The political culture nurtured in this environment automatically determines the relative importance of people and organizations in accordance with this "gold standard" to inform their interactions. An informal rank is attached to almost every individual and organization that is equivalent to bureaucratic grades used in the government. A ranking mentality contributes to the political system's difficulty in inter-agency coordination. An entity of lower rank seeking cooperation with an entity of higher rank faces a daunting challenge. Many analysts attribute the well documented communication problems between the People's Liberation Army (PLA) and the Ministry Foreign Affairs to the large gap in their respective ranks. The PLA's Central Military Commission is of equivalent rank to the State Council, China's cabinet, while the Foreign Ministry is a mere ministry under the State Council. For the Foreign Ministry to liaise with the PLA, it must report up to the State Council, which may have to report further up to the Politburo in order to secure PLA's cooperation.

In another example of the distorting influence of rank, state-owned enterprises sometimes outrank the party boss and the chief executive of the locale where they are based. It is impossible for the local government to issue binding orders to them. The rank system can also impede effective regulatory oversight when regulators share the same bureaucratic rank as entities they are charged with regulating. For example, while China's banking regulator, the China Banking Regulatory Commission (CBRC), has ministerial rank, and China's five largest state-owned banks are also ranked at a quasi-ministerial level. The cadres heading these organizations are all senior party officials managed by the organization department of the communist party. Ranking in this case tends to dilute the oversight of CBRC of the banks.

(Continued)

(Continued)

One solution periodically proposed for some of these rank-related governance problems is to abolish administrative ranks for the executives of SOEs, financial institutions, universities and other organizations unrelated to public administration. In 2000, a central government commission issued provisional policy requiring large and medium-sized SOEs to give up administrative rank, but only the cities of Shanghai and Guangzhou have shown any interest in implementing it. Giving up the official rank means to give up a wide array of associated privileges and the career opportunities within the party-state.

A long-time challenge for the US–China relationship has been that China treats U.S. Cabinet secretaries as of equivalent rank to Chinese ministers whereas in fact these ministers are far down in the intra-party pecking order. The creation of the US–China Strategic and Economic Dialogue (S&ED) allowed the United States to bypass the rank system and find a way for the US Secretaries of the Treasury and State to deal directly with their real counterparts above the ministerial level. The US Secretary of Defense, however, is still hosted by the Chinese Minister of Defense, who is only the third most senior uniformed member of the CCP's Central Military Commission.

agricultural economy enabled the development of similarly stable and enduring networks of village self-governance based upon kinships and surnames and presided by village elders and the gentry. Such a human ecology naturally resisted innovation and was incapable of adaptation to radical change. The imperial exam system channeled the best of China's brain power to the careers of scholar-officials to form a class of literati with high social standings. This is a system of equilibrium difficult to unravel from within. It took massive external shocks to break it up and transform it. The Opium Wars of the mid-1800s sent this ancient empire into a prolonged period of revolutions to produce the rising China we see today.

Table 1 presents a summary model of the patterns of traditional China.

Table 1. A Model of Traditional China

	Key characteristics	Cultural/Ideological Bonding	Resulting Patterns of Social change (or the lack of it)
State	Centralized Bureaucratic Authoritarian	Human agents: the gentry officials/ literati/intelligentsia (Confucian scholars in contrast to hereditary aristocracy)	*Cycles* The dynastic cycle The Agricultural cycle (around the lunar calendar) The family cycle
		Hierarchically organized roles and rules that are well-specified, accentuating the dominance of the state; Rigid, authoritarian but integrate the three on the left well to form a highly stable order (as long as the economy remains stationary)	
Economy	Agrarian Labor-intensive Stationary		*Main Disequalibrating Variables* Ever-worsening Land-population ratio Organizational capability of rebels/ revolutionaries
			Main Driver of the Dynastic Cycle Ever-increasing misery of the peasantry Secret societies, religious sects, peasant rebellions and uprisings Local warlords
Society*	Familial Tribal Native land Nation		

* Individual's main relationships of self-identity in descending order.

Main Readings:

Boxed Essays 1, 3, 7, 8.

Key Issues and Relevant Readings in the Book:

- Patterns of traditional China [Sections of Story 7 on Chinese culture and history].
- Class hierarchy of traditional China [Tb 1.1 (p. 171)].
- Public intellectuals [Tb 1.2 (p. 130)].
- Family relationship and its cultural expressions [*Story 4*, Qi Yun narrates the mutual obligations between parents and children pp. 62–63, 73, 90; Tbs 1.3 (p. 29), 1.4 (p. 38)].
- Political culture and legacy of the Traditional China:

  — The dynastic cycle.
  — The "mandate of heaven" and political legitimacy.
  — "Middle-kingdom" mentality [Tb 1.9].
  — The Century of Humiliation.
  — Moral dilemma in the political culture.
  — Authority relationship [Tbs 1.5 (p. 163), 1.6 (p. 184); Story 5; Story 7, esp. the Rolls-Royce incident].
  — The CCP's peasant root [Tb 1.7 (p. 78); Story 3, esp. the story of Gao Qili].

- The struggle for China's future: the CCP versus the KMT.

Exercises:

a. Go online and consult a library to construct a timeline of modern Chinese history since the Opiun War; pay special attention to the Revolution of 1911, the May 4th Movement, the Communist Revolution, and the Cultural Revolution.
b. Name five great Chinese dynasties.
c. Describe the patterns of stagnation of the Imperial China.
d. Draw a list of salient characteristics of the traditional Chinese culture.

Some Further Readings:

— Jenner, WJ, *Tyranny of History: Roots of China's Crisis.* Penguin Press, 1992.
— Johnson, David, Andrew Nathan and Evelyn Rawski. *Popular Culture in Late Imperial China.* University of California Press, 1985.
— Metzger, Thomas A, *Escape from Predicament: Neo-Confucianism and China's Evolving Political Culture.* Columbia University Press, 1977.
— Rankin, Mary Backus, *Early Chinese Revolutionaries: Radical Intellectuals in Shanghai and Chekiang, 1902–1911.* Harvard University Press, 1971.
— Spence, Jonathan, *The Gate of Heavenly Peace.*Penguin Books, 1982.
— Pye, Lucian, *Mandarin & Cadre: China's Political Cultures.* University of Michigan Press, 1988.

STUDY UNIT 2

THE CONTEXT OF "THE GREAT
CHINESE REVOLUTION"

T he Great Chinese Revolution" is the title of a book authored
by the great Sinologist of Harvard University, John King
Fairbank. It captures the essence of Chinese history in the
past 150 years. A revolution is a thorough transformation of one
state of affairs into a radically different one, from one order to
another in a relatively short span. What the Chinese revolution has
to achieve is both clear and daunting. It was clear that the highly
developed and super-stable agrarian civilization of China could not
withstand the onslaught of the Western industrial capitalism that
"have battered down the Great Wall of China" (Karl Marx), flooded
the Chinese market with cheaper and better products than those
produced by the indigenous handicraft industries, and thereby
caused the disintegration of the "natural economy." Whatever the
initial resistance offered by the Empire was quickly overcome by
the far superior military force of the Western industrial powers.

The late Qing reformers knew what China needed urgently for
its survival was the Western weaponry — the marvels of modern
technologies and engineering, and a modern military. However, this
would entail a new education system (the imperial exam system
was abolished in 1905) that produced talents and skills entirely different from the classic Confucian scholars, which in turn called for a
modern culture and mindset to accommodate and facilitate the
introduction of a new mode of production, which in turn required a
new government system and a different social structure. To achieve
the above China must free itself from the subjugation by foreign
imperialist powers. In other words, the Great Chinese Revolution

must simultaneously be a nationalist revolution, a political revolution, a social revolution, a cultural revolution, and an economic revolution. Given China's enormous size and vast historical inertia, such a revolution has to be long, protracted, and exceedingly bloody.

1. A Nationalist Revolution

The nationalist revolution in China aimed to fulfill two major tasks: to overthrow the rule of the alien Manchu minority and to rid China of its semi-colonial status marked by the concessions and spheres of influence of the imperialist powers on its territory, as well as by the unequal treaties forced upon China after its military defeats. It meant regaining national pride and dignity, and revenging the humiliation suffered at foreigners' hands. After the 1911 Revolution got rid of the Manchu imperial court, China fought eight years (1937–1945) to drive out the Japanese imperial army; being a member of the allied forces that emerged victoriously at the end of World War II, China finally did away all the foreign concessions and unequal treaties; by 1949 when the communists came to power, all foreign troops left Chinese territory.[1] It was no wonder that, to the Chinese people, one of most memorable proclamations of Mao Zedong was the one made at the founding of the People's Republic of China, "Henceforward, the Chinese people have stood up!" It is also small wonder that the "China Dream" recently proclaimed by Xi Jinping, the State President and the 5th generation CCP leader, is defined as "national rejuvenation" — to regain China's status as a premier power in the world. Generally speaking, China's nationalist revolution has been exceptionally successful.

2. A Political Revolution

The 1911 Revolution overthrew the imperial court and replaced it with a rudimentary republican form of government. It was a landmark event in Chinese history but the Revolution was far from

---

[1] Except a small contingent of Soviet navy in Danlian and Qingdao, upon the request of the new regime that had no navy of itself own to defend its shorelines.

complete. Local warlords left over from the Qing Dynasty continued to rule their regions as if under the imperial court. Several attempts at restoration of the imperial system were made, including one by the president of the new republic, General Yuan Shikai, who negotiated the abdication of the Qing Court and was subsequently made the President of the new republic in exchange.

While the revolutionaries were united against the Qing Court, they had very different visions for the future form of government. The course of least resistance was of course to incorporate the old elite of the imperial era — the bureaucrats, the gentry, the landlords and so on, into the new state. This was the course taken by the successive warlord governments in Beijing and, to a lesser extent, by the Nationalists led by Chiang Kai-shek. A limited bourgeois democracy, gradually installed under the tutelage of a strong military state, and free-market capitalism were the vision of this limited and gradualist version of political revolution.

The communists, on the other hand, pushed for a more radical revolution that empowered the vast rural masses to overthrow the old social order as well as the traditional ruling elites. With the backing and guidance of the Soviet Union, they mobilized workers

"Soviet" government officials; second from the right is Mao

in urban centers on strikes and peasants in rural areas for land reforms. With the support of the masses, they attempted to establish a government of workers and peasants. The red radicalism alienated important constituencies in the Nationalist coalition government and led to break up of the first KMT-CCP cooperation brokered by the Soviet Union. The Nationalists massacred the Communists, forcing the latter to flee to the countryside to recoup and regroup. Mao Zedong, one of the founders of the Chinese Communist Party (CCP) pioneered the Soviet-style government in selected locales where enemy forces were weak, usually the border regions between provinces in mountainous areas. These areas under communist rule were called revolutionary bases (*geming gengjudi*). Having subdued the local warlords and nominally unified China, the Nationalist Government turned its troops against these red base areas and eventually forced out the peasant Red Army and sent it on the legendary Long March (October 1934 to October 1936) in search of a new sanctuary, which they eventually found in a poor and remote region in the northwest centered on

Communist generals during World War II

Mao declared the founding of the PRC on Tiananmen on October 1, 1949

Ya'nan. By then, the Red Army was reduced to a shadow of its previous strength.

The massive Japanese invasion into the heartland starting from July, 1937 forged the second KMT-CCP cooperation in the War of Resistance against Japan (1937–1945). The communist troops stayed behind the enemy line waging guerrilla warfare while the Nationalist troops faced the frontal assaults of the Japanese Imperial Army. The communists greatly expanded their armed forces during the war, taking advantage of the KMT's preoccupation with the Japanese invaders. After the surrender of Japan in 1945, the KMT-CCP armed contest resumed. Riding on high popular support, the communists eventually defeated the Nationalists and established a communist state in 1949.

The record of the communist system since 1949 is a checkered one to say the least. It has taken on many of the repressive features of the imperial autocracy, brought national disasters during the Mao era and failed in the reform era to bridge class divisions and the widening income gap as it proclaims to eliminate. When it is intermingled with a market economy in the reform era, the system has proven enormously fertile for corruption and injustice, inciting waves of mass protests. Political reform has been an issue since the end of the Cultural Revolution but suppressed by the authorities for the sake of the rule of the Communist Party. As such China's political revolution is still an unfinished historical mission. However, it appears to have lost the sense of direction in the first decade of the new century. (Essay 4)

2.1 Base area. The Maoist peasant revolution is known for two things: armed struggle and encircle the urban centers with rural base areas before finally capturing the cities. Mao's Red Army established many base areas around China, usually in remote places where enemy forces were weak. Some of these places are poor and backward even today. The communists redistributed farm land, set up their own governments (the Soviets) and developed their armed forces that eventually become powerful enough to take over the entire country. Xi Jinping's father helped to start one such base area in northern Shaanxi centered on Yanan, which later became the main base of the Chinese communists before they took power in 1949.

3. A Social Revolution

A social revolution fundamentally changes the class structure of a society and alters the relative positions of and power and wealth distribution among the classes. Often, new classes are created while old ones mutate or die off. Generally speaking, the upheavals that punctuated the dynastic cycle at the end of a dynasty were not social revolutions because they did not transform the social structure of the imperial China. The peasant economy continued; the imperial court, the literati, the gentry, and the landlords continued to rule, albeit with a new set of individuals. The 1911 Revolution broke off the dynastical cycle precisely because the patterns of China's imperial past could no longer sustain themselves under the relentless onslaught of modern capitalism from abroad. China's traditional social structure founded on the subsistence peasant economy that generated little surplus was a main obstacle to the industrialization deemed necessary for national self-preservation.

A social revolution, not another peasant rebellion such as the Taiping Uprising (1850–1864) that almost toppled the Qing Dynasty — very likely to start another dynastic cycle — was therefore called for. A main difficulty that Chinese revolutionaries faced was where to find the energy source to wage the revolution. Because China's industrialization was not endogenous — it was brought in by foreign imperialists, the classes representing the modern industrial sector, the bourgeoisie and modern industrial workers were both weak due to the limited size of the modern industrial sector that was also dominated by foreign capital. Social support for the revolution must be sought elsewhere. The KMT enlisted the support of the old elites, which had the undesirable (from the perspective of the revolution) consequence of preserving the old social order. The communists tapped into the enormous pent-up frustration of the peasant masses who were always on the brink of starvation, and channeled it away from the dynastical cycle to serve revolutionary objectives.[2]

The communists embarked on the road of armed struggle after breaking up with the KMT in 1927. They established numerous "revolutionary base areas," set up their own governments, and started land reform to gain the support of the peasant masses. They staffed their governments and the officer corps of the Red Army with radicalized peasant youths and controlled them with the highly disciplined Leninist party organizations.[3] By mid-1950s, the landed class and the traditional gentry were decimated, foreign and domestic capitalists were expropriated, and millions of "class enemies" and counter-revolutionaries were physically eliminated. The nationalization of industries and the rural collectivization of the late

---

[2] See Mao's instrumental class analysis of 1925. "Analysis of the classes in Chinese Society." English translation of this article can be found online on many websites.
[3] Franz Schurmann. *Ideology and Organization of the Chinese Communist Party.* Berkeley, CA: University of California Press, 1967.

1942 年，中国士兵守卫着 "飞虎队" 的飞机

A Chinese soldier guarding fighters of "Flying Tiger", an American volunteer airforce to fight the Japanese in 1942

1950s wiped out the economic foundation of property-based social stratification. By the time Mao passed away, China had a very simple social structure in which only three broad social categories were distinguishable: peasants, workers, and cadres. None of them resulted from spontaneous social development because of the CCP's long standing policy of restricting mobility across these social categories. They were regimented into the rural communes and the numerous *danwei* (work unit) created by the party-state for the planned economy. (Essay 2)

The communist-led social revolution was thorough in demolishing the old class structure but failed to create a new one conducive to industrialization until the reform era. The communists derived their strength from successful organization and attempted to replace the old social order they had destroyed with a new one based on its organizations to ensure an egalitarian society. However, the monstrous bureaucratic hierarchy of the party-state itself became the hotbed of a privilege-based new ruling class. Mao sought to destroy this class by launching a "cultural revolution" (the "continuous revolution" in Maoism) that not only shook up the party-state hierarchy but also attempted to create a new mankind free from the grip of the "four olds," (i.e., old ideas, habits, customs, and culture). The most obvious weakness of the egalitarian society attempted by Mao was the lack of entrepreneurship and innovations necessary for a modern industrial economy. It also failed to cultivate a large size of middle class professionals, entrapping the masses in poverty and stagnation. Ideological bias against intellectuals (i.e., well-educated people) played an important role in China's continued backwardness and was carried to the extreme during the Great Proletarian Cultural Revolution (1966–1976).[4]

4. A Cultural Revolution

The concept of a cultural revolution is a tricky one: cultures are taken-for-granted assumptions, values, habitual ways of thinking and behavior and hence normally immune to revolutionary change. For example, the Renaissance that ended the Dark Age in Europe took almost three centuries to run its course.

Nevertheless, the transformation from an agrarian subsistence economy to industrial economy does entail if not require a cultural transformation.[5] The revolutionaries of China of all persuasions believed to varying extent that China's backward cultural traditions were obstacles to modernization. From time to time, they attempted to speed up cultural modernization. Translation of Western classics, the establishment of modern institutions of education, sending students abroad to study science, technologies and engineering etc. were started in earnest in the late Qing Dynasty. By far, the most successful attempt at was the May Fourth Movement of 1919, which grew out of the patriotic student protests against the Versailles Treaty that transferred the possessions of the defeated Germany in Shandong province to Japan without even consulting the Chinese government. China's ineptness in foreign

---

[4] Social change in the reform era is dealt with in Essay 1.
[5] This is the essential argument of modernization theory.

relations triggered a profound introspection on its cultural traditions to identify the sources of China's weaknesses. The movement attacked Confucianism, initiated a vernacular style of writing, and promoted science and democracy. It also spawned the "New Culture Movement." Numerous newspapers and magazines were published to stimulate new thoughts and set new trends. The left wing intellectual leaders of the movement such as Chen Duxiu and Li Dazhao were influenced by the success of the Russian Revolution of 1917, which contrasted sharply with the failure of the 1911 Revolution in China to change the social order and improve the conditions of the nation. With the help of the Comintern[6] they founded the Chinese Communist Party in Shanghai in 1921.

The KMT regime's "New Life Movement" in the 1930s and the 1940s, despite its fascist undertone, nevertheless carried on the momentum of cultural renewal. The CCP carried on the May 4th tradition with various movements of "thought reform," believing that the Chinese revolution could not be carried on without reforming the people. In the era of armed struggle, the Chinese Red Army adopted the commissar system of the Soviet Red Army to impose ideological control on the soldiers and indoctrinate the peasant new recruits. The Yan'an Rectification (1942–1945) was the CCP's first large-scale thought reform campaign.[7] After the founding of the PRC, land reform and rural collectivization were followed by several "socialist education" campaigns in which "work teams" of CCP cadres were sent to the countryside to solve problems, to rectify the work style of rural base-level cadres who were often abusive, to propagate socialist ideas and to eradicate old ideas, habits, customs, and culture — the "four olds" (Story 2). Both Western bourgeois culture and Chinese traditional culture were rejected in favor of creating a new proletarian culture and a "new man"

---

[6] Communist International, an organization of communist parties around the world created by Lenin in 1919 and later controlled by the Stalin regime till 1942. Its mission was to spread the Bolshvik Revolution around the world. The Chinese Communist Party was founded initially as a branch of the Comintern.
[7] Like all the subsequent ones, the Ya'nan thought reform campaign was also used by the top leaders of the CCP as a tool for intraparty power struggle.

exemplified by role models such as Lei Feng and Jiao Yulu.[8] Class struggle entering into the arena of culture and ideology constituted Mao's "Continuous Revolution."

The Great Proletarian Cultural Revolution (1966–1976) that lasted for a decade was a radical movement that shut down schools, slowed production, turned people against one another in civil war-like upheavals, and virtually severed China's relations with the outside world. It was proletarian because it was a revolution of workers, peasants and students against party officials. It was cultural because it meant to alter the values of society in line with the communist ideology. The CR threw the entire country into chaos, brought down and disgraced millions of cadres and intellectuals and destroyed most local state establishments and replaced them with "revolutionary committees" dominated by radicals. It turned children against parents, masses against cadres, subordinates against superiors and created tragedies for millions of families and individuals in the name of class struggle to keep the Maoist revolution alive. A whole generation of youth lost their opportunities for formal education and was sent to the countryside, the remote regions, and high mountains to settle down there and be "re-educated" by peasants.[9] In the cities, factory workers were dispatched as "working class propaganda teams" (gongxuandui) to take charge of schools and "rescue" the school children from the grip of the "bourgeois intellectuals" who dominated the institutions of education. Scientists, engineers, professional experts as well as cadres were sent to do manual labor on farms, to raise pigs, and to clean toilets. China fell even further behind the capitalist industrialized powers and the national economy was on the brink of collapse.

The Cultural Revolution achieved Mao's goal of eliminating his political opponents but failed spectacularly in its cultural and

---

[8] Lei Feng, a soldier do-gooder, has been the perennial role model meant for everybody since the early 1960s while Jiao Yulu, a hardworking, thrifty, people-loving, and devoted county-level cadre also of the 1960s, is recently brought back by Xi Jinping, apparently in a attempt to serve as the role model for cadres again.
[9] Referred to as the "Sent-down Movement" (1968–1976) and the young urbanites involved are commonly called the "sent-down youth."

刘少奇邓小平陶铸
从党中央滚出去！

Cultural Revolution Poster

ideological objectives. Instead, it left many people dead and many more traumatized. Ironically, the disaster of the radical Cultural Revolution paved the way for the far-reaching reforms in the post-Mao era that made China an economic powerhouse. It is this on-going market-based economic revolution that is transforming the Chinese culture and introducing new ideas in ways, speed and magnitude that has never happened before (Essay 1). But of course, the various attempts at reforming the culture in the preceding 100 years have also contributed to it by diluting the cultural traditions. The revolutionary upheavals destroyed their class base and institutional underpinnings.

5. An Economic Revolution

The ultimate goal of the Great Chinese Revolution is to transform the economy and bring China into the modern industrial age, and move along with the advanced nations into the post-industrial age. An economic revolution is both the starting and the ending points of China's great transformation.

China's modern economic transformation started with the inroad of foreign capitalism on the coastal port cities after China's door was forced open by the Opium Wars and the unequal treaties in the aftermath. The defeat prompted the first wave of industrialization effort in the form of bureaucratic capitalism under the banner of "Self-strengthening Movement" launched by reformist ministers of the late Qing. Modern shipbuilding, armament manufacturing, railways, steel making industries as well modern textile and other light industries were introduced in major cities. Foreign capital, on the one hand, undermined the foundations of China's "natural economy" and wrecked the handicraft industries both in the cities and in the peasants' homes, and on the other it hastened the growth of a market economy in towns and in the country. The destruction of the natural economy created a commodity market for capitalism while the bankruptcy of large numbers of peasants and handicraftsmen provided it with steady supply of labor. Some merchants, landlords and bureaucrats began investing in modern industry in the latter part of the 19th century, under the stimulus of foreign capitalism. At the turn of the 20th century, China's national capitalism took its first steps forward. During the First World War, China's national industry expanded further, taking advantage of the preoccupation of the imperial powers with their war efforts in Europe.

Overall, however, during the Nationalist period (1927–1949) China's modern industries were weak, subjugated under foreign capital and the bureaucratic state, and disrupted by the Japanese invasion, the frequent in-flights among the local warlords, and the decades' long civil war between the Nationalists and the Communists. At the founding of the PRC, China remained a country of impoverished peasantry. The modern sector was small and confined to major coastal cities and Manchuria.

Economic development under Mao is characterized by "more haste, less speed." Mao believed that the Western imperial powers would not allow China to become an industrialized country in the capitalist world economy dominated by them; China had to join the Soviet Bloc and embrace the Stalinist model of endogenous industrialization. State planning and squeezing the rural economy for surplus as the capital for industrialization in urban areas were the two pillars of that model. The CCP announced the first five-year plan in 1953 to speed up industrial development with massive aids from its treaty ally Soviet Union. The nationalization of foreign and the KMT's bureaucratic capital, the collectivization of light and handicraft industries as well as the rural economy ensured the concentration of major resources in the hand of the state for a planned economic development.

However, as a master revolutionary, Mao soon grew impatient with the Soviet-style bureaucratic planning and launched the disastrous Great Leap Forward in 1958. The Great Leap Forward was designed to overcome the backwardness of China's agriculture, industry, and technology. It was to be achieved through use of the vast manpower mobilized by local cadres and party organizations in massive production campaigns. Unrealistic production targets were set, which were further expanded when production quotas were passed down the party-state hierarchy. Steel production was to be increased by setting up small-scale "backyard furnaces," and agricultural output was to be raised by combining the collective farms into communes. About 26,000 communes were created, each composed of approximately 5,000 households. The preoccupation with raising steel production channeled the main energy of rural areas to "backyard furnaces" to the negligence of the crops in the fields. A great famine ensued that claimed estimated 30 million lives, by far the deadliest in world history. The steel produced by the backyard furnaces was of low quality, practically useless, and the quantity fell short of the targeted goal.

In humiliation, Mao retreated to the backstage and allowed his deputies Liu Shaoqi and Deng Xiaoping to clean up the mess. Liu and Deng scaled back Mao's radical policies, reduced the size of the communes, dissolved the practice of collective dining, allowed the peasant households to lease the collectivized farmland to engage in family-based production as they had done for centuries. Private plots for family use were also restored. The countryside did not fully recover till 1965. In May, 1966 Mao launched the Cultural Revolution in part to bring down Liu Shaoqi and Deng Xiaoping. Economic development was once again disrupted.

With deteriorating living standards amidst incessant political and ideological campaigns, the population grew increasingly disillusioned with Mao's "Continuous Revolution" towards the end of the Cultural Revolution. Premier Zhou Enlai, a moderate who managed to get along with the radicals, resurrected the slogan of "four modernizations" (agriculture, industry, national defense, and science and technology) in 1973, in an apparent attempt to reorient the nation toward economic development. After Mao's death in 1976, the "four modernizations" became the centerpiece of the CCP's policies and programs. It legitimized the Dengist reforms at the initial stages in the late 1970s and led to the repudiation of the Maoist revolutionary orthodoxy. In 1984, the CCP Central Committee officially declared the Cultural Revolution "unprecedented national devastation."

In contrast to the Maoist ideological lunacy, the Dengist reforms were distinguished by pragmatism. A saying widely attributed to Deng goes "It does not matter if a cat is white or black, as long as it catches mice." The mouse that Deng was after was China's modernization. Toward that end, Deng was willing to try all means and go all lengths as long as the ruling position of the communist party was not in jeopardy. The post-Mao policy making is frequently characterized as "crossing the river by feeling for the stepping stones." After a brief period of recentralization of power to end the Cultural Revolution chaos, the new leadership in Beijing encouraged local policy initiatives to speed up production and deliver material betterment to the people after decades of stagnating and, for many, deteriorating living standards.

In hindsight, the Dengist reforms in the 1980s till late 1990s followed three basic lines: decentralization, marketization, and opening up to the outside world. The main objective of decentralization was to motivate local governments and enterprises to pursue growth and the main approach to it was subcontracting. The central government signed contracts with the provinces to fix the amount of revenues the latter were obliged to remit to Beijing for several years. The provinces were allowed to manage their own economies and keep the revenues generated above the contract obligations. The provinces in turn followed similar schemes to subcontract with the cities and prefectures etc., all the way to enterprises in urban areas and to the households in rural areas. The initial success came from the countryside: leasing farmland to the peasant households led immediately to a boom in agricultural production. The surplus farm products after fulfilling the obligation to the state and the household consumption had to be sold, which in turn revived the rural free markets. (see Essay 1)

The Stalinist model of development put emphasis on heavy industries such as steel making and machine building etc. These industries claimed the bulk of the nation's investment capital. Added to this, the Cultural Revolution disruption led to the negligence of the light industries and a general scarcity of consumer goods. The revival of the market made new entries to the production of consumer goods extremely profitable. The result was a feeding frenzy that saw the dramatic rise of the so-called township and village enterprises (TVEs). These were small-scale businesses started by peasant households as well as by county, township, and village governments to meet the enormous pent-up demand in the consumer markets. Both the technologies used and the management were crude, but by 1994 the TVEs rose to contribute nearly half of China's total industrial output. Private businesses also re-emerged in this context.

Meanwhile, China opened its door for foreign direct investment (FDI) and later on adopted the strategy of export-led growth that was credited for the enormous success of the East Asian newly industrialized economies (NIEs), namely, Japan, Taiwan, Hong Kong, South Korea, and Singapore. Taking advantage of China's cheap, disciplined and relatively skilled labor force, as well as the accommodating local governments, the NIEs and many Western nations relocated their manufacturing to China. In the 1980s and 1990s, most foreign-invested firms produced for the export markets. Soon China became the largest recipient of FDI in the world and its foreign trade to GDP ratio reached as high as 70% in the middle of the first decade of the 21st century. China became the "factory of the world," flooding the world market with cheap "made in China" products. Persistent trade surplus allowed China to accumulate enormous foreign reserve ($3.3 trillion by December, 2012), a large part of which was invested in the US treasury bills, making China, the largest developing nation, the largest creditor of the United States, the largest developed nation. FDI brought many other benefits to the Chinese economy such as new technologies, new products, new business models and management know-how. Besides rapid growth, the Chinese economy is upgraded and becomes world-wide competitive.

The success of the TVEs, private businesses and foreign firms put great pressure on the state-owned enterprises (SOEs), which generated a net loss throughout the 1990s. In the late 1990s and early 2000s, the Chinese government carried out a massive operation to "restructure" the SOEs. Most of the small and medium-sized were privatized and the large central government-owned SOEs were consolidated into 117 giant corporations (March 2012 figure). In 2012, 79 of them made the list of Fortune Global 500 (second only to the United States). These giants became enormously profitable, taking advantage of their monopoly positions and privileged access to credit, technology, raw materials and state subsidies.

Tens of millions of workers were laid off during the SOE restructuring. Assets stripping and other forms of corruption by SOE managers and their government supervisors were widespread. The dissolution of the rural commune in the early 1980s revealed the magnitude of the under-employment problem in rural China. Peasants began to leave their native villages in droves in search of non-farming opportunities in cities and the coastal regions where the economy was booming. The number of "migrant peasant workers," as they are dubbed, reached 250 million in 2012, constituting the grandest rural–urban migration in human history. It has completely transformed the social landscape and created a consumer market that is potentially largest in the world. It is this potential market that continues to lure foreign investors to China. The three decades of rapid economic growth is primarily driven by investment and export. The contribution of domestic consumption to GDP growth is relatively small. The 2008 financial crisis that dramatically weakened world demand and the pressure from the West — China's traditional export market — for China to "rebalance" its economy (i.e., to reduce or eliminate the trade surplus) highlighted the external vulnerability of the Chinese economy. The Chinese government has ever since been trying to change China's growth model from export-led to domestic consumption-driven.

Arguably, the economic revolution is the most successful of the five revolutions undertaken by China. It started in the mid-19th century, experienced brief spurs in the late 19th century and in 1920s but was repeatedly disrupted by civil wars, foreign invasions, and revolutions. It finally took off in the post-Mao reform era and is on its way to make China the largest economy in the world again. When China achieves its dream of modernization and regains its pre-eminence among the nations of the world, the Great Chinese Revolution will have fulfilled its historical mission and run its full course. From that historical perspective, China is unstoppable, carrying enormous historical inertia forward. The more relevant question for the rest of the world is whether China, when regaining a GDP share of a quarter to a third of the world's as it enjoyed in the first half of the 19th century, will also resurrect the "middle kingdom" mentality and become indifferent to the outside world; or will it have learned the Western ways to be intimately engaged with the world at large.

But many problems and puzzles remain about China. In particular, the so-called "China model" is highly unconventional and defies common sense in many ways. Chief among these is that the Chinese economic "miracle" took place in a context of communist party rule and the persistence of many institutions created in the Mao era for the planned economy. It is to this structural context that we will turn in Study Unit 3.

Main Readings:

Boxed Essays 7, 11

Key Issues and Other Relevant Readings in the Book:

- Self-strengthening movement.
- The 1911 Revolution.
- The May 4th Movement (1919).
- The Red Army and the revolutionary base areas [Tb 2.1 (p. 218); Story 2].
- The Great Leap Forward and the great famine [parts of Story 7].
- The Cultural Revolution.
- The "planned economy" [Essay 1 (1); Essay 2 (1)].
- Socialist education movement [Tb 2.2 (p. 14); Story 2].

Exercises:

a. Write a two-page biography of Deng Xiaoping.
b. Why is the Chinese revolution such a long drawn out one? Compare it with the American or French Revolution.
c. What was the social basis for the 1911 revolution? Why is it called a political revolution but not a social one?
d. What was the respective class base of the CCP and the KMT: how did it affect the policies and strategies of the two parties? Would the Nationalist policy achieve the goals of the Chinese revolution?
e. What does "Political power comes from the barrow of a gun" mean?
f. Find out what are Chinese "literati" and the role this class of people play in the society and politics of traditional China.
g. Explain the difference between democracy and the massline of the CCP.

Further Readings:

— Bianco, Lucien. *Origins of the Chinese Revolution, 1915–1949*. Stanford University press, 1971.
— Fairbank, John K. *The Great Chinese Revolution, 1800–1985*. Harvard University Press, 1987.

— Wakeman, Frederic. *The Fall of Imperial China.* Free Press, 1977.
— Li, Lincoln, *Student Nationalism, 1924–1949.* SUNY Press, 1994.
— Thaxton, Ralph. *Salt of the Earth: Peasant Protest and Communist Revolution in China.* Berkeley, CA: University of California Press, 1997.
— Bernstein, Thomas P. *Up to the Mountains and Down to the Villages: The Transfer of Youth from Urban to Rural China* (New Haven, etc.: Yale University Press 1977).

STUDY UNIT 3

THE STRUCTURAL CONTEXT
(THE POLITICAL SYSTEM)

A communist polity is commonly characterized as a party-state: the close intertwinement of the organizations of the ruling party with the state apparatuses. However, a fuller description of the Chinese political system should include four entities: the party, the government, the people's congress and the people's political consultative conference.[1] These four exist in tandem at all the five levels of the political hierarchy — the capital, the provinces, the municipalities, the counties (including county-level cities or city districts), and the townships (or street administrations in urban areas). In the capital, the "gang of four"[2] consists of the party center of the CCP, the State Council (the central government), the National People's Congress (NPC) and the Chinese People's Political Consultative Conference (CPPCC). In the following sections, I will provide a concise description of these four bodies at the highest level in Beijing and the relationship among them as a snapshot that the reader can roughly apply to the local states at the remaining four levels. All the stories in this book take place in a structural context constituted by these four bodies at one level or another.

---

[1] The military is obvious very important as the ultimate source of the CCP's power, but is omitted in this discussion because it does not normally involve in the daily politics on the civilian side.

[2] The original reference to the "gang of four" (*sirenbang*) was the four Maoist radicals purged after Mao's death: Jiang Qing (Mao's wife), Zhang Chunqiao, Wang Hongwen, and Yao Wenyuan.

10.6 As a vanguard Leninist party, members of the Communist Party, especially cadres, are expected to serve as the moral exemplar for the people. There is no denying there are party members who are morally exemplary and righteous. However, under a single party rule where power is unchecked and ineffectively supervised, corruption is inevitable. Rampant corruption is ruining the party's reputation, discrediting even those who are morally exemplary.

1. The Party Center of the CCP

The Party center (*zhongyang*) refers to the central party authorities consisting of several organs. The Central Committee (CC) of the CCP consists of 200 or so members plus 150 or so alternate members. It is in theory elected by the National Party Congress that convenes once every five years. The locus of power in the CC is the 25-person politburo but the apex of political power in China is the seven-person Politburo Standing Committee (PBSC).[3] In other words, at the top is a collective leadership; each PBSC member has an equal vote in decision making but one of the seven also serves as the General Secretary of the Party. This person is therefore the first among equals. This arrangement is in part a response to the personal dictatorship of Mao, who's unchecked and absolute power built around his personality cult brought one disaster after another upon the nation.

The National Party Congress elects the CC, which in turn elects the Politburo and its standing committee. It also elects two other bodies: the Central Discipline Inspection Commission (CDIC) and the Central Military Committee (CMC). However, because both are chaired by a PBSC member (the latter generally by the General Secretary) they are in effect subordinate to the PBSC. Members of the PBSC also head the government, the NPC and the CPPCC. In other words, all political power concentrates in the PBSC.

The work of the PB and the PBSC are supported by the Central Secretariat, which runs the daily party affairs on behalf of the PB, and

---

[3] Historically, the number of people on the PBSC varied from 5 to 11.

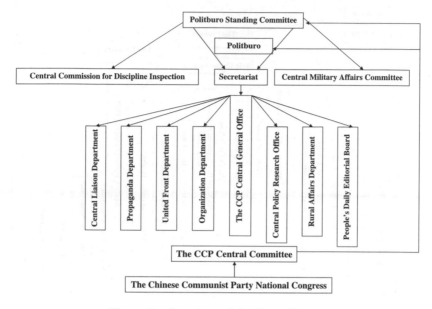

Figure 2.   Structure of the Party Center.

Source: Author's compilation

by the Central General Office and several functional departments. The structure of the party center is shown in Figure 2.

2. The State Council

The second of the "gang of four" in terms of the real power wielded is the State Council (SC) or the central government. It consists of the Premier, four vice premiers and several state councilors. Public administration at the SC is distributed among many ministries, commissions and other functional agencies. The 2013 State Council, for example, consisted of 74 ministries, commissions, specialized agencies and public organizations such as think-tanks and academies. Figure 3 is an abridged presentation of the organization structure of the State Council.

The Premier is supposedly elected by the NPC but in fact derives his power mainly from his membership on the PBSC. Similarly, the vice premiers, state councilors and ministers are all

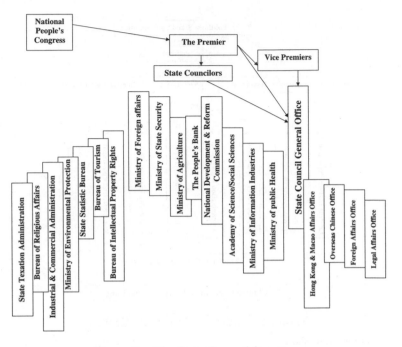

Figure 3.   The State Council Structure.

Source: Author's compilation

supposedly elected by the NPC. In reality, the NPC deputies (mostly CCP members) have to vote on a list of personnel appointments prepared by the CCP. The SC is the bastion of Chinese bureaucracies. It vastly expands the bureaucratic state of the imperial China, which normally had only six ministries in charge of defense, treasury, personnel, ritual, engineering, and judiciary. In part, the expansion was caused by the interlude of the planned economy in the Mao era when most economic activities were run by the state. Seven rounds of State Council reform in the reform era (up to 2013) have eliminated all the industrial ministries and established the basic regulatory institutional framework for a market economy. But state intervention in the marketplace is still extensive, due in large part to the existence of an extensive bureaucratic establishment. Further reform to simplify the government structure and scale back the state's role in the economy is expected.

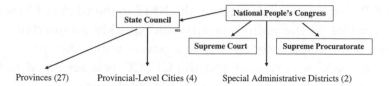

Figure 4. Formal Relationship between NPC and State Council, Supreme Court, Supreme Procuratorate and the Provinces.

Source: Author's compilation

3. The National People's Congress

According to the PRC's Constitution, the NPC is "the highest body of power" in the land. It passes most important laws but is more than a legislature as commonly understood. It elects the Premier of the SC, the Chief Justice of the Supreme People's Court, and the Inspector General of the Supreme People's Procuratorate and supervises the work of these three bodies. (see Figure 4) The NPC has a five-year term and convenes once every year in March. Its 3000 or so representatives are elected by the provincial people's congresses and other electoral units. When the NPC is not in session, the Standing Committee consisting of 150 or so full-time law makers takes charge of the routine legislative affairs. Like the US Congress, the NPCSC is also divided into subcommittees. The Chairman of the NPC, as mentioned above, also sits on the PBSC of the CCP, exercising the leadership of the Party over the legislature. Because most of the NPC deputies and Standing Committee members are CCP members who are required to toe the Party line and obey Party disciplines, the NPC is widely regarded as the rubber stamp of the Communist Party.

4. The Chinese People's Political Consultative Conference

The CPPCC is the least powerful of the "gang of four" and is defined as an "advisory body" to assist the rule and broaden the base of support for the CCP. As a matter of fact, the CPPCC was the first legislature of the PRC established in 1949, as a result of the united front the CCP built with eight other political parties in a common struggle against the Nationalist Government. But after the CCP won the Civil War, drove the KMT to the island of Taiwan, took control of the entire country and quickly consolidated its power, it no longer needed to share power with other parties. In 1953, the NPC was created and the CPPCC was relegated to the status of an advisory body and a united front organ.

The chairman of the CPPCC is also a member of the Politburo Standing Committee and, like the NPC, it also has a standing committee divided into subcommittees in charge of different areas of affairs. Each year, the CPPCC convenes at the same time as the NPC. However, unlike the NPC, the CPPCC cannot pass laws — it can only make recommendations or proposals to the SC and the NPC. The CCP is still the largest party in the CPPCC but the percentage of its members is not as high as in the NPC, but high enough to ensure the CCP's control over that body. With marketization and globalization of the Chinese economy, the Chinese society becomes increasingly pluralistic. Influential social elites (business people, public intellectuals, artists, scientists, engineers and experts in other fields) have emerged outside the political establishments. Many of them do not want to join the CCP which regards them as potential oppositions. The CCP has adopted a strategy of herding them into the CPPCC either as independents or as members of the other parties housed in it. The strategy has been relatively successful and gradually the CPPCC became the bastion of China's social elites, just as the CCP is the bastion of China's political elites and the NPC of the economic elites. The participants in the CPPCC's annual conference are more outspoken than their counterparts in the NPC but have less impact. Both bodies are gaining importance in China's political life as a result of increasing pluralism in the Chinese society. The CPPCC also has a five-year term concurrent with that of the NPC.

5. Mechanisms of Integration

In the Chinese political system, a politician's status is not determined by the government office he or she occupies; instead it is determined by his or her standing within the Communist Party. The highest position one can hope for is a seat at the Politburo Standing Committee. Each member of the PBSC is assigned a different portfolio. Take the

PBSC of the 18th Party Congress for example, of the seven members one is the Party's General Secretary, State President and the Commander-in-chief of the armed forces; the second is the Premier in charge of the government and public administration; the third one is the chairman of the NPC; the fourth the chairman of the CPPCC; the fifth heads the Party's Central Disciplinary Inspection Commission; the sixth is responsible for media, propaganda and party affairs, and the seventh is the executive vice premier to assist the Premier to run the State Council. In other words, the seven people occupy the top positions of all the most important political bodies. Interlocking appointments between the Party and the state is an important mechanism of political integration at all levels of the state hierarchy.

A second mechanism of integration is the extensive Party organizations in the SC, the NPC, and the CPPCC. Individuals hold key positions of these bodies are all CCP members. Party groups (*dangzu*) are embedded in all important state organs and serve as the locus of decision making. For example, each ministry of the State Council has a party group made up of the minister, vice ministers and the chiefs of important departments. Decision making in the ministry is in fact decision making inside the Party. As shown in Figure 8 on page 249, the SC had 64 party groups in the various ministries, commissions, and other type of government agencies. The standing committees of the NPC and the CPPCC are also led by a party group consisting of the top officials in these bodies.

On tasks that cut across the bureaucratic divisions of a "leading small group" (LSG) — a task force of sort — is set up with members drawn from the relevant departments. The level of authority of the group is determined by the status of the person who heads it. The highest level LSGs are usually headed by PBSC members. For examples, the Foreign Affairs Leading Small Group is headed by the General Secretary of the CCP; the Financial and Economic Affairs Leading Small Group is headed by the Premier. As indicated above, both are PBSC members.

The Central Organization Department (COD), the human resources department of the CCP, is in charge of the management of all state officials at the provincial-ministerial level and above.

With the approval of the PB or PBSC it screens and appoints officials, moves them around in different positions or transfers them
among different provinces or ministries, and puts them through
the various training programs in the Party school systems and
academies of public administration. A basic policy of the CCP is
"the Party controls cadres": all important personnel decisions have
to be made by the Party.

The general office (GO) system also plays a critical role of coordination in the Chinese political system. The CC, the SC, the NPC,
the CPPCC and all the ministries, commissions and other government agencies have a general office of their own. The GO's functions
include (1) staff support, (2) logistic support, (3) information filter-
ing, (4) monitoring and supervision of subordinate bureaucracies,
(5) policy research, (6) coordination of policy implementation, (7)
mediation between leaders and the led, (8) house-keeping for leaders, (9) act as go-between and communicate between members of the

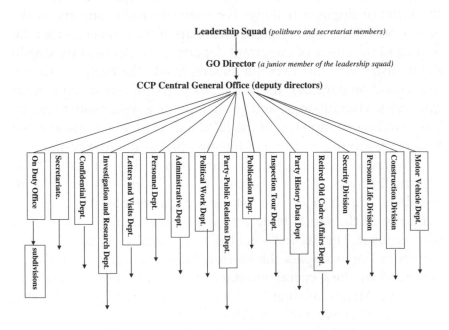

Figure 5.   Central General Office of the CCP.

Source: Author's compilation

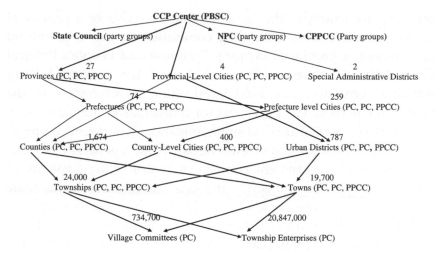

* PC (first): party committee; PC (second): People's Congress, PPCC: People's Political Consultative Conference.

Figure 6. Overall Political Structure.

leadership squad, and (10) training future leaders. GO directors are at the center of operation of the political system and have broad exposure to all aspects of its operation; they know the leaders they serve intimately and are aware of the very complicated politics going on at the top of their organizations. They are, therefore, best prepared to take leadership positions in the future. In fact, this position is often used to groom future leaders.

The large number of meetings, conferences, document flows, study sessions, and party propaganda also play an important role in maintaining Party unity and coordinate party affairs. Figure 5 illustrates the structure of the general office of the CCP Central Committee. The GOs in other organizations at both the central and local levels are similar in structure and functions.

6. Applying the Snapshot Downward

Applying the afore-described political structure at the highest level as a snapshot, we get the basic picture of the political structure of the provinces, municipalities, counties and townships. Taking a province, for example, the "gang of four" consists of a provincial party committee with a standing committee on top, a provincial government, a provincial People's Congress and People's Political Consultative Conference. The members of the provincial Party standing committee also hold interlocking appointments in the other three bodies. The provincial (or municipal, county, township etc.) party committee also has an organization department, a propaganda department, a united front department, a general office etc. The provincial government consists of basically the same set of bureaucracies as the ministries and commissions etc. in the State Council. Party groups are also embedded in these bureaucracies as well as in the PC and PPCC to ensure the dominance of the Party. Invariably, the provincial party secretary is the number one and the governor (usually also the deputy provincial party secretary) number two in the province. Figure 8 on page 249 depicts the parallel hierarchy of the party and the government (the people's congresses and the political consultative conferences are omitted), from which we can see the total domination of the party over the government. Figure 6 describes the entire political structure of China together with the numbers of political units at each level of the hierarchy.

Main Readings:

Essays 2, 5. Boxed Essays 6, 8, 10, 13.

Key Issues and Other Relevant Readings in the Book:

- The "gang of four": CCP, SC, NPC, CPPCC.
- The Communist Youth League [Tb 3.1 (p. 15)].
- Department of Letters and Vists [Tb 3.2 (p. 363)]
- Officials producing figures and figures producing officials [Tb 3.3 (p. 73)].
- Retired senior cadre affairs bureau [Tb 3.4 (p. 104)].
- The "planned economy" [Essay 1 (1); Essay 2 (1)].
- Local states [Essay 3 (1, 5); Essay 4].
- Mechanisms of integration [Tb 3.5 (p. 49)].
- Term and age limits [Tb 3.6 (p. 59)].
- Cadre promotion [Tb 3.7 (p. 96)].
- Changing role of NPC [Tb 3.9 (p. 149)].

Exercises:

a. Why is the communist regime in China called "party-state"?
b. Describe the mechanisms by which the CCP control other bodies of the state, such as the military, the State Council, the People's Congress etc.
c. What is the role of *danwei* in the Chinese system?
d. Compare the American and Chinese political systems: Are there similarities and what are the major differences?
e. Describe the relationship between the National People's Congress and the State Council, the Supreme People's Court and the Supreme People's Procuratorate.
f. What is "party group" and *"leading small group"*?
g. Elaborate on the role of the "general office" in the Chinese political system.
h. What does the "Bureau of Retired Senior Cadre Affairs" do? What does its existence tell you about Chinese politics?

Further Readings:

— Wei, Li. *Chinese Staff System: a Mechanism for Bureaucratic Control and Integration.* Institute for East Asian Studies, University of California, 1994.
— Jiang, Jinsong. *The National People's Congress of China.* Beijing: Foreign Language Press, 2003.

STUDY UNIT 4

THE CHINESE COMMUNIST PARTY

B y any measure, the Chinese Communist Party (CCP) is the largest political party in the world. In June, 2012, its membership stood at another all-time high of 83.43 million, more than double from the 37 million in 1978 when the post-Mao reform era began. It rivals the population of a major nation. Were it a nation, the CCP would have ranked the 17th most populous in the world. The percentage of Party members in the population had also inched up from less than 0.9% in 1949 when the CCP came to power to almost 6% in 2010.

Membership-wise, today's CCP is very much a product of the reform era. Figure 7 indicates that at the end of 2008, Party members who joined the Party in the reform era (after October 1976) took the lion's share of the total Party membership — 72.29% or 54.89 million. In comparison, the revolutionary generation (those who joined the Party before October 1, 1949, had shrunk to less than 1% (0.97%, or roughly 73,000). The Cultural Revolution generation (those who joined the Party between 1966 and 1976) accounted for 16% and those who joined before the Cultural Revolution, 11%.

The growth of Party membership has stabilized in recent years at around 2.5% per annum. However, the growth of the CCP carries with it tremendous momentum and is set to continue in the foreseeable future. By June, 2012, the CCP had 4.03 million grassroots organizations. A basic mandate by the Party constitution of these grassroots organizations is recruiting new members regularly, and even if each of these grassroots organization recruits only one new member per year, the net growth of the Party would be well over two million.

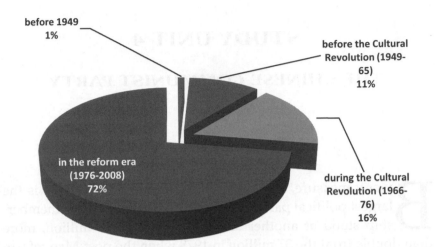

Figure 7.   Membership Composition by Time Period Joining the Party (2008).

Source: COD "Intra-party statistics communiqué, 2008"; *People's Daily*, July 7, 2008.

9. Leninist Party

Also called a "vanguard party," a Leninist Party is typically made up of an elite group of dedicated revolutionaries. It is a highly organized and disciplined party practicing the so-called "democratic centralism." Before a policy or a decision is made, extensive discussions and consultations are allowed but once a decision is made, the party authorities demand unconditional obedience from party members. The Russian revolutionary Vladimir Lenin (1870–1924), saw the possibility of mounting a successful communist revolution with a group of highly organized and dedicated revolutionaries to substitute for the weak proletariat in the agrarian Russia of the early 20th century. The success of the Bolshevik Revolution of 1917 encouraged the forming of Leninist parties in other parts of the world.

Functionally, the Leninist vanguard party provided to the working class the political consciousness (through indoctrination

(Continued)

(Continued)

and organization) and the revolutionary leadership. Once in power, however, a Leninist party tends to form a privileged ruling clique that monopolizes power, organizations and resources, turning into a ruling class not unlike the ones it overthrew during the revolution. A Leninist party is an organization party; in other words, it is not necessarily class-based. Its organization methods tend to influence the way it rules the country. A communist regime is usually a party-state, with party organizations intertwined with the state apparatuses. A Leninist party also attempts to extend its organization networks into all politically significant spaces in the society and the economy and tries to brainwashing the entire population. The term "totalitarianism" refers to this total domination.

Joining a Leninist vanguard party involves an extended period of trial and grooming, and an elaborate process of screening, approval and swear-in rituals. The candidate is mentored by existing party members who also must sponsor the candidacy. The party is usually an exclusive elite club, especially the leading cadres.

The organizations of the ruling party are like giant fishnets that span the entire social landscape of China, penetrating every corner of the economy and society in addition to tightly gripping state power. Table 2 indicates the extent to which the various categories of organizations in China are penetrated by the CCP at the grassroots level. On the surface, it appears the Chinese state remains very much a party-state and the CCP seems to continue to live in its past legacy in a time capsule. However, the market has fundamentally eroded this organization structure and altered the nature of the Party's grassroots organizations; it is redefining the meaning of being a Party member. To understand the impact of the market, we need to look first at the basic characteristics of the communist rule.

Table 2.   The Rate of Party Coverage at Grassroots Level.

	Total Number of Administrative Units		Total Number of Party Organizations		Rate of Penetration (per cent)	
Townships and Towns	34,324		34,321		99.99	
Communities (*Shequ*)	79,000		78,000		98.74	
Villages	606,000		605,000		99.83	
Enterprises	2,634,000		595,000		22.59	
State-owned		249,000		216,000		86.75
Private		2,385,000		380,000		15.93
Non-profit organisations*	578,000		464,000		80.28	
Colleges/Universities		1,622		1,622		100.00
Research Institutes		7,982		7,765		97.28
NGOs **	81,000		12,000		14.81	

* Shiye danwei. ** minban feiqiye danwei.

Source: Central Organisation Department: *"Dangnei tongji gongbao"* (Communiqué of Intra-party Statistics). *Xinhua News Agency*, July 1, 2009.

Basic Characteristics of Communist Rule

The CCP has retained the basic structure of a Leninist party. It is organized as a giant pyramid, with committees, branches, groups and other types of Party organizations both in and outside the government. Figure 8 depicts the overall organization structure of the party-state. It shows that, above the grassroots level, the overall structure of the Party (the right side above the village level) closely parallels the structure of the government (the left side above the village level), with Party cells embedded in government bureaucracies. As a general rule, the Party (i.e., its committees at various levels) makes major policy decisions while the government implements those decisions. The Party groups (*dangzu*) embedded in the government bureaucracies ensure that Party's policies get implemented. At the grassroots level, Party cells also penetrate virtually all organizations of significant size or importance in society (to be followed in the boxed essay on *danwei* on page 250).

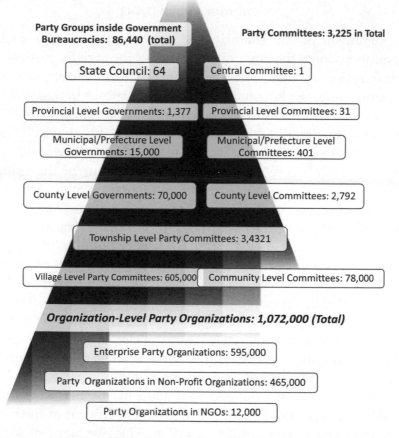

Figure 8.   Party-State Hierarchy.

Source: Press release by Wang Qinfeng, deputy director of the Central Organisation Department of the CCP on 24 June 2011, http://cpc.pepole.com.cn/GB/74838/137931/225181/index.html

However, the flipside of the micro-rule of the CCP is the dependence of Party organizations on *danwei* for power and prestige. A Party cell is "in power" only when it runs a functional organization (*danwei*). These organizations are in turn the "carriers" (*zaiti*) of Party organizations. It was the durability or permanency of *danwei* in the pre-reform era that undergirded the stability of Party organizations at the grassroots level. And, it is the erosion of *danwei* by market forces in the reform era that throws these organizations off balance.

10. *Danwei* (Work Unit)

Communism is also characterized by "micro-rule." The Party controls not only the government but also, through its grassroots organizations, almost all other organizations in society, such as factories, schools, hospitals, research institutes, villages, urban communities, units of the military, and so on. These organizations are customarily referred to as *danwei* (or "work unit"). The Party cells resident in *danwei* used to be (in many cases still are) the "leadership core" running *danwei* on behalf of the ruling party. The power and prestige of the Party organizations are derived from their control over public, corporate and other types of administration at the national, local, as well as grassroots levels. In other words, the CCP rule consists of not only its control over state power but also the micro-level domination of *danwei* by Party cells. In the Mao era, most *danwei* were either created or incorporated by the party-state, allowing the latter unchallenged authoritative claims over them. The embedded Party cell represented the interests, objectives and policies of the party-state; they allowed the authority of the Party to reach from the top of the government to the shop floor of a factory.

The individual's dependency upon his or her work unit used to be total. Because of the Maoist suppression of the market, the Chinese work unit took on an extensive array of social functions and was responsible for key aspects of the lives of its members. It strived to provide some or all of the following services to its members: employment, schools for the children of the employees, medical care facilities, housing, grocery stores, barbershops, sports and entertainment facilities, public baths, transportation, security service, cafeteria or dining halls, and even the employment of the younger generation of *danwei* members, all being either *danwei*-subsidized or of member-only access. Because of the very limited opportunities of cross-*danwei* mobility in the Mao era, the Chinese work unit had a

(Continued)

(Continued)

tendency to become a self-contained miniature society. This "organized dependency" of individuals upon their *danwei* and through *danwei* upon the entire communist system was an effective leverage with which the Party exercised domination over the entire population. To a great extent, such institutional arrangement is designed to run a planned economy. *Danwei* were embedded in the structure of the party-state and functioned as the implementers of the planning directives issued by the planning apparatuses of the party-state to allocate resources in the absence of the market.

While the term *danwei* remains in use today it is more properly used to refer to an era when the individual is a life-long member rather than an employee of an organization or in the context of party-state organizations and state-owned enterprises.

Main Readings:

Essay 2; Boxed Essays 8, 9, 11, 13.

Key Issues and Other Relevant Readings in the Book:

- Size, growth, and organization structure of the CCP.
- The use of role models [Tb 4.1 (p. 66); 10.6 (p. 234)].
- Changing social base and social composition of membership [Essay 2].
- The "first hand" or "squad leader" [Tb 4.2 (p. 48)].
- Personnel dossier [Tb 4.3 (p. 16); Story 2].
- Massline [Tb 4.4 (p. 353); 7.6 (p. 11); Essay 4(1)].
- *Danwei* as control mechanism [Tb 4.5 (p. 131)].
- The rule by edicts/documents [Story 7 (1); Tb 4.6 (p. 123)].
- Cadre training [Tb 4.8 (p. 136)].
- Micro-rule and organized dependence.
- "The Party controls cadres" and "the Party controls talents."
- Red aristocracy (princelings).
- Status quo interests [Essay 5].

Exercises:

- What are the main characteristics of a Leninist party?
- Describe the organizational structure of the CCP.
- Write a two-page essay to describe the circumstances that led to the founding of the CCP in 1921.
- Describe the "micro-rule" of the CCP.
- What are the major effects of marketization on the Party?
- Why does the CCP continue to grow? What factors are driving this growth?

Further Readings:

— Dirlik, Arif. *The Origins of Chinese Communism*. Oxford University Press, 1989.
— Guillermaz, Jacques. *A History of the CCP, 1921–1949*. Random House, 1972.
— Walder, Andrew G. *Communist Neo-Traditionalism: Work and Authority in Chinese Industry*. University of California Press, 1988.
— Gore, Lance LP. *Chinese Communist Party and China's Capitalist Revolution: The Political Impact of the Market*. Routledge, 2011.
— Zheng, Yongnian. *Chinese Communist Party as Organizational Emperor: Culture, Reproduction and Transformation*. Routledge, 2010.

STUDY UNIT 5

THE MAO ERA

The Mao era of the PRC (1949–1976) was a turbulent period filled with great revolutionary experiments. During the armed struggle with the KMT for political power, the CCP adopted a policy of united front to get as many social and political groups on its side as possible. To make itself appealing to the capitalists, petite bourgeoisie, the reformist intellectuals, enlightened gentry and part of the landlord class in rural areas, it promised a coalition government that would encourage capitalist development and establish a broad-based democracy. Riding on popular support, the CCP defeated the KMT and established the People's Republic of China.

However, as soon it consolidated its ruling position, the Party under Mao began to retract from the promised it made to other classes and political parties. It established one-party rule and launched ambitious programs to build a planned economy and transform the entire society and culture. Mao instigated numerous political and ideological campaigns to pursue his utopian vision of building a communist society. The two major events in the Mao era of lasting impact are the Great Leap Forward (1958–1960) and the Cultural Revolution (1966–1976).

The Great Leap Forward (GLF) is a mass campaign-style development drive found in many communist countries. In China, the GLF pinned the hope for rapid industrialization on making use of the massive supply of labor and new organizations for production. The regime under Mao also sought to avoid the social stratification of the Soviet model of development. At a Politburo meeting in August 1958, it was decided that the people's communes would become the new form of economic and political organization in rural China. By the end of the year, approximately 25,000 communes had been set up, with an average of 5000 households each. The communes were relatively self-sufficient co-operatives where wages and money were replaced by "work points" (see Tb 5.5 on page 10). The commune system was aimed at generating the surplus for the industrialization in cities; it also ensured the provision for urban workers, cadres and officials.

Mao saw grain and steel production as key pillars of economic development. In the August 1958 Politburo meetings, it was decided that steel production would be set to double within the year. With no personal knowledge of metallurgy, Mao encouraged the establishment of small backyard steel furnaces in every commune and in each urban neighborhood. Huge efforts on the part of the masses were made to produce steel out of scrap metal. To fuel the furnaces, the local environment was denuded of trees and fire wood was sometimes taken from the doors and furniture of peasants' houses. Pots, pans, and other metal artifacts were requisitioned to supply the "scrap" for the furnaces so that the wildly optimistic production targets could be met. Many of the male agricultural workers were diverted from the harvest to help the steel-making drive. The output however consisted of mostly low quality lumps of pig iron of negligible industrial value.

In the communes, a number of radical and controversial agricultural innovations were promoted at the behest of Mao, including close cropping, whereby seeds were sown far more densely than normal on the incorrect assumption that seeds of the same class would not compete with each other. Altogether, these untested "innovations" generally led to decreases in grain production rather than increases. In a dash toward the communist utopia, rural collective dining facilities were established for the peasants and household kitchens were abolished; family life was partially dissolved. The result was that, while crop yield was down, food wastages were up. Meanwhile, local leaders were pressured into falsely reporting ever-higher grain production figures to their superiors. These doctored figures led to higher state procurement quotas of grain and even increased export of food. A massive famine ensured in which an estimated 30 million people perished, by far the largest in world history. The hierarchical, upward-oriented communist system lacked effective feedback loop to correct its mistakes. Mao simply blamed bad weather for it and refused to change course. Even today, the CCP has not faced directly with this monumental episode in its history and drawn adequate lessons from it.

The Great Proletarian Cultural Revolution, commonly known as the Cultural Revolution, took place from 1966 through 1976. Set into motion by Mao Zedong, then Chairman of the Chinese Communist Party, its stated goal was to advance communism in the country by removing capitalist and traditional cultural elements from Chinese society, and to impose Maoist orthodoxy upon the entire population. The revolution marked the return of Mao Zedong to power after the failed GLF.

Mao alleged that bourgeois elements were infiltrating the Party, the government and the society, threatening to restore capitalism. He maneuvered to remove the "revisionists" (those party members no longer believing in communism) by mobilizing mass rebellions against those in positions of power. China's youth responded to Mao's appeal by forming Red Guard groups around the country. The movement spread into the military, urban workers, rural peasants and the rank-and-file of the Communist Party. It resulted in widespread factional struggles in all walks of life. In the top leadership, it led to a massive purge of senior officials who were accused of taking the "capitalist road," most notably Liu Shaoqi and Deng Xiaoping. During the same period, Mao's personality cult grew to

Cultural Revolution poster, with Mao at the center

5.1 The "four big democracies" of the Cultural Revolution (1966–1976): "Big airing of views, big-character letters, big debates, and big criticisms." People were called to rebel against their bosses using these tools. Indeed, these four "freedoms" brought down for a time all authorities except that of Mao. Big (or mass) criticism turned violent and claimed many lives.

immense proportions. Millions of people were persecuted in the violent factional struggles across the country, and suffered a wide range of abuses including public humiliation, arbitrary imprisonment, torture, sustained harassment, and seizure of personal property. A large segment of the population was forcibly displaced, most notably the transfer of urban youth to rural regions during the "Sent-down Movement" that lasted till 1979. Historical relics and artifacts were destroyed. Cultural and religious sites were ransacked.

The ferocity of the mass revolts and madness went beyond Mao's expectations; so was the widespread factional fighting. The energy released by the Cultural Revolution indicated the pent-up frustration and anger among the population against the rule of a rigid and repressive bureaucratic state and the lack of freedom of expression etc. The chaotic situation eventually led to Mao's decision to send the military to restore order and take over public administration. Mao officially declared the Cultural Revolution to have ended in 1969, but it persisted until his death in 1976, with many more political campaigns and purges. Mao and his radical supporters introduced a wide range of reforms to create a more egalitarian society, such as the "bare-foot doctors" that extended universal healthcare to the rural masses; a system of cadres engaging the masses, living and working among the masses for a few months each year; regular criticism and self-criticism sessions for ideological and moral purification; the "re-education" of urban educated youths by relocating them in the countryside to live with the peasants; the shortened formal k-9 education with an emphasis on practical knowledge and skills and so on. Most of the Maoist reforms associated with the Cultural Revolution were abandoned by 1978. Although the Cultural Revolution has been regarded officially as a disaster ever since, Mao Zedong's egalitarian ideal and wariness of the re-emergence of a privileged ruling class increasingly resonates with the masses today, who are fed up with corruption and lopsided income distribution. The popularity of Bo Xilai's Chongqing Model is an example. (Essay 4)

Mao's enduring appeal among the masses is derived from many of the features of Maoism. *Maoism* is officially referred to as Mao Zedong Thought in China. It inherits the Marxist ideology about class struggle as the locomotive of history. Mao's main contribution to the communist revolution was his strategy of mobilizing the impoverished peasant masses to engage in armed struggle against perceived class enemies, and of building revolutionary base areas in the countryside where the communists could nurture and expand their forces till they became strong enough to take over the urban centers where the enemy's forces were strongest.

11. The Tenets of Marxism

Marxism is an economic and sociopolitical worldview and a critique of capitalism. In the mid-to-late 19th century, the intellectual tenets of Marxism were inspired by two German philosophers: Karl Marx and Friedrich Engels. Marxism is based on a materialist understanding of history, taking as its starting point the necessary economic activities required by human society to provide for its material needs. To produce for these material needs, humans enter into certain relationships with one another. The form of economic organization, or mode of production, is understood to be the basis from which the majority of other social phenomena — including social relations, political and legal systems, morality and ideology — arise. These social relations form the superstructure, for which the economic system is the base. As the forces of production (most notably technology) improve, existing forms of

(Continued)

(Continued)

social and political systems become inefficient and stifle further progress. These inefficiencies manifest themselves as social contradictions in the form of class struggle, which is regarded as the "locomotive of history" by Marx.

Marxism holds a teleological view of human history, which passes through in successive stages "primitive communism" (the hunter–gatherer society where everyone shares everything because of the lack of surplus), the slave society, the feudal society, the capitalist society and will eventually arrive at a communist society. The passage from one stage to the next represents major upgrade of the forces of production following major changes in the relations of production. The driving force is class struggle, e.g., between slaves and aristocracy, between feudal lords and peasants, between capitalists and the proletariat. According to Marxist analysis, class conflict within capitalism arises due to intensifying contradictions between socialized production performed by the proletariat, and private ownership and private appropriation of the surplus value (profit) by a small minority of capitalists. To increase their profit margins, capitalists would reduce labor costs, which in turn reduces the total demand for their products, resulting in periodic economic downturns or crises. The "enmiserization" of the proletariat will eventually lead to a social revolution to overthrow the capitalist system and the establishment of socialism, a socioeconomic system based on cooperative ownership of the means of production, distribution based on one's contribution, and production organized not for profit but for directly satisfying human needs. Karl Marx hypothesized that, as the productive forces and technology continued to advance, socialism would eventually give way to a communist stage of social development. Communism would be a classless, stateless, humane society based on common ownership and the principle of "From each according to his ability, to each according to his needs."

(Continued)

Later, Marxists such as Lenin, Stalin and Mao believed the inevitable historical progress could be sped up by launching a revolution to seize control of the means of production and introduce state planning. The great communist experiment of the 20th century ended in grand failure with the collapse of the communist regimes in Eastern Europe and the disintegration of the Soviet Union in the early 1990s. The Dengist reform is a retreat from such radical approach in order to allow history to take its own course. This entails re-introduction of capitalism and market economy.

According to Marxism, continuous development of the means of production is the ultimate purpose of class struggle. Under Mao, that goal was pursued through first wrenching power from the exploiting classes — landlords, capitalists and the gentry-officials, and then organizing mass production campaigns to promote the economy. These mass campaigns were made possible by nationalization of industries and collectivization of agriculture. Thus between the late 1950s and mid-1970s, the entire population was reorganized by the party-state, regimented by the urban *danwei* system and the rural communes. The state took control of the means of production and ran the economy and society by administrative fiat and mass mobilization.

The Maoist egalitarian development based on the elimination of exploitation was to be achieved also through the inculcation of certain prescribed values in party members and, by extension, in society as a whole. These included selfless dedication to the common good and fervent commitment to ideal social behavior. Mao believed a "new socialist man" must be created to achieve the communist utopia, and it had to be created through a "cultural revolution" that rid society of the remaining influences of the exploitative social system that the 1949 Revolution overthrew.

This is the so-called "continuous revolution under the dictatorship of the proletariat."

The Maoist radical approach to development failed on both accounts. By the time of Mao's death, the country had been in continuous chaos of the Cultural Revolution (1966–1976); factory production had slowed down or halted; schools were closed and government officials, scientists and engineers were sent to do manual labor. The national economy was on the brink of collapsing. The new regime under Deng Xiaoping had to repudiate the radical elements of Maoism through a policy of "emancipating the mind." (i.e., liberalization) Officials as well as scholars debated publicly over issues such as the value of the commune system, the need for market in a socialist economy, the historical impact of humanism, and even the current relevance of Marxism-Leninism. Student demonstrators in the 1980s went beyond what the CCP could tolerate by questioning the leadership of the Party. The pro-democracy demonstrations of spring 1989 were dealt with a bloody crackdown. The ensuing national focus on rapid economic development for the following two decades also created massive income gap and class divisions to challenge the ideological foundation of communist rule. Because Maoism played such a central role in the CCP's history and the success of the communist revolution, the Party could not renounce it. Its revolutionary appeal actually increases recently with increasing popular resentment to income polarization and widespread corruption.

Main Readings:

Study Unit 2, sections 2.4 and 2.5. Boxed Essays 2, 11.
Relevant sections of Story 7.

Key Issues and Other Relevant Readings in the Book:

- The Great Leap Forward and the Great Famine.
- The "four freedoms" of the "big democracy" of the Cultural Revolution [Tb 5.1 (p. 256)].

- Maoism and "continuous revolution."
- "Socialist education" [story 2; Tb 5.2 (p. 14)].
- Collective dining halls.
- Charisma of Mao [Tb 5.3 (p. 120)].
- The Little Red Book [Tb 5.4 (p. 18)].
- The work point system of the rural commune [Tb 5.5, (p. 10)]

Exercises:

a. Write a two-page biography of Mao Zedong.
b. Write an essay analyzing the reasons of the continued appeal of Maoism.

Further Readings:

— Tsou, Tang. *The Cultural Revolution and Post-Mao Reforms*. University of Chicago Press, 1986.
— Daubier, Jean. *A History of the Chinese Cultural Revolution*. Vintage Books, 1974.
— Dittmer, Lowell. *Liu Shao-Ch'i and the Chinese Cultural Revolution*. University of California Press, 1974.
— MacFarquhar, Roderick and Michael Schoenhals. *Mao's Last Revolution*. Belknap Press of Harvard University Press, 2006.

STUDY UNIT 6

POST-MAO REFORM AND DEVELOPMENT

Main Readings:

Topical Essay 1; Stories 4 and 5; Boxed Essays 4, 6, 14.

Key Issues:

- The East Asian developmental state [Essay 3].
- Gradualist reforms.
- Marketization and decentralization [Essay 1].
- The township and village enterprises (TVEs)
- GDPism [Tb 6.1 (p. 94)].
- Investment-driven growth.
- Political multiplier effect [Tb 6.2 (p. 138)].
- Fake FDI.
- Attracting commerce and investment [Tb 6.3 (p. 103)].
- SOE reform [Tbs 6.4 (p. 64)].
- Political consequences of decentralization [Tb 6.5 (p. 174)].
- Contract responsibility system [Tb 6.6 (p. 47)].

Exercises:

a. What is "East Asian developmental state"?
b. Find out what the CCP refers to as "primary stage of socialism."
c. Describe the manner in which the market was revived in the immediate post-Mao era.
d. What were the two major reform thrusts in the 1980s?
e. Why did the TVEs suddenly flourish during the 1980s and early 1990s?
f. Describe the role local governments play in promoting economic growth in their locales.

g. What is "GDPism?" Describe the incentives for local states to pursue economic growth.
h. Find out some local development models other than the Chongqing and Guangdong models. (Essay 4)
i. How did China become the "factory of the world? "

Suggested Readings:

— Shirk, Susan. *Political Logic of Economic Reform in China*. University of California Press, 1993.
— White, Lynn. *Unstately Power: Local Causes of China's Economic Reforms*. M.E. Sharpe, 1998.
— Gore, Lance LP. *Market Communism: the Institutional Foundations of Post-Mao Hyper-Growth*. Oxford University Press, 1999.
— Cheung, Peter; Jae Ho Chung; Zhimin Lin eds. *Provincial Strategies of Economic Reform in Post-Mao China: Leadership, Politics, and Implementation*. M.E. Sharpe, 1998.
— Oi, Jean C. *Rural China Takes Off: Institutional Foundations of Economic Reform*. University of California Press, 1999.
— Lardy, Nicholas. *Integrating China into the Global Economy*. Bookings Institute, 2002.

STUDY UNIT 7

SOCIAL TRANSFORMATION AND
STATE–SOCIETY RELATIONS

As an area of inquiry, state–society relations focus on the interactions and interdependency between the state and the society. From its origins in the Weberian tradition of political sociology, work on state–society relations shares a predilection for large-scale generalizations about the state and its relation to society. However, work in numerous fields, from public policy and public administration to local governance, political culture and economic sociology, reveals important dimensions of state–society relations that can rarely be fully grasped by means of the traditional state–society dichotomy, which has given way to more nuanced, more complex conceptualizations of the relationship between the two. Predominantly state-centered approaches have increasingly yielded to greater attention to society and its dynamics.

In one influential account (Migdal, 1997), a "strong state" is what makes the difference for effective policy. But a "strong society" is crucial to building an effective state. In an era of increasingly complex state activities, an expanding line of research has incorporated a disaggregated conception of the state and its relations with society. A further line of state-centered analysis has focused on state–society relations at the local or regional level.

Joe Migdal, in the introduction to *State Power and Social Forces* reveals some basic tenets of the "state in society" literature. First, states vary in their effectiveness based on the relationships they have with society. It is a misconception to assume that states are always the central actors in societies. Second, states are not black boxes but must be disaggregated in a comparative way to reveal the social contexts in which they operate. Third, social forces and states are both contingent on specific empirical contexts. Empirical contexts vary greatly among polities. Fourth, states often empower social forces and vice versa. State–society competition is not always a zero sum game and interaction among diverse groups can be mutually beneficial as well as mutually destructive.

In the case of China, the study of state–society relations can profit a great deal from the insights offered by analyses of the political culture. Confucianism, for example, attempts to culturally regulate state–society relations not as a dichotomy but as gradual incorporation of relationships from individual to the family to the community and to the nation or "all under heaven" (*tianxia*).

Main Readings:

Essays 2 and 3; Story 6 and relevant parts of Stories 3 and 6; Boxed Essay 10.

Key Issues:

- The erosion of the *danwei* system [Essay 2 (2)].
- Market and individual autonomy [Tb 7.1 (p. 157)].
- The incipient class structure [Essay 2; Story 3].
- Income gap [the story in the Introduction; Essay 3 (2)].
- Peasant migrant workers [Essay 3 (3,4)].
- Privileged class [story 7; Tb 7.2 (p. 117)].
- The era of "dad contest" [Tb 7.3 (p. 164)].
- Petitioning (Shangfang) [Tb 7.4 (p. xvii)].
- Moral degradation and money worshiping [Story 7; Essay 5; Tb 7.5 (p. 177)].
- Convergence of political, social and economic elites [Essay 5].
- The masses and the vanguard party [Tb 7.6 (p. 11)]
- Innate source of democracy [Tb 7.7 (p. 27)]

Exercises:

a. What is driving social change in China?
b. Describe the emerging new class structure and patterns of stratification in the Chinese society today.
c. What are the main emerging classes in the Chinese society? What have been CCP's strategies to deal with them?

d. Do you see the Chinese capitalist class an adversary to the communist regime? Why?
e. Find out the CCP's "four cardinal principles" and comment on them.
f. Find and draw a list of the most common causes of social protests in China.
g. How has the power distribution between the state and the society changed during the reform era? What are the political implications?
h. Find out the causes of income disparity in China; do they differ from those in a mature capitalist society?
i. Why do you think that the state–society confrontation is intensifying in China?
j. Do you see revolution potentials in today's China?

Suggested Readings:

— Pearson, Margaret. *China's New Business Elite: Political Consequences of Economic Reform.* University of California Press, 1997.
— Perry, Elizabeth and Mark Selden, eds. *Chinese Society: Change, Conflict, Resistance.* Routledge, 2000.
— White, Gordon, Jude A. Howell, and Shang Xiaoyuan. *In Search of Civil Society: Market Reform and Social Change in Contemporary China.* Oxford University Press, 1996.
— Chan, Anita, *China's Workers: Exploitation of Labor in a Globalizing Economy.* M.E. Sharpe, 2001.
— Gries, Peter Hays and Stanley Rosen, eds. *State and Society in 21st Century China: Crisis, Contention, and Legitimation.* Taylor and Francis, 2004.
— Migdal, J. S. *Strong Societies and Weak States: State-Society Relations and State Capabilities in the Third World.* Princeton, N.J., Princeton University Press, 1988.
— Migdal, J.S. *State in Society: Studying How States and Societies Transform and Constitute One Another.* Cambridge; New York, Cambridge University Press, 2001.
— Migdal, J.S. "Studying the State" in Mark I. Lichbach and Alan S. Zuckerman, eds., *Comparative Politics: Rationality, Culture, and Structure.* Cambridge and New York: Cambridge University Press, 1997.
— Migdal, J.S., A. Kohli, et al. *State Power and Social Forces: Domination and Transformation in the Third World.* Cambridge England; New York, Cambridge University Press, 1994.

STUDY UNIT 8

POPULAR PROTESTS

In imperial China, revolts and rebellions were predominant forms through which the peasant masses expressed their anger and conveyed their desperation and dire situations. They generally did not seek reforming the system but demanded better treatment under it. Traditional public intellectuals injected into large-scale peasant movements the notion of "mandate of heaven" to justify replacing an old dynasty with a new one. Protests aimed at reforming the existing system is relatively new. They started with a group of enlightened scholar-officials and public intellectuals of the late Qing dynasty which expanded into ever-widening social circles and eventually led to the 1911 Revolution to end the imperial era. The ensuing Republic of China had to be improved with reforms. As a result, popular protests in the modern, reformist sense began. The most notable is the May 4th Movement of 1919. Students were the most politically active group in these protests. In addition, strikes of industrial workers, movements for land reforms in rural areas became common in the 1920s through 1940s and were often instigated by the CCP. However, when the CCP gained power, these were banned.

In the Mao era, partly because of the closure of the pressure valves and partly because the CCP's reigning philosophy of class struggle, the political and ideological campaigns sanctioned by Mao tended to be violent; they tended to be revolutionary rather than reformist. In a sense, popular protests were hijacked by mass campaigns instigated by Mao. The Cultural Revolution, for example, can be regarded as top-down manipulated mass protests. The devastation of the Cultural Revolution re-opened some of the pressure valves that allowed non-revolutionary protests to emerge. To be sure, the CCP continues to deal heavy-handedly with any threats to its rule (e.g., the bloody crackdown at Tiananmen in 1989) but it also begins to tolerate and positively respond to protesters with legitimate claims.

Mass protests in the reform era become spontaneous and pervasive. After Tiananmen they usually evolve around mundane bread-n-butter issues such as the loss of jobs or benefits by SOE workers, excessive fees and levies on the peasants, wages and working conditions, official corruption, incidents of social injustice, land grabbing, forcible demolition of homes and businesses, property disputes, pollution and environmental degradation etc. The widening income gap and the rise of the privileged class controlling both wealth and power are also an important source of mass discontent and protests. The protesters often conveniently resort to the Maoist egalitarian and revolutionary ideals. According to official statistics, "mass incidents" that involve 10 or more people in protests are numbered in the hundreds of thousands per year in recent years. The CCP has so far been able to keep these as isolated and localized events but the cumulative discontent in society and the spread of the social media may change that, just as we have seen in the Arab Spring of 2011–2012. With increasing social stratification and pluralism in society, social conflicts and the demand for political participation are both on the rise. Popular protests are expected to become "normalized." (See also the Boxed Essay 5 on page 113)

Main Readings:

Essay 3; Story 6; Boxed Essays 5, 12, 14.

Key Issues and Other Relevant Readings in the Book:

- Mao's continued appeal [Stories 2 and 7; Essay 4 on Chongqing model; Tbs 8.1 (p. 167); 5.3 (p. 120)].
- Stability maintenance [Boxed Essay 12 on page 271].
- Land grabbing and forcible demolition [Boxed Essay 14 on page 281; Tb 8.2 (p. 86); 8.3 (p. 101)].

Exercises:

a. Search online to find out a few recent incidents of mass protests in China. What are they about? How did the government (local and central respectively, if applicable) respond?
b. Analyze the political functions of Mao's manipulated mass rebellions such as those during the Cultural Revolution. How do they differ from spontaneous popular protests in form as well as in results?
C. Research and reconstruct the Wakan protest of 2011, explaining the key issues involved and the political significance of that incident.

Further Readings:

— Moody, Peter R *Opposition and Dissent in Communist China.* The Hoover Institute, 1977.
— O'Brien, Kevin and Lianjiang Li. *Rightful Resistance in Rural China.* Cambridge University Press, 2006.
— Zhang, Junhua and Martin Woesler, eds. *China's Digital Dream: the Impact of the Internet on Chinese Society.* European University Press, 2004.
— Zheng, Yongniom. *Technological Empowerment. The Internet, State and Society in China.* Stanford, Calif., Stanford University Press, 2008.

12. "Stability Maintenance" (*weiwen*)

The CCP has closely followed Deng Xiaoing's dictum that "stability is paramount." Maintaining social stability is the top priority of both the central and the local governments. The central government holds the local leaders responsible for the social unrest or "mass incidents" that occur under their watch with the dreaded "one-vote veto." (*yipiaofoujue*) That is, no matter how much the local government has achieved in other areas, including economic growth, the top local leaders will be punished (stripped of position or demoted) if the number of "mass incidents" took place in the region under their watch exceeded a pre-specified limit in a given period of time. Similarly, too many petitioners coming to Beijing from their locales will also count against them.

(Continued)

(Continued)

This incentive structure motivates the entire government establishments to invest heavily in "stability maintenance" (*weiwen*). The police and security forces are upgraded; a comprehensive set of institutions are created, including a *"weiwen* leading small group" usually headed by the local party boss, and a specialized "stability maintenance office" to coordinate the actions of relevant branches of the government. Contracts and pledges are signed between upper and lower level governments to preserve social tranquility. The local governments will go any length to keep up the appearance of a stable society. That they send their agents to intercept the petitioners from their locales and put them into the so-called "black jail" is widely reported; brutal crackdown and excessive use of police force on protesters are also well-known. However, lesser known is the extent to which local governments are willing to spend their way out of trouble to make peace with the protesters. They pay them hush-money; it is also known that some local governments treat the would-be petitioners to five-star hotels, offer to pay airfares for the petitioners already in Beijing to return and even pay for their sightseeings along the way. In 2011, the estimated total spending on "stability maintenance" exceeded for the first time the national defense budget.

On the other hand, local governments are also a main source of mass protests. They pocket handsome profits from land acquisition and real estate development. Because legally all land is owned by the state, local governments can acquire land at a nominal or below-market price and sell it at many times higher to developers. It is also the behind-the scenes protector of local polluting enterprises. According to some estimates in 2010, nationally, land transfer funds accounted for 76.6% of local government revenues. This means that without the income from land sales, most of local government finances would collapse.

(Continued)

(Continued)

Polluting enterprises in many areas, especially in poor areas, are supported by the local governments because they are big tax payers. Therefore, local governments are often the real culprits in the disputes and protests caused by land acquisition and industrial pollution. In that sense, "stability maintenance" is a self-defeating purpose; the ballooning costs will eventually make it unsustainable.

STUDY UNIT 9

ELITE POLITICS

E lite politics refers to the pattern of interactions among political elite in pursuit of power, status and influence, including the norms, formal and informal rules governing such interactions. Chinese elite politics has undergone remarkable changes since the Mao era and yet considerable continuity persists underneath the change. Chinese elite politics is informed by two main sources: the Chinese cultural tradition and the history and the structural context of the Party. As mentioned before, the Chinese have, under the influence of Confucianism, developed a moralistic political culture that accentuates interpersonal relations based upon a familial imagery as well as a status hierarchy; it values loyalty, patronage and mutual obligations. Status is often based upon seniority while loyalty cumulates around charismatic authority. Deep ambivalence exists over the forever unfulfilled ideal of "virtuocracy" — in which the right to rule is derivative from personal virtues. Abstract ideological or philosophic principles are often overwhelmed by practical considerations of human relations. It is a culture of shame rather than a culture of guilt.

As a Leninist vanguard party, the CCP enforces party discipline and protects the authority of party leaders. Unity even if only at surface level is paramount and open factionalism is a taboo in intra-party politics. "Splitting the party" is the ultimate sin. The Party is strictly hierarchically organized with clear chains of command. Despite the rhetoric of "democratic centralism," both personnel control and operation mode are top-down. Cadres are upward rather than downward accountable. Intra-party election is in general a sham.

The decision rule within the party is consensus-based. Within this power structure, the dominant form of power struggle used to be ideology-based purge. It is life-and-death struggle resulting often in physically eliminating the political opponents (often charged with counterrevolutionary, revisionist, capitalist roaders, black gang etc.). In the name of class struggle, there were no rules to follow and rights protection to rely on. Individual party members had to seek to be affiliated with powerful figures higher in the party hierarchy as patrons to attach his or her loyalty. Informal factions inevitably formed within the Party. One of the roles of the paramount leader was to balance out the various factions to exalt his own position.

The devastation and trauma of the Cultural Revolution has prompted substantial changes within the Party. Many rules, norms and institutions are introduced to govern intra-party politics. Factional struggle becomes less brutal. Campaign-style rectification for a long time fell out of favor until recently, when Xi Jinping revives it as a draconian measure against the rampant corruption within the Party and to shore up his authority, although it is far from clear whether he will be successful in this. With the institutionalization of the age and term limits, and with the opening up of alternative opportunities by the market economy, the career ladders within the Party are less congested.

Factionalism persists; in fact with increasing pluralism within the Party and in the society at large it is expected to grow and even become open and institutionalized. Selectively persecuting cases of corruption has become a heavily used weapon in elite politics. Commonly identified factions within the Party include the princeling faction consisting of the offspring of the revolutionary generation CCP leaders, the Youth League faction and the provincial party boss faction. The "Shanghai Gang" of Jiang Zemin is dying out.

Main Readings:

Essay 5; Stories 3 and 7; Boxed Essays 1, 3, 8, 13.

Key Issues:

- Purge and political campaigns.
- Succession politics [Story 4 and 7].
- Consensus decision rule [Tb 9.1 (p. 58); Story 7].
- The role of staffers (*mishu*) and the staffer gang [Tbs 9.2 (p. 63), 92 (p. 127); Story 7].
- Factional politics.
- Positional power [Tbs 9.4 (p. 173), 1.5 (p. 163); Story 7].
- Post-Mao institutionalization [Boxed Essay 13 on page 278; Tb 3.6 (p. 59)].

Exercises:

a. What are some of the major institutional changes in the cadre system introduced in the reform era?
b. Why is the rule of law so difficult to implement in China? Is it possible at all in China's political system and why?
c. What are the main status interests groups and how do you think they will affect further reforms?
d. Why is the Chinese system so corrupt, and yet is capable of generating rapid economic growth that has lasted for three decades?
e. Would you have become corrupt had you grown up and lived in China?
f. How would you clean up corruption while preserving the rule of the CCP—as the CCP has been trying to do?

Suggested Readings:

— Lieberthal, Kenneth and David Lampton, eds. *Bureaucracy, Politics, and Decisionmaking in Post-Mao China*. University of California Press, 1992.
— Scalapino, Robert A, ed. *Elites in the People's Republic of China*. University of Washington Press, 1972.
— Fewsmith, Joseph, *Elite Politics in Contemporary China*. M.E. Sharpe, 2001.
— Kampen, Thomas. *Mao Zedong, Zhou Enlai & Chinese Communist Leadership*. Nodic Institute of Asian Studies, 1999.
— Lampton, David M and Sai-cheung Yeung. *Paths to Power: Elite Mobility in Contemporary China*. Center for Chinese Studies, University of Michigan, 1986.
— Lieberthal, Kenneth & M Oksenberg, *Policy Making in China: Leaders, Structures and Processes*. Princeton University Press, 1988.

13. Post-Mao Political Institutionalization

Political institutionalization refers to political actions being increasingly constrained by formal and informal rules or norms. It usually manifests as increasing adaptability, complexity, autonomy, and coherence of political organizations and the willing acceptance of the prevailing rules by the members of a political community. The successive post-Mao CCP leaderships have introduced a wide range of incremental reforms that have increased the level of institutionalization of political life in China. The cadre retirement age and term limits are universally implemented. A comprehensive system of cadre training, evaluation and promotion are introduced. Other reforms include local and grassroots elections, making power succession at the top more rule-based, rebuilding the legal system destroyed during the Cultural Revolution, firmly embracing principles of meritocracy, reforming the mass media etc. Although with limited success, intra-party democracy is being explored; efforts are made to increase the communication channels with the general public. The CCP has substantially reformulated its ideology to adapt to and accommodate the changing socioeconomic reality. There are also increasing differentiation and functional specialization of institutions within the regime. All these increase the stability of the political system and enhance the regime's level of acceptance to the people. As a result Chinese elite politics is more rule-based and less brutal now. The less lop-sided power distribution within the regime in the post-paramount leader age (after Deng), the increasing pluralism both in and outside the Party, a focus on market-based economic development, and the embracement of globalization etc., all contribute to political institutionalization. Nevertheless, there are large areas in social justice, income distribution, mass political participation, conflict resolution, anti-corruption and so on where institutionalization has lagged far behind.

STUDY UNIT 10

CORRUPTION

Political corruption is the use of power by government officials for illegitimate or immoral gains. Forms of corruption include bribery, extortion, cronyism, nepotism, patronage, graft, sexual exploitation and embezzlement. Corruption may facilitate criminal enterprise such as drug trafficking, money laundering, and human trafficking, though it is not restricted to these activities. A state of unrestrained political corruption is known as a kleptocracy, literally meaning "rule by thieves".

Corruption directly results from unconstrained, unsupervised and unchecked power. Not all corruption is aimed at private gains. In a poorly designed, inefficient system, corruption is often used to make normal, productive transaction possible. Reputable corporations operating in emerging markets with poorly developed legal and institutional infrastructure often face a moral dilemma whether to engage in activities normally deemed as corrupt in order to make doing business possible in that environment. Public officials otherwise clean and with integrity often have to yield to corrupt practices if corruption has become endemic or even part of the culture. Otherwise they would not be able to survive as we have seen in many stories of this book. In China being corrupted is at least as much a problem as being corrupt. Under one-party rule, with the concentration of power in the hands of the party bosses (typical of a Leninist party), with the lack of judicial independence, electoral pressure as well as adequate media supervision, corruption has systemic roots. The CCP is perhaps the most draconian in its anti-corruption campaigns in the world (it sometimes sentences ministerial level officials to death for serious corruption), however, it is

279

unlikely to be successful without radically reforming the political system, a step it is so far reluctant to take for fear of losing power. Meanwhile, powerful *status quo* interests are consolidating within the party-state establishment (Essay 5), further dimming the prospect of political reform. Such conditions tend to call for the emergence of strong leadership at the top, making way for authoritarian politicians.

Main Readings:

Essay 5; Stories 1, 3, and 7 (esp. Zen's Casino case); Boxed Essay 3.

Key Issues and Relevant Readings in the Book:

- Historical sources of corruption [Story 7, esp. Pan Xing's discussion of the Six Ministries].
- Human nature and corruption [Tb 10.1 (p. 56)].
- Public property rights and corruption [Tb 10.2 (p. 180), 6.6 (p. 47)].
- Power-money nexus [Essay 5; Tb 8.6].
- Political culture [Stories 1, 5 and in the Introduction Tbs 10.3 (p. 80)].
- Social and political consequences of corruption [Essay 5].
- Buying and selling official posts [Story 3 (II, VIII); Tb 10.4 (p. 85)].
- Innovative corruption [Story 7].
- Structural inducement [Tb 10.5 (p. 40)].
- Virtuocracy [Tb 10.6 (p. 234)]

Exercises:

a. Find and sort out the types of corruption in stories in this book.
b. Were you a cadre in China, would you be able to maintain personal integrity? Or would you even want to maintain your integrity? Why?
c. Comment on being corrupt and being corrupted in the Chinese political culture.
d. Propose your solutions to weed out corruption and try to convince someone from China that your solutions will work.
e. The story about the Six Ministries traces the deep cultural and historical roots of the rampant corruption we see in China today. Can the same thing happen in your country? If so, will it happen

in the same way? Taking advantage of your comparative perspective as an outsider, what do you think China could do to cure corruption?

Suggested Readings:

— Lu Xiaobo, *Cadres and Corruption: the Organizational Involution of the Chinese Communist Party*. Stanford University Press, 2000.
— Sun, Yan, *Corruption and Market in Contemporary China*. Cornell University Press, 2004.
— Gold, Thomas, Doug Guthrie, and David Wank, eds. *Social Connections in China: Institutions, Culture and the Changing Nature of Guanxi,* Cambridge University Press, 2002.

14. Land Grabbing and Forcible Eviction

In China, the term "land grabbing" refers to the practice of involuntary land requisitions from the citizenry, typically to make room for development projects. In many instances, government authorities working in collusion with private developers seize land from villagers, often with inadequate compensation. The rate of forced evictions has grown significantly since the 1990s, as city- and county-level governments have increasingly come to rely on land sales as an important source of revenue. Forced evictions with inadequate compensation occur in both urban and rural contexts, with even fewer legal protections for rural residents. In most instances, the land is then sold to private developers at an average cost of 40 times higher per acre than the government paid to the villagers.

Under Chinese property law, there is no privately held land; "urban land" is owned by the state, which grants land-use rights for a set number of years. Rural, or "collectively owned" land is leased from the state for periods of 30 years, and is theoretically reserved for agricultural purposes, housing and services for farmers. Under China's constitution and other property laws,

(Continued)

(Continued)

expropriation of urban land is permitted only for the purpose of advancing "public interests", and those being evicted are supposed to receive compensation, resettlement, and protection of living standards. "Public interests" are often ill-defined, however, and abuses are common in the expropriation process. In 2011 and after 12 years of deliberation, China's legislative body passed a new law limiting the use of violence in forced evictions, as well as outlawing demolation at night and during holidays. Under the 2011 regulation, violent law enforcement measures are to be used only in "emergencies," though the term is not defined.

Forced evictions are a common catalyst for organized protests. A number of protests have also made international headlines: Qian Mingqi, a farmer from Fuzhou whose home had been demolished to make room for a highway project, complained of losing 2 million yuan in the forced eviction. After numerous failed attempts to petition the authorities for redress, on May 26, 2011, Qian detonated three bombs at government buildings. He was hailed as a hero by many Chinese internet users, who viewed the attacks not as a form of terrorism but "righteous vengeance." Citizens have also resorted to a variety of semi-institutionalized forms of resistance, including petitioning and litigations to challenge forced land requisitions or to demand better compensation. In the first half of 2004, for instance, China's Construction Ministry reported receiving petitions from more than 18,600 individuals and 4,000 groups over forced evictions and unlawful transfers of land. Numerous lawyers identifying with the *weiquan* (rights defending) movement have taken on cases related to forced evictions and land requisitions, often free of charge.

STUDY UNIT 11

CHINA'S UNRESOLVED ISSUES

Are we witnessing the winding down of the Great Chinese Revolution? When the Chinese president Xi Jinping spoke in his inaugural address in November 15, 2012 about the "China dream" being the "national rejuvenation," his sense of a historical mission is shared by the Chinese people, left and right, at home and abroad alike. National pride is the selling point of his presidency. As is clear from the above account of where China came from and where it is going, "national rejuvenation" is no less than a rebirth of an ancient civilization. However, the competition among the various visions to define the future of China is far from settled. We can gain a better sense of where China stands now by taking stock of what has been accomplished by the Great Chinese Revolution so far.

China's nationalist revolution has been extremely successful. China is no longer under the shadow of foreign powers as a century ago and has become a major, and at times, over-powering actor on the global stage. The proposal of "Chimerica,"[1] absurd as it seems at present, nevertheless reflects the recognition that China is increasingly capable of a role in world affairs on a par with the United States. In contrast with 100 years ago when China was being carved up into many spheres of influence of major powers, repeatedly invaded and forced to cede territories and pay huge war indemnity, today it is unthinkable for any country to invade

---

[1] It is a vision of a new world order, proposed by a Harvard economist, that is hinged upon the condominium between the US and China in managing world affairs.

China. From the Chinese state's perspective, the only remaining issues are unification with Taiwan and stamping out the separatist movements in Tibet and Xinjiang.

The prolonged and torturous political revolution has first deposed the imperial system and then replaced the nationalist republic with a communist system, which in turn has since 1978 engaged in reforming itself incrementally. In other words, the communist system in its existing form is not and should not be the end result of China's political revolution. There are obvious solutions to the key issues of political reform cited above but the CCP leadership has been too fearful of losing power to pursue them. The impasse may, however, be well proven transitory for two reasons: first, the current generation of leadership as well as the cadre corps grew up in the Mao era and are comfortable working within the broad parameters of the communist system; future generations of politicians will be less constrained by the Party's past legacies. Second, the discontent with the system is mounting from both within and outside the CCP and social forces pushing for further political reform will only grow stronger with time.

China's social revolution is thorough in the destruction of the traditional social structure. However, the Mao-era attempt to regimentalize the entire society with the *danwei* system dominated by Party organizations not only produced repression but also retarded the growth of a healthy, autonomous, and self-regulation society that undergirds political stability. Social development in the reform era started from atomized individuals released from the communist institutions; they are regrouped by market forces on the basis of unmitigated self-interests. The new market-based society is still taking shape but several features have emerged. The first is the rapid return of class polarization together with the widening income gap. Secondly, the moral fabric of the new class society is still lacking. Third, money is increasingly wedded with political power to produce a privilege class both in and outside the Party establishment. Injustice, inequality, and lack of basic trust are symptomatic of deteriorating social conditions. (Essay 5) In other words, the rebuilding phase of China's social revolution is far from over and the outcome far from clear.

The road to China's cultural revolution is similarly torturous. Waves of assault on the traditional culture since the late Qing bore fruit only when the social and economic foundations of the traditional culture were decimated. The Maoist interim took the cultural revolution to the extreme but the promoted new communist culture was perched upon an ideological utopia that came crashing down when Maoism was discredited after Mao's death. A crisis of faith has permeated the society and into this spiritual void poured in all sort of values, beliefs, ideologies and religious faiths. The Chinese culture has become more individualistic, materialistic and diversified. The CCP has never given up its attempt to revitalize the official ideology and propagate the associated values, ideals and code of conduct. Various elements of the traditional culture have been revived. However, the culture of consumerism has been the most unbridled. In short, the cultural scene in China is quite messy but also pregnant with many possibilities.

The economic revolution has taken root with China's near double-digit growth for the past three decades. However, the Chinese economy still suffers from some structural problems such as over-reliance on investment and export; the factor markets are still incomplete and state interventions in marketplace still extensive. Although China is the second largest economy in the world, its per capita income still ranks below the median of the world. Resources and environmental constraints pose serious challenges to the long-term sustainability of growth; structural reforms are also imperative.

Therefore, of the five main components of the Great Chinese Revolution, the nationalist and the economic revolutions are by far the most successful. To varying degrees, substantial progress has been made in other areas as well but there is still a long way to go before a healthy state of affairs emerges in those areas. But it has become more clear recently that the ruling CCP tends to stand in the way of national rejuvenation even though it has been the leading force of it. (Essay 5)

Some Key Issues in Political Reform

As a backlash against the disastrous Cultural Revolution, earlier reformers, especially the intellectual forerunners of the reform, attempted to resurrect the legacy of the May 4th Movement that embraced modernization via Westernization. Liberal reformers within the Party in the 1980s such as Hu Yaobang (then Party General Secretary) and Zhao Ziyang (then Premier and later succeeding Hu as the General Secretary) were constrained by the conservative ideologues and the need to defend the ruling position of the communist party. Nevertheless, the liberalism embodied in the political reform programs adopted by the 13th Party Congress in 1988 is still unsurpassed even today, especially in the area of separation of the Party from the government. The Tiananmen movement of 1989 and the ensuing collapse of communism in Eastern Europe and of the Soviet Empire put political reform on hold indefinitely. China's economic success, the disillusionment with the Western neoliberalism and the corresponding rise of nationalism and cultural pride since then seemed to have reduced the pressure for political reform. Some even talked about the "China model" or "Beijing Consensus." Nevertheless, issues such as the rule of law, democratization, freedom of expression, equal rights protection etc. have been smothering underneath the economic boom and become more salient in recent years.

The Chinese communist system has proven remarkably resilient and potent in promoting economic growth. Taking advantage of its immense capability at resources mobilization, China has naturally championed an investment-driven and export-led growth model, sustaining a near double-digit annual growth rate for three decades. However, economic success has created a host of new issues and problems that the current political system is incapable of solving. The first and foremost is corruption. The PRC has acquired the unenviable reputation worldwide for rampant corruption. Underneath the general category of corruption, however, are some distinct issues that require specific attention.

First, although the economic growth is generally market-driven, it is also state-led. The party-state's interventions in the marketplace are extensive. A robust power-money nexus has emerged as the root cause of China's corruption problems. Specifically, large and amorphous role of the state creates many opportunities for rent-seeking; state actors have developed close ties with business elite to form a symbiotic coexistence. Much of the income gap is caused by the unequal access to resources and political power. Better and more clearly defined role of the state in the economy is necessary to effectively tackle corruption and rent-seeking. Further administrative reform and instituting the rule of law are important part of political reform but both run into strong resistance from the *status quo* interests.

Second, the market-driven social transformation has created a more pluralist and stronger society. With the dismantling of the planned economy, people are less tolerant of the repression inherent in the communist system and more vocal and fearless in expressing their minds and demands. New classes and class conflicts have emerged. Rising discontent and mass protests are pushing the limits of the state apparatuses of repression, which has also been beefed up considerably. Stronger society and stronger state inevitably lead to state-society confrontation. The party-state needs to be not only responsive to society but also adaptive to the rising popular aspiration for political participation. Some form of institutionalized democratic accommodation is necessary but the tightly knit system of party-state and party organizations offers too little space for it.

Third, some forms of checks and balances and more effective supervision of power must be created. Unlimited and inadequately supervised power is the fountain head of corruption that erodes equality and social justice, and undermines state credibility and legitimacy. In addition, the dualist structure of party-state makes it hard to rationalize public administration and reduce the size of the state and the state sector in the economy. It also makes political power expansive. The collapse of communism in Europe halted the reforms to separate the Party from the government because of the CCP's fear of party authority and legitimacy being challenged by another independent power center.

Since the late 1990s, the political elite have recaptured the economy to become a privilege class deeply rooted in the market economy. The relative separation of the economic elite and political elite is no more, as is the cultural discrimination against the merchant class. Hence, today's ruling elite are much more difficult to dethrone than those targeted by Mao's Cultural Revolution.

Key Issues:

- Political legitimacy.
- Credibility of public authority [Essay 5].
- Political reforms [Essay 4].
- Status-quo interests [Essay 5].
- State-society confrontation.
- Civil society development [Essay 4].
- Democratic accommodation [Essay 5].

Exercises:

a. What are the problems, if any, do you see in implementing a Western democratic political system on China? Are these insurmountable?
b. In your opinion, in which areas political reforms are most urgently needed and why?
c. How do you assess China's future? Please give clear reasons for your assessment.
d. Search online to find a copy of "The CCP Central Committee's Resolution on Several Major Issues in Deepening Reforms" passed by the 3rd Plenum of the 18th Party Congress on November 12, 2013; analyze and comment on the reform package: what status-quo interests the proposed reform measures are going to run into? Will the Xi leadership be able to overcome them?

Suggested Readings:

— Nathan, Andrew, *China's Crisis: Dilemmas of Reform and Prospects for Democracy*. Columbia University Press, 1990.
— Tsai, Lily, *Accountability without Democracy: Solitary Groups and Public Goods Provision in Rural China*. Cambridge University Press, 2007.

— Zweig, David, *Democratic Values, Political Structures, and Alternative Politics in Greater China*. US Institute of Peace, 2002.
— Ogden, Suzanne, *China's Unresolved Issues*. Prentice Hall, 1989.
— Shirk, Susan, *China — Fragile Superpower: How China's Internal Politics Could Derail Its Peaceful Rise*. Oxford University Press, 2007.
— Pei, Minxin, *China's Trapped Transition: The Limits of Developmental Autocracy*. Harvard University Press, 2006.

PART III

TOPICAL ESSAYS

ESSAY 1: THE GENESIS
OF THE POST-MAO MARKET ECONOMY

The most fundamental change in the past three decades is the establishment of a market economy. However, the post-Mao marketization in China is in many respects paradoxical; it has helped to generate the hyper-growth for a period of over three decades and yet it took place within an ownership structure that remains avowedly "socialist" and under an unabashedly Leninist political regime. The Chinese case is an excellent laboratory to study the development of a market economy. Like the former communist states in Eastern Europe, the Chinese state deliberately eradicated the market as a social evil in pursuit of "continuing revolution" and is now resurrecting and reconstructing it. However, unlike the former Eastern Bloc countries where the communist regimes collapsed, the reconstruction of a market economy in China is presided over and administered by a communist state. Given this and the legacy of a command economy, market development has had to serve the interests of at least part of the cadre class — the most powerful group in the Chinese political economy. Contrary to the common assumption of a dichotomy between market and command, hierarchically situated state actors in China's institutional setup have much to gain by becoming market players. And by their very participation in market exchange, they not only expand the market but create the incentives for further marketization. Once it has gained momentum, market development generates its own political constituencies and reshapes power distribution in society to a point of no return. This essay tells the story of political marketization in China.

1. The Political Revival of the Market

Communism is organized around bureaucratic fiat. The operation of the command economy, and hence the maintenance of the

vanguard party's revolutionary or transformative goals, its ideological visions, organizational cohesion, and the nature of the
political regime, all depend on the party-state's monopoly of
resources and rewards in society.[1] Market suppression in China
had a whole theoretical-ideological edifice built around it in the
form of Mao's theory of "continuous revolution," which deemed
the market to be the embodiment of capitalism and endeavored to
replace it with a planned economy. Market suppression was particularly severe for farm products due largely to the system of "unified purchase and marketing" (*tonggou tongxiao*) imposed on the
peasantry to force the transfer of rural surpluses to urban-indus-
trial sectors through monopoly purchase of farm products at
below-market prices. Table 3 depicts the severity of market suppression in pre-reform China: from 1952 to 1978, while the population and total consumption increased 67.4% and 295.8% respectively,
the total number of commercial establishments (retail stores, restaurants or repair shops, etc.) declined by 72.4% (from 5.5 to 1.52
million); and the average number of people served by each commercial establishment increased from 104.4 to 6,332.5.

Although it has often been noted that China's progress toward
central planning was not as long or as thoroughgoing as in the
Soviet or East European experience (e.g., the plan in China never
covered more than 600 goods, out of which only 200 were managed
in detail, whereas the plan in the USSR covered over 60,000 items),[2]
it does not logically follow from this that China's efforts at market
suppression were any less intense. Paradoxically, the PRC may
have been both more thorough in the suppression of markets and
less thorough in planning than its fraternal socialist republics. The
result of market suppression was a "product" economy (as opposed
to a commodity economy), in which prices were set by a central

---

[1] See Janos Kornai. 1992. *The Socialist System: The Political Economy of Communism*.
Princeton: Princeton University Press, and Zbigniew Brzezinski. 1989. *The Grand
Failure: The Birth and Death of Communism in the 20th Century*. New York: Scribner.
[2] Naughton. 1995. *Growing Out of the Plan: Chinese Economic Reform, 1978–1993*.
New York: Cambridge University Press, pp. 41–42.

Table 3.   Market Suppression, 1952–1978.

(million or million yuan unless otherwise specified)

	1952	1978	Change
Population	574.87	962.59	67.4%
Gross social product (GSP)*	101,500	684,600	574.5%
Total consumption	47,700	188,800	295.8%
Commercial employment**	9.53	9.39	−1.5%
Commercial establishments	5.5	1.52	−72.4%
Retail	4.2	1.05	−75.0%
Food & beverage	0.85	0.12	−85.9%
Other services	0.45	0.09	−80.0%
No. of persons served by each commercial employee	60.32	102.51	−69.9%
No. of people served by each commercial establishment	104.5	6,332.8	5,960.1%
Retail	136.9	9,167.5	6,596.5%
Food & beverage	674.3	80,215.8	11,796.2%
Other services	1,277.5	106,954.4	8,272.2%
Share of commerce in GSP	11.1%	6.4%	−42.3%

* A statistical category used in the place of GDP in the pre-reform era. Roughly, it is the total output of industry, agriculture, commerce, construction and transportation; all in current price.

**People employed in retail, food and beverage and other services such as barbershop, shoe repair and so on.

Sources: Calculated from *Zhongguo guonei shichan tongji nianjian 1991* [*China Domestic Market Statistical Yearbook 1991*], pp. 27, 30, 53 and 54.

plan according to the labor theory of value rather than the market logic of supply and demand. As planning was far from comprehensive, many products were also distributed through nonmarket channels (e.g., the network of work units, or *danwei*). The center of redistributive planning was the State Council, within which the State Planning Commission, the Ministry of Commerce, the Ministry of Materials and Equipment, and the Ministry of Grain all played key roles via their local branches. On the eve of reform, commerce was monopolized by the state via a three-tiered distribution system of wholesale stations and a network of state-owned retail stores and trading companies.[3]

The redistribution system was not only tiered but segmented, not only regionally but sectorally; e.g., the Ministry of Commerce was primarily responsible for urban areas, while rural distribution was under the jurisdiction of the General Cooperative of Rural Supply and Marketing (*gongxiao hezuoshe*). Producers did not produce to meet market demand but to fulfill a plan quota, fighting against the constraint of limited supplies. This created a "seller's market," i.e., a systematic shortage of agricultural and consumer goods, magnifying the importance of the hierarchically organized and controlled *danwei* to supply individual needs, as well as the need to cultivate informal supply channels. This reinforced the traditional cultural reliance on connections (*guanxi*).

The intellectual recognition that an economy based on planning tended to develop certain shortcomings such as an increasing difficulty correlating supply and demand, flagging work incentives or lagging innovation dates back to the period of painful reassessment that followed the debacle of the Great Leap Forward, when some economists revived interest in the "law of value." This economic rethinking found a receptive audience in such key political actors as Liu Shaoqi, Chen Yun, and Deng Xiaoping, who on this basis were willing to experiment with such expedients as limited rural free markets, returning to household production and allocating private plots to peasant households; the expanded use of profit as an index of economic efficiency, the indexing of pay scales to productivity, even consumer surveys, the stock market and industrial trust.[4]

The fact that the market option was available is not a sufficient explanation for its political resuscitation. The favorable political climate was created by the widespread sense in the aftermath of the

---

[3] For a survey of the pre-reform state-owned marketing and distribution system, see Andrew Waltson. 1988. The Reform of Agricultural Marketing in China since 1978. *China Quarterly*, No. 113, pp. 5–13.

[4] E.g., Lowell Dittmer. 1998. *Liu Shaoqi and the Chinese Cultural Revolution*. Armonk, NY: M. E. Sharpe, 2nd edition.

Cultural Revolution and Mao's demise that the drive for socialist purity had reached a dead end. The veteran cadres purged during the Cultural Revolution were rehabilitated and reinstated after the downfall of the Gang of Four, and formed the core of the "reform faction" that supported the restoration of Deng Xiaoping to a leading position at the Third Plenum of the 11th Party Congress in late 1978.

Once back in a position to set the agenda, the reform leadership needed new policy ideas and a way to mobilize a bureaucratic constituency, and the market provided both. The economic corollary of the Cultural Revolution's political bankruptcy was that Mao's focus on "spiritual incentives" had been widely discredited, leaving apathy and cynicism in its wake. As Andrew Watson's analysis shows, market development in the rural areas was initiated accidentally by post-Mao institutional reforms that introduced the rural household contract responsibility system and changed the practice in state purchase of farm products (in particular, the state raised the purchasing price). As a result of increased production incentives, rural output soared. When the sluggish state marketing and distribution system could no longer handle the increased volume, the state changed its long-standing policy and allowed peasants to sell part of their products on the free market (after fulfilling their obligations to the state). As a result, the rapid growth and extension of free marketing was almost inevitable. Market centers were hastily established in villages and urban streets and both individual peasants and collective units began to trade on them. As market institutions developed, producers of all ownership types began to re-orient their production toward the market, and gradually became dependent on it for their operations. Victor Nee also identified the same process by which commercialization leads to specialization of the producers (including the peasant households) and their increasing reliance on the market as the dominant form of transaction.[5]

---

[5] See Victor Nee, "Organizational dynamics of market transition: Hybrid Forms, property rights, and mixed economy in China," *Administrative Science Quarterly*, Vol. 37, No. 1C Mar., 1992), pp. 1–27. His point is that this process shifts power away from state hierarchy. However, we should also note that many of these market participants (including the most powerful ones) are themselves state actors.

In urban areas, the reform leadership's first expedient was a reemphasis on workplace discipline (which Deng also stressed in 1974–1975 during his short-lived first rehabilitation), whereafter they resorted to "material incentives." These provided the discretionary income from which marketization naturally flows, acquiring a self-sustaining momentum with snowballing vested interests behind it. These vested interests were personified in the myriad lower-level bureaucratic entrepreneurs who stood to gain most from marketization, largely because of the continuation of public property rights, which undergirded their political power while also giving them market advantage. The focus was on reshuffling the roles and decision-making powers among state actors, rather than on creating a new class of economic actors outside the state sector. The market and non-state actors were, in the earlier years of reform, a necessary evil to be tolerated rather than indulged. These cadres enthusiastically supported further expansion of the market, generating the paradoxical dynamic of marketization within a Leninist institutional framework.

During the 1980s, the market acted like a giant magnet drawing people into a headlong "plunge into the sea of commerce" (*xiahai*). Commerce became not only a profession but a fashion, and the popular jingle of the day was (of then China's one billion people) "Nine hundred million are in commerce, with another hundred about to commence." As mentioned before, market consists of its participants; the nationwide rush to the marketplace created a tremendous momentum that expanded the market and raised the level of marketization. By late 1980s and early 1990s, the sidewalks of Chinese cities were thronging with small peddlers who came not only from the countryside but from moonlighting urban factory workers, school teachers, and cadres from all kinds of state units. Table 4 depicts a complete reversal of the trend identified in Table 3: between 1978 and 1996, the population increased by 27%, but the number of commercial establishments grew by 1,122%. As a result, the average number of people served by each commercial establishment dropped from 6,332.8 to 65.9. Figure 9 shows the rapid growth of retail sales by ownership category. By far, the

Table 4.   Market Development, 1978–1996.

(million and million yuan)

	1978	1996	Change
Population	962.59	1,223.89	27.1%
GDP	684,600	6,859,380	902.0%
Total consumption	188,800	4,019,597	2,029.0%
Commercial employment	9.39	52.74	461.7%
Commercial establishments	1.52	18.58	1,122.4%
No. of persons served by each commercial establishment	6,332.8	65.9	−99.0%
No. of persons served by each commercial employee	102.5	23.2	−77.4%
Share of commerce in GDP	7.3%	8.4%	15.1%

Source: Calculated from State Statistical Bureau. 1998. *Zhongguo shichang tongji nianjian 1997* [*Market Statistical Yearbook of China 1997*]. Beijing: Zhongguo tongji chubanshe, pp. 14, 20, 73.

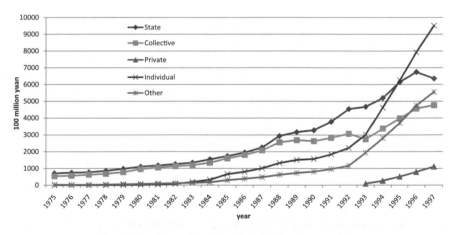

Figure 9.   Growth of Retail Sales by Ownership.

Source: National Statistical Bureau; *Market Statistical Yearbook of China 1998*. Beijing: Zhongguo tongji chubanshe (1998), p. 32.

fastest growing sector was individual ownership, but beginning from a minuscule base it did not overtake state-owned units as first in total sales until 1995.

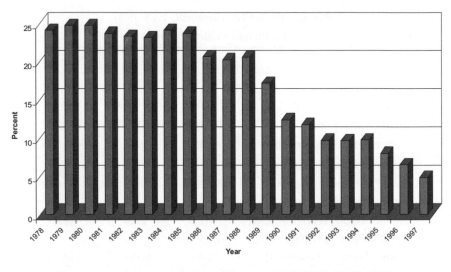

Figure 10.   Average Margins of Return of All SOEs (1978–1998).

(tax+profit/total assets)

Source: China Statistical Yearbook, various issues.

This commercial craze was fueled by the extraordinarily high market profit margins created by the pent-up demand in the pre-reform shortage economy, as well as by the enormous gaps between state-set prices and market-determined ones. In the early 1980s, the free market price for farm products was consistently 40% or more above the state procurement price.[16] Figure 10 shows the average margins of return of all state-owned industrial enterprises (1978–1997). Note the much higher profit margins during the 1980s; presumably the returns in non-state sectors were even higher because these sectors were less constrained by state price controls.

2. Marketization of the State-owned Sector

Largely because of the repressed demand that the market was able to serve, marketization proved successful beyond the wildest dreams of its political sponsors. However, the decisive shift from plan to market came only when state actors became market players. This shift was made easier by the structural characteristics of pre-reform command economy: China had a relatively decentralized system with structural fragmentation and incomplete planning, large numbers of small- and medium-sized enterprises, and a disproportionately large rural sector. In other words, unlike their counterparts in the former Soviet Union, local governments, state-owned enterprises (SOEs) and other state actors faced fewer formal, rigid institutional constraints when redirecting production for the market.

The reorientation towards the market was initiated by the decentralization reforms that were intended primarily to empower and increase the autonomy of lower-level state actors in enterprises and local governments. The typical scheme of reforming the incentive structure of state actors in the economy was to reduce their planned task assignment and allow them to engage in market exchange after fulfilling their plan obligations. However, coming out of the shortage economy of the Maoist era, the market enjoyed a considerable advantage over the plan in rewarding economic entrepreneurship. The enormous price gaps between the free market and state planned procurement for goods and services led to rapid draining of resources from the planning channels into the open market.[6] As a *People's Daily* commentator lamented in January, 1982 that state plans for purchasing fast-selling, scarce goods were not being fulfilled, in part because of competition between factories rushing to production sites to procure raw materials, shopworkers traveling directly to rural areas to buy goods, and even some foreign trade departments participating in the melee, all without any concern for whether or not the local purchase task for state commerce had been completed. By mid-1980s, the typical estimate was that enterprises carrying out planned production could only obtain from the state planning channels an 80% quota of the material supply required to fulfill their planned task; only 80% of this quota could be translated into actual orders at the annual trade

---

[6]According to the State Planning Commission, the planned prices of all commodities in the first half of 1992 were below world market price, among which, crude oil was lower by 77.3%, timber by 66.6%, corn by 59.2%, wheat by 32.4% and copper by 32.7%, while those of domestic market prices were significantly higher: copper higher by 14.5% (21% in 1991), lead by 12.6% (26% in 1991), and soyabean oil by 69.6% (86.7% in 1991).

conference for materials, and only 80% of the ordered materials actually got delivered. In other words, enterprises were frequently forced to secure their material supply from the market at much higher prices and sell to the state the finished products at the planned price. Naturally, this caused widespread resentment and shirking in plan implementation. In addition, state and non-state actors alike rushed in a speculative craze to take advantage of the dual price structure by extracting resources from the planning channels (using their power of office and various *guanxi*) and sell them on the market to generate a profit. Soon it became apparent that state plan was no match for the market; the government repeatedly had to raise its within-plan supply and procurement prices, which eventually converged with market prices to make the plan superfluous.

Decentralization through fiscal and enterprise contracting undermined the plan from another direction as well. Under the contracting system, localities and enterprises had incentives in the intense intrastate bargaining process to reduce the scope of the central plan governing their economic activities in order to increase their discretionary power over resources. Because of the huge initial market returns, these newly autonomous state actors invariably became market players despite the statist tendencies in their market behavior. Yet another facet of state actors turning into market players is the remarkable array of revenue-generating [*chuang-shou*] business ventures started by party-state bureaucracies and other organizations, and the People's Liberation Army units. They start businesses, often using their power of office and state or communal resources under their control, to generate additional incomes for the members of their work units.[7] Although systematic data are impossible to come by, the typical estimate by some Chinese authorities is that over 50% of the total monthly income of

---

[7] However, here the profit motive is mixed with the survival motive: According to author's interviews, stagnant salaries, shrinking budgets and rising inflation have often made the normal operation of and even the subsistence of the members of many units impossible without additional income.

cadres was generated in some forms of moonlighting. For example, by 1993, the Ministry of Railways system (the ministry and its subordinate regional bureaus and sections) had started 46,000 second-line businesses[8] that were independent accounting units. At the end of 1992, the ministries of postal services, telecommunication and transportation had between them 129,000 or so similar enterprises. In 1992, 10% of all new companies nationwide were started by organizations in the Communist Party and the government, and in Liaoning Province alone, party-state organizations (*dangzheng jiguan*) started 3,590 new business ventures. At the end of 1994, the state-run trade unions across the country owned 130,000 businesses.[9] The financial departments and even the tax bureaus in many localities generated an extra income through making short-term loans to cash starving enterprises using state's money flowing through their offices. Almost every *danwei* was involved in several lines of businesses and ran its own secret coffer (*xiaojinku*). Many kept several accounting books to deal with different authorities.

The importance of non-wage income is of course not restricted to the cadre class. In 1995, wage income as a percentage of the total income for all Shanghai residents declined from 59.3% the previous year to 56.1%; the largest item in the non-wage income was listed as "other incomes from their work units." This "second-lining" is perhaps the most striking feature of the Chinese political economy in the reform era, and it is the participation of these state actors in market exchange that removed many political obstacles to greatly quicken the pace of marketization.

Illustrative of the marketization of state actors is the transformation of the material department of the government and its subordinate firms, which formerly comprised the hard core of state planning. Before 1996, all important production materials — coal, steel, wood, cement, oil, machinery and equipment and so

---

[8] That is, outside their official line of business or railway transportation. These include hotels, department stores, restaurants and manufacturing.

[9] *People's Daily* (overseas edition), May 3, 1995.

forth — were in short supply. The brief period of re-centralization after Mao's death in 1976 saw the number of materials under central planning increase from 217 in 1970 to 837 (of which 256 were the so-called first-category materials directly controlled by the State Planning Commission; the rest were allocated by the various ministries).[10] Reforms in the sector not only allowed enterprises in material production and trading the opportunity to pursue the enormous profits created by the gap between the planned price and market price of materials, but also reoriented the well-established state-owned distribution channels to serve the market. In fact, once decentralized and reoriented, state-owned commercial firms and distribution networks have become part and parcel of China's emerging market. By 1987, the numbers of first-category materials were reduced to 27, and all state-own material firms were performing dual roles: profit making as well as carrying out the plan. As can be expected, extra-plan business dealings increased rapidly: from 55.1% in 1987 to 83% in 1991. From 1980 to 1990, all domestic production of materials that fell under plan was reduced: coal from 57.9% to 40.7%, steel products from 74.3% to 41.5%, timber from 80.9% to 21.8%, cement from 35% to 11.8%. The rest of the output was sold by producers on the market (except a small portion distributed under local government plans). In 1988, SPC allowed certain producers of materials under direct state plan to sell at market price as long as the state preserved the right to allocate them (i.e., to decide whom to sell to).

By 1990, 30% of steel and 50% non-ferrous metal produced under state directive plan were sold at the market price. With the profit generated on the market, many state-owned material firms became essentially businesses. Some branched into tourism, real estate, and other sectors, some formed joint ventures with foreign capital to provide direct services for other firms. The marketing and distribution systems of the government's material departments were open to clients of all sorts, including collective and

---

[10] According to state regulation then, market trading of all first category and most second category materials were strictly prohibited.

private dealers. The state-owned specialized materials marketing network of distributors (*wangdian*) used to implement plan only (i.e., to allocate materials according to plan directives) but they were now refurbished to serve market demand. By 1990, there were 40,000 of such specialized distributors nationwide with total sale of 202.9 billion yuan, and market sales amounted to 80% of the total of all state-owned material trading firms. About 45% of the total sale of coal was made on the market, steel was 72%, copper 81%, aluminium 63%, timber 78%, cement 66%, rubber 79%, heavy trucks 82%. By 1995, the ratio of market sales approached 100% for most categories.

3. Marketization and Decentralization

Marketization coincided with decentralization and devolution to lower levels of government and to production units. Governments of all levels gradually adopted pro-market policies in the early to mid 1980s and began to promote market development actively.[11] There were two main benefits of the market to local governments: faster economic growth and expanded revenue base. In addition, as mentioned above, with the rapid shrinking of state planned supply, many localities had to rely on the market to supply the material input for local firms to carry on their normal production.

Initially, most provinces were suspicious of the market; they were still trapped in the leftist thinking of the Maoist era. However, with decentralization and the shift of the CCP's emphasis from ideological purification to economic development, localities are in fact pitted against one another in an intense rivalry to deliver faster economic growth. When a few bold provinces, such as Guangdong, Anhui and Sichuan, took the lead in pro-market reforms and delivered tangible results, others followed suit. As Montinola, Qian, and Weingast's analysis shows, China's *de facto* economic federalism created by decentralization not only allowed the market to flourish in the interstices but forced anti-market local

---

[11] See Dorothy Solinger. *China's Transition from Socialism*, esp. Chapter 10.

governments to adopt pro-market policies.[12] For example, in its report at a conference on urban reform organized by the State Commission on Reforming the Economic System in 1991, Suzhou municipal government listed the benefits of promoting the market as: (a) to secure factor input for production, as the planning channels could no longer supply these with any adequacy; (b) to promote sale of local products when the central government's planning authorities no longer guaranteed their purchase; (c) to promote industries: for example, by building the specialized silk market, the traditional silk industry renowned in this region was revived; (d) to ensure social stability through economic prosperity brought about by bristling market activities; (e) to promote enterprise reform by forcing them to survive on the market; and (f) to break the rigidity of the administrative structure in which enterprises were trapped.

To promote market development, many localities have rushed in a concerted effort to build the infrastructure for market activities. If the earlier development of these markets was characterized by spontaneity, later market centers were creations of the local governments, who often cleared out a piece of land, erected a structure, furnished transport, utility services and police patrol, and then began to rent out spaces to retailers, from whom they could collect taxes and fees. Creating market centers as new growth poles in the local economy became a popular strategy for local economic development, a strategy commonly characterized as "The government sets the stage and the enterprises put on the show." Many wholesale markets were established by local governments as a way to expand their organizational grip over the flourishing private traders.[13] State-promotion, therefore, characterized the pattern of market development in China after 1980. In a more extreme case, in 1993 the municipal government of Zhengzhou, the capital city of Henan province situated on the cross-road of two main railway

---

[12] See Gabriella Montinola, Yingyi Qian and Barry Weingast. Federalism, Chinese Style. *World Politics*, October 1995.

[13] Solinger. *China's Transition from Socialism*, p. 236.

arteries and aspiring to become one of the country's main hubs of commodity trading, ordered all government employees and SOE workers to set up peddler's stands in the weekend fair organized by the government in the central square. The objective, according to the government, was to create an atmosphere of "big city, big commerce" and improve the city's image as a commerce-friendly locale.

Politics in the Party center has similarly played out in favor of the market. The coalition that dethroned Hua Guofeng, Mao's hand-picked successor, was eager to move away from the Cultural Revolution era and search for new directions of economic development. They had little guidance other than a new consensus on the goal of the "four modernizations" (i.e., industry, agriculture, science and technology, and national defense). Lacking a blueprint from the very beginning, the reformers were forced to adopt an incremental approach, but they were willing to allow bold experiments by the localities and let the results guide their policy and institutional choices.

4. Marketization and Central Power

The most important role played by the central state during the early phases of reform was to remove institutional obstacles to marketization. There were two main obstacles to the opening of the market: the vested interests supporting state planning, which resisted marketization by insisting on state monopoly of resources; and Maoist ideology, which regarded the market as the breeding ground of capitalism. As the plan faded into the background in the context of the dynamic described above, the removal of ideological obstacles became crucial, for "mind emancipation" under communist game rules could only be initiated from the top. As early as the 1950s and early 1960s, top planners such as Chen Yun advocated a limited role for the market in the socialist economy. Chen envisioned a "bird-cage economy" in which the state plan laid the framework within which the "birds," that is, enterprises, could have limited space (the market) to hop up and down. The revival of the market early in reform era had much to do with Chen's return to the center stage of economic policy-making in the late 1970's. The 12th Party Congress of 1982 hit upon a scheme in which "plan is the primary, the market is the supplementary" (*jihua weizhu, shichang weifu*). Two years later, the Third Plenum of the 12th Party Congress, in which the "Resolution on Reforming the Economic System" was passed, further developed the scheme into "a planned commodity economy" model,[14] and made it an important task of reform to establish a national market system. The 13th Party Congress of 1987 not only continued the "planned commodity economy" formulation but attempted to reconcile it with the Marxist theoretical edifice by proposing a theory of "preliminary stage of socialism," which was expected to last at least for another hundred years in China. During this stage, according to the theory, because of the low level of economic development, market forces and even private property rights had to be permitted and harnessed to promote the forces of production.

During the post-Tiananmen conservative backlash (1989–1991), a new tune — "the internal unification of the plan and the market" — was played across the land. Although coined by Deng himself, it was used by central planners and other conservatives as a disguised retreat from the market-oriented reforms back to renewed emphasis on state planning, which resulted in a new cycle of re-centralization. The decisive ideological breakthrough came with Deng's famous southern tour of early 1992, when he renounced the traditional ideological dichotomy that equated socialism with state planning and capitalism with the market. That finally cleared the way for the CCP's 14th Party Congress later that year to adopt a "socialist market economy" as the target model of economic reforms.

---

[14] *You jihua de shangpin jingji.* Note here the term "market economy" (*shichang jingji*) is avoided in favor of a "commodity economy" (*shangpin jingji*), indicating the lingering ideological taboo associated with the market and its capitalist tendencies.

Yet beginning with the attempt to reign in the inflation precipitated by Deng's southern tour and achieve a "soft landing," and also motivated by the CCP analysis of the collapse of communism in Europe, the leadership began to place higher priority on the need for central control over the chaotic currents of reform. Particularly since the 15th Party Congress in late 1997, the central government asserted leadership even as the pace of marketization accelerated significantly. If hitherto the zeal among local state actors for marketizing reforms was revenue-driven, the central government seemed to be motivated by the opportunity to build the institutional infrastructure of a market economy as a way of recovering some of the regulatory and revenue power dissipated to the localities during earlier decentralization reforms. This reassertion of central leadership was a consequence of the changed macroeconomic environment faced by bureaucratic actors in the marketplace. On the one hand, the persistent and ever-expanding budget deficit forced the central government to take drastic actions; on the other hand, as diminishing returns to bureaucratic entrepreneurship altered the incentives of cadre participation in market exchange, the state actors became motivated to retreat from the marketplace, allowing greater space for the private sector.

Bureaucratic entrepreneurship has been a potent force in driving China's spectacular growth;[15] but it is effective only when the marketplace is characterized by shortage. Under high market demand, state actors are extremely effective in building production facilities to meet the still crude and unsophisticated demand. However, state actors' capacity to mobilize resources, plus their inherent propensity to protect their own enterprises during an economic downturn, inevitably lead to overproduction or surplus capacity, which in turn drives down or even wipes out profit margins. When the market is no longer profitable for state actors, the enterprises they have built become liabilities, for it is the state which must support and subsidize these loss-making firms and

---

[15] See Lance Gore. *Market Communism*, esp. Chapter 4.

their workers, a proposition that is increasingly unsustainable given the mounting budget deficit.

In addition, broad participation by state actors in market exchange distorts the market and creates abundant opportunities for corruption and rent seeking. During the high-growth years when everybody benefited from the expanding economic pie, this malaise was tolerated or ignored; however, once hard times hit, such deviance became a politically explosive issue, a point well-illustrated by the crisis that brought down the Suharto regime in Indonesia in 1998. In other words, economic slowdown increases both political and economic liabilities of the state, which has hitherto been too broadly engaged in the economy. Economically, the state budget has to support an ever-expanding number of state cadres. Politically, corruption among cadres has become endemic and seriously threatens the legitimacy of the state. Downsizing the state is, therefore, a natural course of action to reduce the political and economic liability. Thus, the underlying causes of China's liberalizing and marketizing reforms late 1990s were very similar to those in other developing countries.[16] Table 5 describes the deficit situation during the two decades since 1978. This should also be considered in the context of declining state revenue as a proportion of the GDP and the manifold increase of administrative expenditure as a percentage of the state budget (Table 6).

To reduce state liabilities, the central government adopted three reform measures that significantly speeded up the pace of marketization. The first was administrative reform, aimed at restructuring the state machine to suit a market economy and, during the process, greatly reduce the number of state cadres and shrink the scope of state participation in the economy; the second was SOE reform, which followed a strategy of "grasping the big ones and letting go of the small ones" (*zhuada fangxiao*), and the third was to further improve the political, legal, and institutional environment of private businesses.

---

[16]See Chaudhry. "The myth of the market and the common history of late development." *Politics & Society*, Vol. 21 No. 3, September 1993, 245–274.

Table 5. State Budget Deficit.
(100 million yuan)

Year	GDP	State Revenue*	Revenue/GDP	Budget Balance
1978	3624.1	1132.26	31.2%	10.17
1979	4038.2	1146.38	28.4%	−135.41
1980	4517.8	1159.93	25.7%	−68.9
1981	4860.3	1175.79	24.2%	37.81
1982	5301.8	1212.33	22.9%	−17.65
1983	5957.4	1366.95	22.9%	−42.57
1984	7206.7	1642.86	22.8%	−58.16
1985	8989.1	2004.82	22.3%	0.57
1986	10201.4	2122.01	20.8%	−82.91
1987	11954.5	2199.35	18.4%	−62.83
1988	14922.3	2357.24	15.8%	−133.97
1989	16917.8	2664.9	15.8%	−158.88
1990	18598.4	2937.1	15.8%	−146.49
1991	21662.5	3149.48	14.5%	−237.14
1992	26651.9	3483.37	13.1%	−258.83
1993	34560.5	4348.95	12.6%	−293.35
1994	46670	5218.1	11.2%	−574.52
1995	57494.9	6242.2	10.9%	−581.53
1996	66850.5	7407.99	11.1%	−529.56
1997	73452.5	8651.14	11.8%	−582.42

*Debt income not included.
Source: State Statistical Bureau. 1998. *China Statistical Yearbook 1998*, pp. 55, 269 and *Market Statistical Yearbook of China 1998*, p. 32.

By the time a buyer's market emerged around 1996, marketization and decentralization had thrown the state planning apparatuses into complete disarray. Like Humpty-Dumpty, no amount of effort could reassemble it to reassert central planning. Illustrative of the futility of the attempts to reinstate planning control was the humiliating failure of the post-Tiananmen round of re-centralization. Therefore, instead of a return to central planning, the central

Table 6.   Growth of State Administrative Expenditure in Total State Expenditure.
(100 million yuan)

Year	Total State Expenditure	Administrative Expenditure	Share in Total State Expenditure
1978	1122.1	52.9	4.71%
1979	1281.8	63.05	4.92%
1980	1228.8	75.53	6.15%
1981	1138.4	82.63	7.26%
1982	1230.0	90.84	7.39%
1983	1409.5	103.08	7.31%
1984	1701.0	139.8	8.22%
1985	2004.3	171.06	8.53%
1986	2204.9	220.04	9.98%
1987	2262.2	228.2	10.09%
1988	2491.2	271.6	10.90%
1989	2823.8	386.26	13.68%
1990	3083.6	414.56	13.44%
1991	3386.6	414.01	12.22%
1992	3742.2	424.6	11.35%
1993	4642.3	535.8	11.54%
1994	5792.6	729.4	12.59%
1995	6823.7	872.7	12.79%
1996	7937.6	1040.8	13.11%
1997	9233.6	1137.2	12.32%

Source: State Statistical Bureau, *China Statistical Yearbook* (various issues).

government attempted to regain its position by building up the institutional infrastructure (fiscal, legal as well as regulatory) of a market economy, and pushed to dismantle the state's microeconomic management apparatus built for the command economy as a way to weaken localism and correcting market distortions. In March 1998, Premier Zhu Rongji's government launched an ambitious reform program of overhauling state bureaucracies. The target was to cut both the personnel and institutions of the central government by half in three years. By October 1998, most industrial ministries of the State Council had been abolished, their macro-economic regulatory functions repackaged into a new super-ministry — State Economic and Trade Commission, and the SOEs attached to them reassigned to the localities or become independent operations. The personnel of the State Council were reduced by 47%. Three ways have been designed to marketize the industrial ministries at both the central and local levels: (1) to turn them into business entities (corporations, enterprise groups, holding companies etc.) that are stripped of their government administrative functions; (2) to turn them into semi-official trade associations or business councils, and (3) to turn them into macro-regulatory agencies.

By 1996, the returns of SOEs in most industries were negative. As a result, as soon as the 15th Party Congress put forward the reform line of "grasping the big ones, letting go of the small ones," local governments were in a selling frenzy to get rid of their loss-making SOEs. The change of attitude among the localities was so dramatic that the central government had to step in to curtail the fire sale. SOE reform had also stripped SOE workers of their privileges of state sector employment, privileges the state found itself no longer able to pay for. Workers now had to contribute to the housing fund, their medical care, pension plans and other insurance; not only their life employment tenure was history, tens of millions of them were laid off and relegated to the vicissitudes of the marketplace. In effect, labor, even in the privileged state sector, had been marketized, notwithstanding all the CCP's Marxist principles.

Finally, after the 1987 "theory of the preliminary stage of socialism" removed the ideological obstacles to private ownership, a 1999 amendment to the Constitution granted private businesses equal status with the state and collective sector firms in China's market economy. To the state, the benefits of a vigorous private sector are manifold: it generates employment when the state needs it the most to head off social unrest; it provides a new growth engine when bureaucratic entrepreneurship is faltering; its ups and downs do not increase the political and economic liability of the state the way the SOEs do. Privatization helps the state to marketize its liabilities.

5. Conclusions

When institutional economists talk about choice between forms of transaction (i.e., market versus hierarchy), the assumed objective is simple and straightforward — to maximize profit and minimize transaction costs. However, when talking about such choices in a communist context, something much bigger is at stake. The market is not simply a place where people exchange money for products, for a rudimentary market of this type existed even under the plan. According to Victor Nee's theory of market transition, the logic of marketization means embracing a set of rules of the game that alters the nature of society as well as the polity.[17] Marketization diminishes the importance of the state hierarchy in resource allocation and dispensing rewards in society. It threatens the communist order by ushering in a different set of organizing principles that are based on contractual relationships between relative equals (on the spot of exchange), by offering a new set of opportunities for rewards, and by draining resources from state command. Therefore, all communist regimes are inclined to suppress the market as a political imperative. This fact raises the question of the post-1978 reform epoch: Why did those in a political position to stop a process that undermines their interests fail to do so?

This essay has shown that the decisive push towards marketization comes from within the party-state, and that, contrary to the conventional dichotomy between market and command, hierarchically nested state actors found much to gain in pushing the market oriented reforms. The Dengist reinterpretations of Marxism define markets as fully compatible with socialism in its early stages; market and plan are no longer mutually exclusive. In the context of the

---

[17] Victor Nee. "A theory of market transition: From redistribution to markets in state socialism." *American Sociological Review*, 54 (October, 1989), p. 663.

relaxation of political and ideological constraints, cadres suddenly found it possible to orient production toward either plan or market depending on the relative rewards. The participation of state actors in market exchange not only expanded the market but created a self-sustaining dynamic for further market expansion, in accord with the institutional dynamic of path dependency. The question is thus why it was in the interest of the Party leadership to opt for marketization in the first place.

The party-state is no monolith; its cadre class consists of groups with diverse orientations. The benefits of marketization have always generated its advocates within the elite, even in the pre-reform period. The failure of Mao's continuous revolution shifted the balance of power away from the ideologues in favor of the pragmatists, and the post-Mao politics of post-mortem succession also necessitated new directions in economic development. The Dengist coalition pushed for market-oriented reforms as a way of building constituent support both within the party-state and among the populace at large. While local governments and lower-level state actors prospered from initial market participation, the central authorities also reaped the benefits of the ensuing growth in both political and economic terms. At a time when the regime's radical ideals were being replaced by developmental objectives as the new rallying cry, the more marketized regions and sectors were delivering clearly superior developmental results; anti-market ideologues were soon marginalized in this dynamic. Policy and institutional choices were both clearly in favor of the market.

Rapid growth, especially along the coast, created a dynamic and rapidly changing economy, the complexity of which rendered it hopeless to continue state planning. Changes in the transaction cost structure of the economy (especially the information costs of monitoring and control) continued to erode the capacity of state bureaucracies or the apparatus of the command economy to a point of no alternative to further marketization. When market returns were high, there was a synergy between the state (especially local governments) and enterprises to pursue market opportunities. After two decades of rapid growth, intensified competition cut the profit margins perilously thin and increased market risks. The burdens to support and subsidize the state sector become increasingly unbearable, creating incentives for the state to "let go of the small (SOEs)" in an attempt to marketize its burdens. Under these circumstances, the central government, responding to its diminished authority and control due to prior decentralizing and marketizing reforms, attempted to regain its authority not by resurrecting the plan but by accommodating the market: it resorted to building up the regulatory and institutional infrastructure of a market economy in order to reassert its authority and rein in the localities. In sum, the dynamics of politics and economics conspire in support of further marketization. This is the genesis of China's market economy.

ESSAY 2: THE POLITICAL IMPACT OF THE MARKET

It is only natural that a party so massive in size and with its grass-roots organizations so extensively embedded in the society should be profoundly affected by a market-driven socio-economic transformation. Marketization has unleashed a multitude of forces that are pulling apart the Party's grass-roots organizations. One of the most significant market-driven social changes is the re-emergence of classes. Figure 11 describes the 10 social strata identified by Chinese sociologists in the early 2000s. They are hierarchically ordered in accordance with their respective social status in the Chinese society. Needless to say, the remergence of classes will have profound political impact, first and formost on the CCP.

1. General Impact

What the post-Mao reform has done politically is, first and foremost, the dismantling of the organized dependency. The Party's power is premised upon its monopoly of resources and opportunities through the *danwei* system. The emergence of the market as a competing mechanism of resource allocation undermines this monopoly. Marketization drains resources from Party control, develops new resource base and opens up new opportunities outside the organization grip of the Party. The individual can now have career and a life outside the party-state control; he or she no longer needs to rely on the party-state for a job, a living quarter, for vital supplies such as food, clothing, health care, education services and so on — he or she can satisfy these needs readily and without hassle from the market. Marketization causes the unloading of many of the roles performed by *danwei* to the market and the corresponding transfer of resources from within the *danwei* system to the open market.

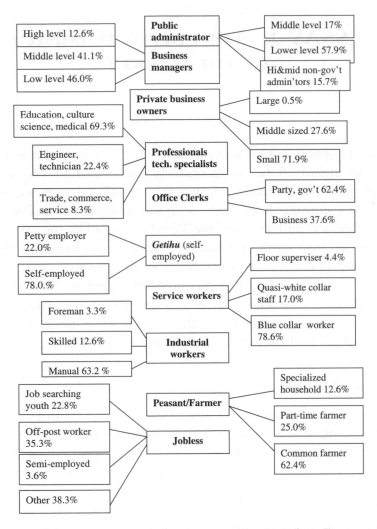

Figure 11.   Ten Social Strata Emerging in the Reform Era.

Source: Constructed from chapter 1 of Lu Xueyi et al. eds. *Social Mobility in Contemporary China*: Beijing: Social Sciences Literature Press, 2006.

A state-owned enterprise (SOE) producing for the market ceases to be a *danwei* in the classic sense; it is transformed into a business that hires and fires workers on a regular basis in response to market conditions. It is detached from the supply network of the

A peasant migrant worker family in big city

party-state and must struggle for survival in the competitive marketplace. The market has thus replaced state planning as the main mechanism of resources allocation in society and thereby changed the rules of the game. The result is either the disintegration of *danwei* or their transformation into market-based organizations, melting down the institutional foundation of the Party's micro-rule and throwing the millions of the Party's grassroots organizations off balance. For without controlling the administration and resources of the "carrier" organizations, it would be difficult for Party cells to attract new members; nor would they be able to uphold the strict organizational hierarchy and discipline that is the trademark of a Leninist party. It is especially true of the CCP today when value or ideological consensus is no longer attainable in a pluralizing society. Without the rewards afforded by the administrative power and resource control of the carrier organizations, the Party is short on leverage over its members and therefore cannot count on their loyalty to maintain the Party's organizational integrity.

Inevitably, the increasing importance of professionalism, the technical and technocratic competence, and entrepreneurship — the

essential ingredients of modernization — diminishes the importance of Party membership in an individual's career success. The
development of the job market also undermines the CCP's control
over human resources. In short, the loss of its monopoly over
resources and rewards in society has caused a subtle but fundamental change in the relationship between Party organizations and
Party members. The Party has to compete with multiple sources of
rewards to attract a following.

2. Impact on the Party in Rural Areas

One of the consequences of the market-driven socio-economic
transformation is the massive exodus of labor force from the rural
areas. For 30 years, the younger, better-educated and more talented
villagers have been migrating in droves to pursue non-farming
opportunities in cities and the coastal belt. The result is a massive
bleeding of the rural human resources. In many areas of the major
labor-exporting provinces (such as Jiangxi, Sichuan, Hunan, Anhui,
and Henan), the countryside is virtually abandoned to the old, the
sick, women and children, and in some areas large quantities of
farm land have been left idle because of labor shortage. The bleeding also dries up the candidate pool of new Party members and
creates a shortage of younger Party members to staff village-level
Party organizations. In addition, an "old party secretary syn-
drome" was widely reported from rural China. It refers to the phenomenon of one person serving as village Party secretary for
decades (such as the one in Wukan village, Guangdong, where a
recent large-scale peasant protests attracted worldwide attention).
These old Party secretaries attempt to block the younger and more
talented people from joining the Party for fear of being disposed.
For they usually have few marketable skills or business talent;
guarding jealously whatever meager benefits vested in their positions is their only option.

The rural Party is also facing stiff competition from revitalized
kinship, religious and even criminal organizations. Many village

Party branches are captured by these organizations or become sub-servient to their interests and objectives. Village elections have also introduced a new dynamic into village politics that tends to deplete the legitimacy and authority of the village Party.

3. Impact on Party Organizations in Business Enterprises

The presence of Party organizations inside SOEs is the legacy of the micro-rule of the CCP in the planned economy era. However, once they are transformed into businesses operating in the marketplace, even SOEs are forced to play by market rules and adopt market practices and institutions. This tends to diminish Party organizations in businesses. Party organizations are often marginalized if they cannot reinvent themselves and find a role that contributes to business survival. Cutting back on base-level Party organizations and personnel is widely reported.

Unlike *danwei*, businesses are inherently unstable; they are in perpetual flux and can go bust anytime. Their instability causes unsustainability of Party organizations embedded in them. In private businesses, the capitalist owners are wary or even hostile to the organizational presence of a communist party; when forced to allow Party organizations to be set up in their firms, the own-ers often seek to serve concurrently as Party secretary and monopolize Party positions with their families or friends. For these reasons, the rate of Party penetration is the lowest in private businesses as shown in Table 2 on page 248. Furthermore, the Party secretaries and Party affairs staff seek to evolve their careers in the direction of business executives, engineers, technicians, or other professionals that would allow them to develop marketable skills; by doing so they neglect Party work. The development of the labor market puts considerable constraints on the Party's practice of appointing enterprise cadres (managers) because market competition tends to enforce the market criteria of human resources over the Party's political and ideological standards for appointment and promotion. The existence of market opportunities has also caused many SOE cadres to bolt from the Party's control into the human resources market — a "brain drain" from the Party.

The CCP has dealt with these problems with a strategy of "mutual penetration and interlocking appointments," that is, top executives sitting on the Party committee and top Party personnel joining the management team or chair the board. Predictably, the Party secretaries and Party affairs workers will always focus on the business side of their appointments to the negligence of Party work; Party organizations are thus effectively assimilated into business management. The political meddling by the CCP in enterprises has resulted in perhaps the most complex corporate governance structure known — the so-called "three olds plus three news" (*lao san hui, xin san hui*). The governance of the SOEs is a hybrid of three old communist institutions (the Party committee, the trade union, and the conference of workers' representatives) and three new capitalist institutions (Board of directors, Board of supervisors, and Shareholders Conference).

4. Party Organizations in the Mobile Population

The disintegration of the *danwei* system has created a mobile society. China's mobile population consists of not only migrant peasant workers but also increasingly the professionals and white-collar workers of urban origin. There are millions of CCP members among them who have lost contact with their home Party cells. The communities where they relocate themselves are part of the new social spaces created by the market. The greatest challenge of party-building is the fluidity and anonymity of these communities of strangers. Local Party authorities often do not have a clue as to how many Party members live in these communities and how to reorganize and reincorporate them into the organization hierarchy of the Leninist Party.

On their part, these Party members often do not have the incentive to be reconnected to the Party — they enjoy the freedom of living in anonymity and are glad to be rid of Party disciplines and obligations such as Party meetings and studies sessions. Local Party authorities often have to use the police registries to find out who are Party members in their community, or to lure them from their hideouts with free services such as job referrals and consultancy — Party organizations have little leverage over these mobile members who make a living on the market.

Party cells formed out of total strangers who follow different career trajectories and divergent daily routines are but a shadow of the Party cells in a stable *danwei*. The footloose attribute of Party members in the community and their lack of organic relations to each other, as well as the absence of a solid organizational base that *danwei* used to provide, are constantly eroding whatever has been accomplished in community party-building.

5. The Party and College Students

One "bright spot" for the CCP is its apparent success in recruiting college students. In 2008, for example, matriculated college students accounted only for 1.6% of the national population but contributed to 38% of new Party members. In contrast, peasants constituted 55% of the population but contributed only 20% of new Party members. A college student is 67 times more likely to be recruited into the communist party than a peasant. College students are also among the most active in the Chinese society in seeking Party membership.

In spite of the impressive recruitment results, party-building on college campuses is also deeply impacted by the market environment. College students seeking to join the Party are motivated by diverse considerations, many at odds with the Party's principles and objectives. For college students whose future are wide open with many possibilities and contingencies, membership in the ruling party is one of many factors to consider when making post-graduation career plans. Party membership may give them some advantages in certain careers. And for a successful career with the party-state, which is still the most desired career choice among college graduates, it is a prerequisite.

"Job advantage" is one motive for joining the Party found in many studies conducted by Party affairs researchers in China. The rapid expansion of college enrolment following the Asian financial crisis in 1997 began to exert enormous pressure on the job market four years later. In 2010, 6.2 million fresh college graduates entered the job market; adding the graduates of previous years still on the job market, as many as 10 million college-educated young people are active on the job market currently. College graduates who are CCP members tend to be quicker in finding jobs and often better jobs too. Many employers, including not only SOEs and the state-owned non-profit organizations but also private and foreign businesses, seem to have developed a preference for Party member graduates. There is a simple reason for this phenomenon: the CCP's elitist approach to party recruitment. By the time college students' graduate, most of the best and brightest among them have been herded into the Party through a long process starting from the elementary school — good students win prizes and these prizes in turn attract Party recruiters. As a result, Party membership becomes a reliable indicator of quality — not necessarily ideological or political quality, but quality in terms of knowledge, skills and leadership capability. It is a strange twist in the spontaneous adjustment of the job market to the communist polity.

6. The Market's Continuous Challenges to the CCP

The impact wrought on the organizations of the CCP by the market-driven social transformation is serious, pervasive and of long-term significance. The transition to a market economy is melting down not only the "iron rice bowl" but also the micro-rule of the CCP's grassroots organizations; there is no longer a stable base of "carriers" for them to continue their traditional form of existence and operation. Marketization has created a completely new socio-economic reality to which the CCP has to adjust its rule.

In a fluid and fast-changing market environment, the CCP faces the challenge of finding new forms of existence and new ways of exercising power. While an extensive organizational infrastructure is necessary to run a planned economy, a market economy has its own mechanisms for economic transactions. Party organizations under a unified leadership and clear chains of command at least in theory can play a role to integrate the national economy and coordinate economic activities in a planned economy; in a market economy, however, such organizations serve no apparent purpose other than an ill-considered fear of losing power. The Party's effort at rebuilding and maintaining an expansive network of grass-roots organizations that penetrates every corner of society is costly and in many cases, simply impossible. With the dismantling of the "organized dependency" and the transformation of the incentives of Party members, these organizations can no longer be expected to deliver the same service or loyalty to the Party. Instead, they increase the Party's exposure to the society at a time when the Party is widely subject to criticism of corruption.

Size is no guarantee for the perpetuation of the Party's rule. Table 7 demonstrates that many of the former communist regimes had much higher party-member to population ratios in the mid-1980s but collapsed just the same. Quantitative expansion cannot counterbalance the qualitative changes in Party members and the deterioration of Party organizations. Party members' views, values, identities and incentives are now shaped more by the market than by Party indoctrination, and Party organizations at the grassroots level increasingly stand on shifting sand. The CCP needs to carefully reconsider the model of its rule — it should not only rule more effectively, but also rule more cost-effectively.

Table 7.   Size Comparison of the Ruling Communist Parties in the Mid-1980s.

Party	Size of Membership (10,000)	As Share of the Population (%)
Korean Workers' Party (North Korea)	320	16.0
Communist Party of Romania	350	15.4
Communist Party of Czechoslovakia	167	15.4
Socialist Unity Party of Germany (East Germany)	330	13.8
Communist Party of Bulgaria	93	10.4
League of Communists of Yugoslavia	220	9.5
Hungarian Socialist Workers' Party	87	8.2
Communist Party of the Soviet Union	1,900	7.0
Communist Party of Cuba	70	6.4
Polish Unified Workers Party	212	5.7
Albania Party of Labor	14	4.7
Mongolian People's Revolutionary Party	8.8	4.6
Chinese Communist Party*	4,775	4.2
Communist Party of Vietnam	220	2.9
Lao People's Revolutionary Party	8.4	1.7

*CCP figures are for 1987.

Sources: *Xiandai zhijie zhengdang*, Beijing: Qiushi chubanshe, 1989, cited in Rang Yihui. 2002. "An Exploration on Controlling the Number of Party Members." *Hunan School of Management Journal*, No. 3, pp. 92–93.

ESSAY 3: INDUSTRIAL RELATIONS MANAGEMENT AS THE DEVELOPMENT OF THE DEVELOPMENTAL STATE IN CHINA

Effective management of industrial relations is a pre-requisite of sustained economic growth and social progress. Labor movements can be immensely disruptive as witnessed by the history of industrialization in the West in the 19th and early 20th centuries. However, widespread strikes and protests eventually led to expanded suffrage and progressive legislations in Western democracies to regulate the labor practices of businesses and protect worker's rights. These legislations, many have argued, have in effect saved capitalism. After 30 years of market-oriented reforms that have produced not only rapid economic growth but also enormous income gaps and massive dislocation of workers, China appears to have arrived at a historical juncture when an institutionalized solution is called for to its mounting labor problems. Labor has become a key issue in China's development.

1. Labor and the Developmental State of East Asia

It is no longer fashionable to talk about the "East Asian developmental state" after the 1997 Asian financial crisis put spotlight on its many weaknesses such as corruption, cronyism, and distortions caused by state intervention in the marketplace. The 2008 Wall Street meltdown has rehabilitated somewhat its reputation by lending credence to the argument that the Asian crisis was not primarily caused by the inherent weaknesses of the state but by rampant speculations in the under-regulated global capital market — the same forces that led to the 2008 Wall Street collapse.

Nevertheless, applying the "developmental state" model on China has always been problem-ridden. A main difficulty encountered by researchers is the fact that much of China's developmental initiatives take place at the local level by local states; that as a continental sized country with a long history there are great varieties and complexities across the regions and that the local states are often engaged in intense competition for market, capital and human resources. The fragmented nature of Chinese state under economic decentralization, the complex central–local relations, the intense competitions among localities, the cross regional diversity in developmental polices, strategies, and institutions and above all, the communist polity, are powerful reasons making the case against adopting the concept of the developmental state in China.

Nevertheless, the role and capability of the Chinese state, including local states, to promote economic growth is undeniable. Students of the developmental state have either explicitly or implicitly invoked the notion of "strategic capacity" as its defining feature. After all, the whole idea of the developmental state is hinged upon the state's ability to guide market forces to achieve developmental objectives. This ability in turn is derived from some structural characteristics of the state. Evans emphasizes two conditions that give the state such capability in his concept of "embedded autonomy": internal cohesion and external connection.[1] Internally, the developmental state is well organized (usually in the form of a competent bureaucracy) to maintain a "corporate cohesion" that enables it to pursue objectives larger than its constituent individuals and agencies. Externally, it is strategically embedded in society so that it is able to create synergy with key social groups or classes to successfully implement developmental policies and programs. This strategic capacity can conceivably emerge from different cultural and social environments, under multiple initial conditions and with diverse institutional arrangements. For example, Meiji Japan consciously followed the development model pioneered by Bismarck's Germany and even today there is considerable resemblance between Japan and Germany in areas such as

---

[1] Evans, Peter. 1995. *Embedded Autonomy: States and Industrial Transformation*. Princeton, N.J.: Princeton University Press.

corporate structure and the role of the state. There is no apparent reason that such capacity cannot emerge from the sub-national level, or even from individual agencies in a larger predatory state establishment as "pockets of excellence".

What makes the Chinese case interesting and relevant is the state's recent effort to establish an institutional framework for labor management in response to the fundamental changes in the larger social, demographic and macroeconomic environment. This effort is aimed not so much at quelling labor agitations than at clearly defined developmental objectives. It is intended to consolidate the state's strategic position *vis-à-vis* both labor and capital and to expand its policy and institutional options. As such the Chinese case offers us a rare glimpse of the process of state capacity building that is largely absent in the literature.

2. Chinese Labor at a Historical Juncture

The wave of labor unrests in 2010 precipitated by the infamous 'twelve jumps' at the Foxconn factory in Shenzhen[2] was extraordinary. The spontaneity and contagion of the strikes and the unusual responses by both the capital and the state mark a watershed in China's industrial relations. Both domestic and international forces coalesced to create a historical juncture — possibly a defining moment for industrial relations in China. On a global scale, China has emerged as the "factory of the world"; countries at all levels of development as well as all businesses that deploy their productions globally have a keen interest and varying stakes in the costs of manufacturing and the stability of industrial relations in China. The fact that labor unrests immediately became headline news worldwide testifies to the global dimensions of Chinese labor.

The 2010 strike wave came with an opportune timing, when the renewed pressure on China from the West about its currency

---

[2]In a span of a few months in 2010, 12 young workers of Foxconn, the world's largest contractor of consumer electronics, committed suicide by jumping off buildings, which ended in 10 deaths and two serious injuries.

A peasant worker looking at a flashy city he has helped to build but cannot become a legal resident of.

peg to the US dollars was coupled with the commitment of the G20 at Pittsburgh Summit in June 2009, with China on board, to "rebalancing" the global economy. It was anticipated that the global economy emerging from the financial crisis of 2008 would no longer be the same. In particular, it seems unlikely that the American market, having long been fuelled by credit-based consumption and staggering national debt, will return as a reliable market for China to continue its export-led economic growth. The burst of the housing bubble seriously eroded the purchasing power of the American people and the financial crisis also taught the American consumers a bitter lesson about the importance of saving. Household savings rose sharply despite the hardships experienced by the ordinary American families.[3] Jobs became the central

---

[3]Government data showed that the household savings rate rose to 6.9% in May, 2009, the highest since December 1993. The savings rate in April 2008 before the

issue in US domestic politics and labor standards rose in importance in the trade relations between the US and China. Much of the
same can be said about China's relationship with the European
Union. The Chinese government realized more acutely than ever
before the vulnerability and unsustainability of over-reliance on
export as the engine of growth. Table 8 illustrates the contribution
of the three drivers of the economy to the growth rate of each year
in a span of thirty years. Only export dipped into the negative
territories.

Domestically, three structural forces are redefining the position of labor. First, the widening income gap has become politically
destabilizing. According to the World Bank China's Gini coefficient
reached 0.47 in 2010[4] but independent studies put it well above 0.5.
Politically destabilizing aside, the lack of disposable income among
the working masses hamstrings the government's effort to shift the
centre of economic growth from export to domestic market by
expanding domestic consumption. Second, after 30 years of high-
powered growth based mainly on labor-cost advantage and relatively low-end industries, and as soon as the worst of the financial
crisis appears to have passed, labor shortage, which had been on
and off ever since 2004, came back to haunt China's coastal export
bases where businesses just began to pick up. Third, now that
China replaced Japan in 2010 as the world's second largest economy, it became imperative for the government to upgrade the
economy in order to escape the dreaded "middle-income trap" and
lay the foundation for the next phase of industrialization. Labor
shortage provided the impetus for wage hikes to force businesses
up the value chain. The audacity and the extraordinary demands
of the strikers in Guangdong and elsewhere reflected labor's
stronger bargaining position as a result of the above three.

---

crisis was zero. (cited by Rich Miller and Alison Sider in their article, "Surging
U.S. Savings Rate Reduces Dependence on China", *Bloomberg* (June 26, 2009).
Available at http://www.bloomberg.com/apps/news?pid=newsarchive&sid=
aome1_t5Z5y8 (accessed on September 3, 2010)
[4] According to the Macroeconomic Institute of the National Reform and
Development Commission, reported by *China Daily* on May 12, 2010.

Table 8. Three Components as Share of GDP and Contribution to GDP Growth.

Year	Final Consumption Expenditure		Gross Capital Formation		Net Export of Goods and Services	
	Share of GDP (%)	Contribution to Growth rate (%)	Share of GDP (%)	Contribution to Growth rate (%)	Share of GDP (%)	Contribution to Growth rate (%)
1978	39.4	4.6	66.0	7.7	−5.4	−0.6
1980	71.8	5.6	26.4	2.1	1.8	0.1
1985	85.5	11.5	80.9	10.9	−66.4	−8.9
1990	47.8	1.8	1.8	0.1	50.4	1.9
1995	44.7	4.9	55.0	6.0	0.3	—
2000	65.1	5.5	22.4	1.9	12.5	1.0
2001	50.2	4.2	49.9	4.1	−0.1	—
2002	43.9	4.0	48.5	4.4	7.6	0.7
2003	35.8	3.6	63.2	6.3	1.0	0.1
2004	39.5	4.0	54.5	5.5	6.0	0.6
2005	37.9	4.3	39.0	4.4	23.1	2.6
2006	40.0	5.1	43.9	5.6	16.1	2.0
2007	39.2	5.6	42.7	6.1	18.1	2.5
2008	43.5	4.2	47.5	4.6	9.0	0.8
2009	47.6	4.4	91.3	8.4	−38.9	−3.6
2010	36.8	3.8	54.0	5.6	9.2	0.9

Notes: (a) Three components of GDP by the expenditure approach are final consumption expenditure, gross capital formation and net exports of goods and services. (b) Contribution share of the three components to the increase of the GDP refers to the proportion of the increment of the each component of GDP to the increment of GDP. (c) Contribution of the three components to GDP growth refers to the growth rate of GDP multiplied by the contribution share of the three components.
Source: *China Statistic Yearbook 2011.*

Figure 12 documents the quarterly changes in the ratio of job openings over job seekers based on data provided by employment agencies in China's major cities. It shows a remarkable upward trend from 2001 before a sudden drop in the fourth quarter of

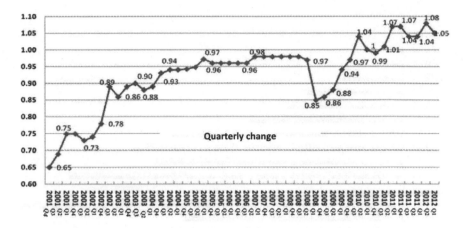

Figure 12. Job Supply and Demand Ratios from Q1, 2001 to Q2 of 2012.
Source: China employment website, available at http://www.chinajop.gov.cn/DataAnalysis/
content/2012-07/31/content_725849.htm (last access 15 Feb. 2013).

2008 — thanks to the Wall Street meltdown. But it climbed up
quickly from the first quarter of 2009 on to reach 1.04 by the first
quarter of 2010 — for the first time in 10 years, there were more jobs
than job seekers in China's manufacturing sector. Labor shortage in
China appears to have a demographic root. Figure 13 describes the
age structure of the Chinese population in 2008. It shows that the
population peaked at the 40–44 age-group, followed by a trend of
declining age cohorts, which forecast a dwindling labor force in
future. An additional factor to be taken into consideration is declining labor participation rate, which is associated with the generational change of China's labor force, in particular, the 242 million
peasant migrant workers.[5] Second generation peasant workers are
no longer willing to work as their parent generation for low wages.
It is noteworthy that the spring 2010 strike wave started from the
affluent areas and hit the prestigious foreign companies first.

Persistent low labor compensation constrained domestic consumption. Figure 14 describes the trend of the total urban wage bill

---

[5] Figure provided by Premier Wen at his annual NPC press conference on March
14, 2011. According to Wen, more than 50% of the income of the Chinese peasantry
now comes from non-farming sources.

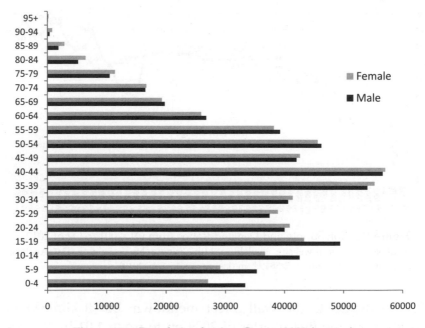

Figure 13. Population by Age Group, 2008 (person).
Based on a survey with a sample size of 1,178,521, or 0.0887% of the population.
Source: China Statistics Yearbook 2009.

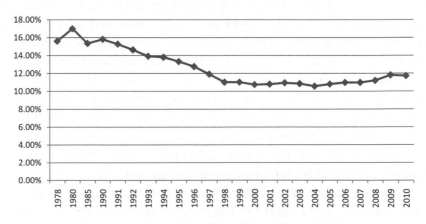

Figure 14. Total Urban Wage Bill as Share of GDP.
Source: China Statistics Yearbook (various issues).

as a percentage of GDP during the reform era (1978–2010). In the initial stages of the reform, it moved up between 1978 and 1980, from 15.61% to 16.99%, and then declined all the way to 10.57% in 2004 before slowly climbing back to 11.72% in 2010. The result is that domestic consumption as a share of GDP generally declined in the reform era as shown in Table 8 and graphed in Figure 15. In comparison to the Unites States where domestic consumption accounts for 70% and export only 10% of the GDP, in China the corresponding figures are 42% and 35% on average in the 2000s.

Neither the demographic trend nor the labor participation rate can be easily altered. With the bargaining position of the Chinese workers strengthening, a shift in industrial relations to reflect this new balance of power is inevitable. In other words, China's labor problems are rooted in fundamental structural forces that no short-term quick fixes such as the deployment of riot police can solve. Faced with mounting labor unrests, the central government took advantage of the new strength of labor to push for its developmental agenda. It showed unusual leniency during the 2010 labor unrest, generally allowing the strikes and protests to run their course. Heated discussions and protests in the cyberspace were

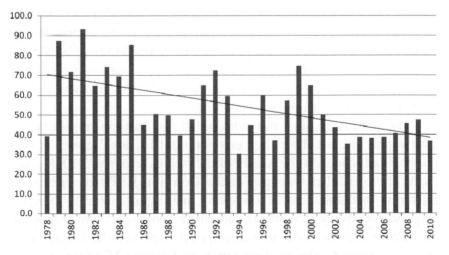

Figure 15. Final Consumption as Percentage of GDP.
Source: China Statistics Yearbook (various issues).

also permitted to rage on relatively unrestrained by the official censorship, which has always been super-sensitive to the destabilizing implications of public discussions.

3. Shifting Developmental Policy and Strategy

In the long-run, it is highly advantageous to have a large and stable domestic market as the main engine of its economy. It will alleviate the pressure from abroad on China's foreign exchange policy, trade balance, labor and environmental standards etc., reduce its external vulnerability, and expand its soft power as a major destination market for the exports of other countries, just as the United States has enjoyed since the end of World War II. To achieve this, the issue of income disparity will have to be addressed. Social justice aside, China cannot increase domestic consumption and size up its domestic markets without pushing up income from the bottom — it will have to boost the disposable income of the majority of the population. Increasing the share of labor remuneration in the national income, a top policy objective in the 12th Five-year Program (2011–2015) reaffirmed by the new leadership team sworn in at the 18th Congress of the CCP in late 2012, is considered a key determinant whether China can escape the middle-income trap and successfully change its growth model from export-led to domestic consumption-driven. At stake are the long-run sustainability of economic growth, political stability and national economic security. This realization largely explains the government's unusual leniency toward the strikers of 2010.

The paradigm shift has dominated the national political discourse and altered the policy environment for local governments and their officials. At the height of the strikes in early 2010, *People's Daily*, the official newspaper of the Communist Party, published blistering articles against company managers, urging them to respond positively to workers' "justified demands." On 29 August, 2010 Premier Wen took the unusual step of personally bringing up the wage issue to the visiting Japanese Foreign Minister, emphasizing that the root cause of labor unrests in some Japanese firms in China was "wages being too low." The 18th Party Congress (November 2012) formally adopted a Japanese-style "income doubling program", pledging to double both GDP and per capita income by 2020 from 2012. The Japanese program adopted in the 1960s is credited with laying the foundation of the Japanese "miracle" in the following decades. In 2010, China launched a new round of minimum wage hikes. Pressured by the central government as well as labor shortages, the provinces competed to raise the local minimum wages. By January 2011, all 31 provinces had lifted the legal minimum wage. The raises were generous too: 10% at the minimum and 37% at the high end, with a national average of 22.8%. To compete with other provinces for labor, 11 provinces launched another round of minimum wage hikes in the first half of 2011.

Nevertheless, it has never been the government's intention to encourage labor movement, let alone to allow it to grow into an independent political force like the Solidarity of Poland. The state's commitment to labor is limited by its strategy of economic development in which the strength of labor is to be taken advantage of, not appeased. Labor demands are carefully balanced out with other national priorities and harnessed to serve the political and economic objectives of the state. For this purpose, not only new policies are needed but also a suitable labor management system must be developed.

4. In Search of a Chinese Model of Industrial Relations Management

The intended change of growth model entails a broad range of institutional reforms, of which labor management is an integral part. Institution building in labor management provides us with valuable insights into the process of the development of the developmental state.

The Chinese state seeks legitimacy as well as popularity; it desires social tranquility and harmony; it wants to remain in control of all politically important social spaces and, after decades of export-led growth, it wants to expand the domestic market and upgrade the economy to put China's growth on a more sustainable base for the long haul. Uncontrolled labor unrests threaten to derail all these. But settling labor disputes by "class struggle" is not an option despite the CCP's long history of labor agitation before it came to power in 1949. The CCP needs capitalists to realize its modernization ambition. It wants a system of managing industrial relations that not only can maintain social stability but also is capable of handling the complexity and fluidity inherent in a transitional economy, of accommodating diverse objectives, and of balancing the interests of different parties without coming down to a show of force. Labor agitation today, like the peasant movements during the revolution, is regarded an energy source to be harnessed to promote the party-state's interests and objectives.

That both the central and local states are intrinsically involved in economic development has been extensively documented by researchers. The two, however, are involved in somewhat different ways. The central government's interests and objectives are not

always congruent with those of local states. But neither is a neutral arbitrator in labor affairs. Their relationship with both labor and capital is shifting with their changing policy objectives. Between labor and capital, local governments have since the 1990s regularly sided with capital, regardless of whether it is private, foreign or state-owned. They, always stakeholders and often stock holders as well, typically dealt with labor strife with heavy-handed restraints on labor in their efforts to maintain a favorable local investment environment. Maintaining a steady influx of investment is key to local economic growth. GDP growth still remains at the top of the agenda of most local governments but now it increasingly has to be balanced with other objectives, such as labor tranquility, social justice, environmental protection and so on. Many of these objectives are imposed on local governments by Beijing and may or may not be consistent with local interests. But in a unitary political system in which the careers of the local leaders are controlled from above, local cadres have to respond to the criteria their superiors use to gauge their job performance. Too many labor protests under one's watch may dim his or her career prospect. An institutional framework needs be created to accommodate diverse interests, objectives, and concerns of many parties. In a typical trial-and-error approach, the Chinese government has concentrated on two things in labor management: establishing a multi-tiered "tripartite coordination mechanism" and implementing collective contract.

The so-called "tripartite coordination mechanism" refers to a framework of consultation, deliberations and negotiation on labor issues, with employees, employers, and the government (via its labor department) as the three parties. While tripartism is the standard approach to industrial relations promoted by the International Labour Organization, its transplantation to China is producing some unexpected outcomes, in part because genuine unionization of workers is non-existent and neither are employers well organized. Of the three parties, the government is well endowed with not only political power but also organization resources, including the long-established official labor union (i.e., All-China Federation of Trade Unions or ACFTU) and the quasi-official business association: China Enterprise Confederation and China Enterprise Directors' Association, collectively referred to as CEC-CEDA (*qilian*).

The ACFTU is one of the three old "mass organizations" that are an integral part of the Communist Party's "united front."[6] It has been dominated by the CCP since its founding in 1925 as part of the CCP-led labor movement. Mainly funded by state budget instead of union dues, the ACFTU is organized into a gigantic national pyramid that parallels the structure of the party-state, with local chapters in all provinces, cities, counties etc. Every business of significant size is required to set up an enterprise union to be affiliated with the local chapter of the ACFTU. In 2009, ACFTU claimed to have 31 provincial-level federations, 10 national industrial unions and 1,324,000 or so grassroots union organizations (inside 2,753,000 or so enterprises and other organizations) affiliated with it, and a total membership of about 169,940,000.[7] Its president, Wang Zhaoguo, was a member of the CCP's Politburo and Vice President of the National People's Congress. Prior to this, he also served two terms as the director of the CCP's United Front Department.

The CEC-CEDA is much younger — it was created at the beginning of the post-Mao reform era as part of the effort to increase the autonomy of state-owned enterprises (SOEs). Its current president, Chen Jinhua, was a former director of the once powerful State Planning Commission. CEC-CEDA used to comprise mainly of SOEs and SOE executives but recently began to extend its reach into the fast-growing private sector. In 2009, the CEC-CEDA claimed 436,000 corporate members across the country. Like the ACFTU, the CEC-CEDA also has local chapters that parallel the administrative structure of the state. While both are closely tied to the government, the CEC-CEDA is closer to an NGO than the ACFTU, which has developed a more extensive organizational infrastructure than the CEC-CEDA, in part because of its much

---

[6]The other two are Women's Association and Communist Youth League.
[7]Data extracted from ACFTU official website at http://www.acftu.net.

longer history with the CCP. These two organizations are designated by the Communist Party as the sole representative of labor
and capital respectively to participate in the tripartite deliberation
on labor issues. A strict ban is enforced on competing organizations
such as the independent union the Honda striking workers
demanded in early 2010.[8]

Together with the labor department of the government (i.e.,
Ministry of Human Resources and Social Security[9] and its subsidiaries in the local governments) the three have formed "deliberation
councils" at various levels and locales to coordinate labor policies
in ways that accommodate or balance the interests and concerns of
labor, capital, and the government. For example, these councils can
set guidelines for collective bargaining, deliberate and make recommendations to the local government on local minimum wages,
labor standard, and other related issues.

The political philosophy behind this institutional framework
is not one of confrontation and balance of power as in the West.
The government envisions that collective bargaining under this
framework should serve to "ensure the unity between the workers
and the enterprises so that the two can share the risks, join force to
overcome difficulties and achieve common prosperity."[10] It is
hoped that such institutional arrangement will not only buttress
social stability but also give the state enough policy flexibility
to weather the ups and downs of the global economy. The main

---

[8] In response to the workers' demand for setting up their own union, the management of the Honda parts factory circulated a flier among the workers, saying it
was beyond their authority to recognize such a union and asked workers to
submit a detailed application for an independent trade union to the government;
see 'A Labour Movement Stirs in China' (*New York Times*, June 10, 2010).
[9] In particular, its Department of Labor Relations and Department of Mediation
and Arbitration Management.
[10] See "Circular on implementing group contracting and carrying out the 'rainbow
program'", Ministry of Human Resources and Social Security, No. 32 (2010), available at: http://www.law-lib.com/law/law_view.asp?id=314714 (last accessed
on March 25, 2010). It is issued in the name of the National Tripartite Council but
by the MHSS.

policy objectives of the tripartite council currently is to help the
government establish a "mechanism for regular wage increases"
that is in some way tied to the business performance, and to implement group contracting, which is to be renegotiated periodically
through collective bargaining.

The Chinese labor law requires the employer to sign a contract
when hiring a worker. So far the contract is signed, if at all, predominantly on an individual basis. The terms of the contract are
set by the employer, presumably within the provisions of the law.
The employees, especially the unskilled ones, are left in a vulnerable position and frequently abused. For example, they are forced
to work long hours, often under hazardous working conditions,
and live in cramped and regimented quarters. Many are not paid
on time or at all. The weak bargaining position of individual workers is considered the root cause of the decade-long stagnation of
wages before 2004, even in the most prosperous regions of China
where the cost of living rose rapidly. Implementing group contract
through collective bargaining[11] presumably will level the playing
field for the contracting parties. But how did it work out in
reality?

5. Representing Labor and Capital

In the reform era, the official trade union has effectively evolved
into two distinctive parts with different interests and bargaining
positions: the supra-firm union and the enterprise union. The former, being on government payroll and part and parcel of the
party-state establishment, naturally stands with the government
on most policy issues. The economic growth-minded local governments are usually pro-big business and the government affiliated union is expected to help ensure labor tranquility. Naturally,

---

[11] The Chinese rendering — *jiti xieshang* is significantly milder than the English
term "collective bargaining." A more literal translation would be "collective consultation." The choice of term reflects a desire for the contracting parties not to
engage in a zero-sum struggle.

the latter is often seen by workers as siding with the management. This has led to its marginalization: to the government it is a minor department; workers never really regard it as representing their interests, and the employers of private firms are by instinct wary of it. For decades it has languished for lacking a clear role and often serves as a half-way stop for party-state cadres who have been nudged aside in politics or are on their way to full retirement.

Enterprise unions, to the extent they exist at all, are usually worse off, especially those in private firms. They are usually set up with the help of the local chapter of the official union.[12] They do not lack a definable role but are, in general, powerless to play any role. Because union officials are also employees, they often live too much in fear of antagonizing the boss to get involved in labor agitation or to put up a fight for labor rights. Unions in private firms are often further neutralized by the fact that the owner, the boss, or their trusted others often serve concurrently as the head of the union. A few provinces have experimented with direct election of enterprise union leaders but it never took off as a general practice. Genuine unionization always presents complicated political problems for the ruling party. Each tripartite council oversees collective bargaining at the enterprise level, where actual contracts have to be negotiated between the employers and the employees case by case because different firms face different situations. However the lack of union leadership at the firm level makes collective bargaining difficult if not impossible. To address this problem, the ACFTU and the local governments have to find ways to provide creditable protection for enterprise union leaders. The ACFTU, for example, was test-running in 2010 a program to send its own agents — people on the union (i.e., government) payroll — to private firms to provide union leadership.[13]

---

[12] In the late 1990s and early 2000s, there were major drives by the CCP to unionize all businesses.

[13] The ACFTU allocated 10 million *yuan* to this program in ten provinces and municipalities in 2010. (*Workers' Daily*, May 23, 2010)

On the employer side, there has been a tacit division of turf between the two government-sanctioned business associations — the aforementioned CEC-CEDA and the All-China Federation of Industry and Commerce (ACFIC). The ACFIC traditionally has the purview over private and family businesses (*getihu*), while SOEs are the turf of the CEC-CEDA. However, the massive privatization of SOEs at the turn of the century significantly diminished the base of the CEC-CEDA and a turf war is currently being fought between these two. The government has officially designated the CEC-CEDA as the sole organization representing all businesses in the tripartite deliberation council but this may not be the end of the story. The ACFIC has a more diverse membership almost exclusively in the private sector and private entrepreneurs in general identify more with the ACFIC than CEC-CEDA. As a result, the ACFIC is more vibrant in its activities and programs. The government may have to find a way to incorporate the ACFIC into the tripartite platform and give it a voice in labor affairs.[14]

The emerging institutional framework, flawed as it is, is for most workers, positive news nonetheless. For inadequate or half-hearted representation is better than no representation at all. Workers may take heart at the prospect that it is no longer the boss alone who decides how much they get paid and under what conditions they have to work. The participation of the government and the official labor union at least improves their odds of getting a better deal at the table and provides them with additional recourses to address their grievances. The tripartite council also provides the official trade union a new theatre and a definable role. Advocating for labor rights, even if only verbally, lends it legitimacy and gives it a voice. It is being revitalized as a result.

To employers, the government has on the surface gained additional leverage over them. However, their real protection comes

---

[14] e.g., "ACFIC propose to represent (private firms) in coordinating tripartite labor relations", *21st Century Economic Report*, March 4, 2008; available at: http://www.21cbh.com/HTML/2008-3-4/HTML_2U5PAR2BXPJ4_2.html (last accessed on March 25, 2011)

from the natural alliance with the development-oriented local states and from their ability to bribe their way or to vote with their feet. The affinity between local governments and businesses is unlikely to diminish with stronger labor representation, especially in a non-democracy where numbers do not necessarily convey political advantage. SOEs and larger private employers are usually better positioned to gain government support than small and medium-sized businesses; cronyism also works in favor of key businesses in a locale. Nevertheless, the tripartite deliberation council can, as the instrument of the government, exert considerable political pressure on businesses to compromise with workers and accommodate the objectives of the state.

The enterprise union under ordinary circumstances shares the interests and concerns of ordinary workers and hence is in a position of genuine representation, but is ill-equipped to do so. The supra-firm union is, on the other hand, predestined to play the role of a go-between rather than a representative. It is well positioned to mediate among the government, the employers and the employees. Research has also shown that, although never poised to launch or promote large-scale labor movement, the governmental trade union (at least in some locales) plays a role in the arbitration of individual cases of labor dispute. It offers legal assistance to workers and sometimes applies political pressure (taking advantage of its status as a *de facto* government agency) on employers to address workers' grievances. By providing legal consultation and representation, the official trade union is able to use individual cases of labor dispute to advocate for labor rights in general, turning "workers' individual legal mobilization into a form of union action that represents its constituency."[15]

The biggest winner of this institution building is ostensibly the state. It is a classic example of power holding principals crafting institutions to benefit themselves the most. Both central and local states stand to gain from this institutional arrangement, which

---

[15]Chen, Feng. "Legal mobilization by trade unions: The case of Shanghai." *The China Journal*, 2004, pp. 27–45.

they can use to promote diverse objectives. The entire institution-building is couched on interests rather than on rights, giving preference to policy and political flexibility over legal certainty. The government wants to strengthen labor, but only as far as it serves its other objectives. The tripartite council can conceivably serve as an institutional buffer between labor and capital as well as a mechanism of conflict resolution that allows the government to influence the outcome. This institutional arrangement virtually gives the government the final say, given the fact that all the three parties, namely, the labor department, the trade union, and the business association, are of its own creation. The institutional arrangement can be utilized by other parties as well but ultimately it is the state that pulls the string.

As such the Chinese state, like the other East Asian developmental states used to do, creates organizations as a pre-emptive move where spontaneous organizations are likely to emerge. However, excessive state control also means that neither the employers nor the employees are adequately represented in the platform. Instead, a kind of "non-delegated representation" is superimposed on both by the state. Inadequate representation may lead both to seek solutions to labor problems outside the framework and prompt spontaneous development of other forms of interest articulation that may eventually hollow out the official platform. This eventuality may be inevitable when both labor and capital grow stronger and more autonomous as the country becomes more developed. A more sophisticated view of the Asian financial crisis holds that the developmental state had outlived its mandate in East Asia by 1997; it disintegrated in part because of globalization and in part because of its own developmental success that had caused the unraveling of the social coalition that sustained it: both labor and capital became too powerful and indomitable by the state — the former through a middle class revolution that led to democratic breakthroughs and the latter through globalization that greatly enhanced the bargaining position of businesses *vis-à-vis* the state. The Chinese developmental state is not immune to this dynamic.

6. The Development of the Developmental State

The Chinese state is strong, authoritarian, development-oriented (even in the Mao era) and interventionist. It pursues industrial policy mainly on market basis and has so far followed a strategy of export-led industrialization. More importantly, it has shown a keen awareness of changes in the environment and responded strategically as other developmental states in East Asia did. In a list-matching exercise it seems to fit the bill. However, a descriptive model does not add much value to our understanding. The strategic capacity account of the developmental state requires an understanding of the institutional structure and its evolutionary dynamic, not only of the state but also of state-society and state-market relations.

In every rapidly developing economy, there eventually comes a time when institutionalized solutions to the mounting labor problems have to be found. Different countries have come up with different solutions depending on the unique configuration of political forces and the socioeconomic conditions at that historical juncture, as well as on their cultural values and ideological inclinations. In the democratic United States, the massive labor movements in the middle and latter half of the 19th century produced big labor unions and a culture of confrontation for rights; in Latin America, the bureaucratic authoritarian political systems found corporatist solutions; in many European countries, social democracy emerged to balance the interests of the opposing classes; in Japan, part of the solution is life employment in big corporations that bind labor and capital in a commonwealth.

The solution of labor problems in China is also shaped by unique circumstances. The wave of strikes in the spring of 2010 took place at a historical juncture when major macroeconomic and political forces coalesced to push labor to the center stage in an intense struggle among various foreign and domestic parties to redefine the position of labor in the Chinese political economy, as well as China's position in the global production chains. Changes in the world economy are exerting ever greater pressure on China to change its growth model to rely more on the domestic market and, after decades of rapid economic growth fuelled by the seemingly inexhaustible supply of cheap labor from the vast rural hinterland, China's population dividend seem to be ending abruptly, thanks in part to its one-child policy implemented since the 1970s. The time has come for China to come up with an institutional solution to its mounting labor problems.

The post-Mao reforms have dismantled the command economy that privileged the proletariat, leaving the Chinese working masses unprotected, powerless against capital and vulnerable to market forces. To certain extent, what the market-oriented reforms have brought back is a form Dickensonian raw capitalism at the stage of "primitive capital accumulation" that is heavily exploitative and repressive of labor. Having grown cosy with capital and played a key role in ensuring labor docility for three decades, the development-oriented state has concluded that it is time to shift policy priorities. It has pursued multiple policy and political objectives with a simple strategy — boosting domestic consumption. The strategy is intended not only to pacify labor but also to achieve a range of other objectives: to maintain state legitimacy; to head off social unrests by building a "harmonious society"; to alleviate the pressure from abroad on labor and environmental standards and on the exchange rate of the RMB;[16] to mitigate the impact of inflation on the masses; to reduce external vulnerability by changing the growth model from export-led to domestic consumption-based; to upgrade the industrial structure and take development to the next level.[17] For all these purposes, the state needs to shore up labor in order to push up the disposable income from the bottom. Labor management for the Chinese state is political and economic management.

---

[16] In theory, increasing labor costs has the same effect as the appreciation of the RMB of making Chinese export more expensive, but it would benefit the Chinese labor while exporting inflation.

[17] China hopes to replicate what the Singaporean government did in the 1980s: forcing up labor costs so as to force businesses up the value chain. See Lim, Linda Y. C. (1983). "Singapore's success: The myth of the free market." *Asian Survey* 23(6): 752–764.

Pursuing these developmental goals requires a large state capacity. This study has documented the meticulous effort by the Chinese state to gain the market-based state capacity in the case of crafting the institutions for labor management. The Chinese state is autonomous and domineering but it also seeks to be strategically embedded in society with institutionalized linkages such as the tripartite council, which in many ways resembles the "deliberation council" (*shingikai*) of Japan. The Japanese institution brought together government bureaucrats, business leaders and academics to plan for and strategize on business development.[18] It is a defining feature of the Japanese developmental state from which Peter Evan derived his concept of "embedded autonomy".

Upon closer examination, however, the institution patterns in China are quite distinct from the archetypical developmental state despite the superficial similarities. But the Chinese institutions do seem to confer similar strategic capacity that gives China a competitive edge in the world market — an unfair advantage as the West contends. The talk about "the China model" or "Beijing consensus", superficial as it is, is evident of the recognition of such edge from abroad. It may be hypothesized that, because of the deeper state penetration into the economy and the society, the state capacity in China is more encompassing and could be used to pursue more diverse objectives than it is possible elsewhere. But it is also better positioned to extract rent, to distort the market and to repress the people. We do not know to what extents the state building will succeed; nor do we know if the resultant state is a plus or a minus on balance. But it should not be too far off the mark to characterize what we have described in this paper as the development of the developmental state, broadly defined.

---

[18] Detailed descriptions of the Japanese deliberation councils can be found in many studies, e.g., Campos *et al.* (1994); Chalmers Johnson (1982); Johnson, Tyson, and Zysman (1989); Ezra F. Vogel (1979) etc. For its spreading to other Asian nations, see Kaoru Natsuda (2008).

ESSAY 4: CHINA IN SEARCH OF NEW DEVELOPMENT MODELS

The dramatic fall of Chongqing party chief Bo Xilai in mid-March of 2012 is widely interpreted as the end of the leftist "Chongqing model"; the rivalry for the heart of soul of the Chinese Communist Party and China's future has settled decisively in favor of the right — the liberal reformers.

Or has it?

Dubbed the "Guangdong model" and the "Chongqing model," the reform experiments at Guangdong and Chongqing have attracted worldwide attention. Domestically, two ideologically distinct camps — the liberal and the new left — have rallied behind them. Despite the ideological brawl, the substantive reforms in these two locales have their own internal logic that is independent of individual leaders and derived from local conditions to address problems of national relevance. The proclamation of Chongqing's death is premature.

1. The Chongqing Model

The Chongqing model is indelibly branded as "singing red, striking black," that is, mobilizing the masses to sing revolutionary-era songs and busting crime organizations that are often tied to and protected by the local police and politicians. Chongqing did both, in a manner reminiscent of the lawlessness of the Cultural Revolution. However, equating the Chongqing model with just "singing red and striking black" would be a gross simplification. Under the rubric of "building five Chongqings," that is, livable (with affordable housing), commutable (with well-developed systems of transportation), healthy (with a good healthcare system), green (with 80% forest coverage), and safe (with low crime rate), a wide range of programs have been introduced. However, the central thrust of the Chongqing model is "co-prosperity," i.e., to narrow the income gap and promote equality, especially the equality between rural and urban residents.

Six pillars define the Chongqing model. The first is the overhaul of the household registration system that has since the Mao era artificially divided the Chinese people into two status groups: the urbanites and the peasants. Under this program, ten million rural residents will be become urbanites by 2020 and granted with the same benefits as other urbanites in social security, health care, education, housing, and employment opportunities.

The second pillar is the program concerning land-use rights. The central government has an iron-clad policy of maintaining 1,800 million *mu* (about 296.5 million acres) of farmland nationwide. Each acre of land consumed by urban expansion has to be compensated by the same amount of farmland created somewhere else. This is usually done by reclaiming farmland through merging smaller villages, moving peasant households to high rises, and returning land used for rural industries to farming. To allow remote rural areas to benefit from the appreciation of land value in the urban boom, the Chongqing government encourages rural residents to create more farmland. Each acre of new farmland created is issued an acre of "land-development certificate," which can be sold to developers in urban areas. The latter have to purchase a land-development certificate in order to be able to bid for agricultural land of the same size in the suburbs for commercial or residential development. In other words, the reduction of farmland in suburbs is thus compensated by new farmland in rural areas.

The third is the city's public rental housing program. Chongqing plans to build 40 million square meters of public rental flats by 2020 to house about 650,000 families. The targeted low-income groups include mainly the peasant workers, the urban poor, and new college graduates. The fourth pillar is the micro-business program. According to a plan released by the Chongqing party committee in July 2011, the city will create 150,000 micro-businesses by 2015. The government supports these enterprises through capital subsidies, tax rebates, loan guarantees, micro-financing, fee reductions, regulatory exemptions etc. The main targeted groups are college graduates, laid-off workers, returned peasant workers, the disabled, IT engineers, and cultural/artistic innovators. Micro-businesses are targeted because they create more jobs and are the driving force for innovation. The fifth pillar of the Chongqing model is a massive expansion of the state sector, especially in the areas of finance and infrastructure. The city has eight major municipal investment corporations and a assets-management company that have played a dominant role in raising capital and building up the infrastructure in recent years. Between 2001 and 2010, the total SOE assets expanded from 170 billion to 1.2 trillion *yuan*; during the same period, the private sector's share of Chongqing's GDP rose from 38.3% to 61.2%.

The last pillar of the Chongqing model is perhaps most responsible for it being branded a leftist model (apart from "singing red"). In a sense, Bo Xilai has resurrected the Maoist massline: he advocated the so-called "three enters" and "three togethers," requiring all party and government officials as well as civil servants to go to the grass-roots, to rural areas and peasant homes and spend a certain amount of time each year to eat, live, and work together with the poor.

4.4 "Massline" is the Maoist approach to manage the relationship between the communist party and the people. It utilizes grassroots organizations of the party and requires the cadres and party members to engage in extensive consultation, persuasion, and mobilization among the masses. This way, the party is more in tune with the people and its policies more aligned with people's preferences without formal democracy. In April, 2013 the PBSC re-endorsed massline, a year after the fall of Bo Xilai.

Every cadre is required to establish long-term associations with two or three poor households and help them in getting out of poverty. In this way, Chongqing also hopes to root out social unrest at its source.

2. The Guangdong Model

While the Chongqing model is full of twists and turns harking back to the Maoist past, the Guangdong model is relatively straight-forward for foreign observers. Under the rubric of "Happy Guangdong," it emphasizes three main components: the rule of law, political openness, and social development.

GDP growth was the obsession of the province in the two decades after Deng Xiaoping set the goal in 1992 for Guangdong to catch-up with the four little dragons of East Asia in 20 years (in terms of total GDP). Guangdong has since achieved that goal, but during the process accumulated many new social problems. The Guangdong model attempts to tackle these problems not by the "singing red and striking black" but by, first of all, establishing the rule of law. It strives to create a legal framework and governance structure that redefine the role of the government and specify the relationship between state, market and society. Part of it is to streamline and reduce the size of the administrative structure. In a pilot reform carried out in Shunde district of Foshan municipality, 41 government departments and their parallel party structures were folded into 16. In addition, Guangdong abolished the life tenure for civil servants in 2006, the first in the nation. Another part is to have more transparency and more political openness. For example, Guangzhou municipality (the provincial capital) took the lead in 2010 to publicly release its budget. To varying extent, the municipalities in the provinces have also opened up the budgeting, law and policy making process to the public and invited public participation.

Instead focusing on GDP growth, the government will devote most of its resources and energy to deliver services to the citizens and respond to the needs of the people. Such a role requires more citizens' participation, more partnership with the various groups in society in extensive consultation and collaboration on policies and programs. The open-door policy pioneered by Guangdong is shifting from economic opening to the outside world to greater political opening to the society. As then provincial party secretary Wang Yang put it, the political reform in Guangdong is to explore ways to expand orderly political participation by citizens, to search for new forms of democratic election, democratic policy making, democratic management, democratic supervision, and to safeguard the people's rights to vote, to know, to participate, to express, and to supervise. It is also to enable the citizens to perform their duties under the law.

Such a model of governance requires a highly developed civil society. Social development is therefore the third key component of the Guangdong model. Building up the civil society and promoting grass-roots-level self-governance are the defining features of the Guangdong model because they will decide the success or failure of the new governance and social management model Guangdong attempts to establish. The province already has the highest density of NGOs of all provinces, partly because of its highly developed economy and the large size of middle-class professionals. By July 2012, NGOs are no longer required to have a "sponsor" — typically a government-run organization with a party committee, to register.

Wang Yang has also taken measures to make some of the hitherto government-controlled NGOs such as the trade union more autonomous in representing the interests of their constituents. In several workers' strikes in 2011, Wang Yang adopted a hands-off approach, encouraging the trade unions to engage in collective bargaining with the employers despite the misgivings among local officials who feared worker activism and upward wage pressures. The peaceful resolution of the Wukan protest at the end of 2011 and the subsequent election of the protest leaders to top positions in the village is a clear break from the CCP's past handling of such incidents.

3. Local Models as Products of Local Conditions

The Chongqing and Guangdong models cannot be appropriately considered as competing "models" for the entire nation. These two places are at different levels of development and face different problems and challenges. Their respective reform experiments are relevant to different parts of the country even though they address

Table 9.   Chongqing and Guangdong in Comparison.

	Guangdong (2010)	Chongqing (2010)	Nation (2009)
Major cities	21	11	
Counties (cities)	67	21	
Total population	104,303,132	33,034,500	1,334,740 (×1000)
Urban	69,027,813 (66.18%)	11,070,000 (33.51%)	46.59%
Rural	35,275,319 (33.82%)	21,964,500 (66.49%)	53.41%
Migrant	31,281,654 (30.00%)	4,188,300 (12.68%)	8.641%
College educated	8.214%	5.491%	7.295%
Total GDP	45,472.83 (100 mil.)	7,925.58 (100 mil.)	
Primary sector	5.1%	9.3%	10.03%
Industrial sector	49.2%	52.8%	46.3%
Service sector	45.7%	37.9%	43.4%
Per capita GDP	43,596 yuan	23,991 yuan	25,732 yuan

Sources: *China Statistics Yearbook* (2010); Chongqing Statistics Communique (2011); and Guangdong Statistics Communique (2011).

certain common issues faced by China today. However, neither can serve as a model for the entire country. Table 9 lists the contrasting local conditions of Chongqing and Guangdong.

3.1. *Guangdong*

Guangdong's per capita GDP almost doubles that of Chongqing. For decades, Guangdong is the forerunner of Chinese reforms. Three of the four original special economic zones are in Guangdong and major reform policies are either pioneered by or test-run in the province before they are promoted to the rest of the country. It has the largest GDP among all provinces for decades and its economy is among the most marketized. As a result, Guangdong has developed a complex society and accumulated many problems associated with rapid social change accompanying industrialization, including corruption, street crimes, triads, class clashes, strikes and protests, income disparity, social upheavals, and widespread discontent. Upgrading the industrial structure and managing social conflicts are top priorities for the government. Three decades of rapid growth have transformed the socioeconomic landscape and rendered the old administrative structure inept in handling new issues and problems. In particular, the rise of three classes has prompted the reform efforts to build the new governance model described earlier. The first is the rich capitalists who enjoy considerable political backing from the local party-state establishments. The second is a relatively large, autonomous and sophisticated middle class, and the third is a large army of migrant workers that account (together with their families) for 30% of the provincial population.

Because the Chinese market economy grew out of the pre-existing communist system, successful private entrepreneurs often have to either come from the state sector or establish close ties with the local politicians. The resulting marriage between money and power not only is the main source of corruption but also has shaped the basic structure of the *status quo* interests which any further reforms have to overcome.

In contrast, the new middle class (i.e., the white collar workers, professionals, and small business owners in the private sector *etc.*) and the migrant proletariat have evolved largely outside the political structure. Benefiting from the relatively liberal political and economic environment of Guangdong, the middle class-based civil society is more developed in Guangdong than anywhere else in China; it is more organized and more vocal, and has been actively seeking political participation to protect their rights. The large migrant population — or the working class in general — are also inadequately represented and served by the existing political structure. In many industrial towns in the Pearl River Delta, migrants far outnumber the locals but do not enjoy the same rights, services, and protection from the local governments. Conflicts between migrants and the local population and local authorities are on the rise.

The province needs a new governance structure to integrate the fragmented population; it needs to provide more channels of political expression for the new classes hitherto excluded; it requires the rule of law to protect the interests of the diverse groups who are increasingly rights conscious, and it necessitates a more hands-off government to facilitate — not to dictate — the interactions among the relatively mature and autonomous social actors. The Guangdong model as outlined earlier seems appropriate enough.

3.2. Chongqing

In contrast, the development of Chongqing is still at a stage where it is incumbent upon the government to mobilize and orchestrate a catch-up industrialization, as is typical of all late developers. The state naturally falls back on communist traditions and relies heavily on existing institutions (rather than try to create new ones as Guangdong does), for no other system is more capable of mobilization than communism.

Even today, Chongqing's per capita GDP is below the national average (Table 9). When Chongqing was promoted to the 4th provincial-level municipality (ranked with Beijing, Tianjin, and Shanghai) in 1997, it was a rusty old industrial city put in charge of some of the poorest rural hinterlands in China. At the time, 90% of the land area was rural and 80% of the population was peasantry. Dubbed "a mega-city of peasants," 14 of Chongqing's 21 rural counties are still designated as "national poverty counties." In contrast, Guangdong has none.

Chongqing was created in part as a growth pole to lift its hinterland out of poverty. A 2008 research conducted by Chongqing Municipal Academy of Social Sciences describes the social structure of the city as inverse T-shaped. At the bottom are farmers living in extreme poverty plus an urban underclass created by the massive layoffs of SOEs from the city's obsolete heavy industries. Hence, bridging the income gap is the top priority for Chongqing. The most effective way to do so is to bridge the urban–rural divide by allowing the peasants to settle in urban areas and to project the urban growth pole effects far into the rural hinterland. To do this, a massive build-up of infrastructure is required. Chongqing is building a network of highways to integrate all counties within two hours' drive from the urban centers of Chongqing. The large-scale public rental housing construction, the household registration reform, the micro-business program, the large welfare spending etc., are all geared toward that purpose. And all these programs require a strong hand of the state. Sending cadres to remote rural areas can conceivably play a positive role in integrating urban–rural development.

4. Local Models as Approaches to National Problems

The reform experiments in Guangdong and Chongqing are nationally relevant despite their differences. Their experiments address some key problems faced by the entire nation and provide alternative policy options for other provinces. Because Guangdong is one of the most developed provinces of China, many problems it faces now are likely to emerge in other provinces down the line. The solutions that Guangdong has come up with may be more relevant to the future direction of Chinese social and political reforms. The Chongqing model, on the other hand, can be readily enacted by other localities because of its reliance on the existing political structure and the communist political tradition.

The number one challenge for all local governments is managing an increasingly restive society. The market-driven socioeconomic transformation has outgrown the party-state's old structure of social control. New classes have clashed with both one another and with the party-state. Reintegrating the society under a more effective governance structure and accommodating rising demand for political participation are challenges faced by all localities. Chongqing has opted for strengthening the existing structure by reviving the Maoist massline while Guangdong, where the civil society is more developed, has responded with expanding grassroots democracy, broadening political participation, improving governance, and promoting the rule of the law.

Bridging the widening income gap is another top challenge. Both Guangdong and Chongqing have expanded their social security safety nets. However, Guangdong prioritizes growth over redistribution while Chongqing prefers to do more with redistributive policies because of the pressing need of the poor. Guangdong emphasizes equalizing opportunities through legislation and social reforms while Chongqing focuses more on results. Most Chinese provinces also face the challenge of urbanization, in particular, how to eliminate the rural–urban dualism, an enduring legacy of the Stalinist development strategy pursued in the Mao era and a major source of income inequality today. Chongqing has made great strides in reforming the household registration system, introducing the Land Exchange, and building large numbers of public rental flats. Guangdong, on the other hand, tries to upgrade its economy to create better paying jobs for the migrant workers.

Three decades of market-driven but state-led growth have created entrenched *status quo* interests. Corruption is the number one factor alienating the society from the state and a primary cause of social protests. To fight corruption and overcome *status quo* interests, Chongqing has taken draconian measures with its so-called "striking black" campaigns to break up entrenched status-quo interests and enhance public safety. Guangdong, on the other hand, prefers a milder albeit long-term approach of building up the legal system and increasing transparency and democratic participation in policy making. China's social management problems mainly come from two fronts; the first is the demands from the new middle class for better rights protection and greater voice in policy making. The second is the livelihood of the estimated 250 million peasant workers. The Guangdong model is largely a response to the former while Chongqing is mainly to the latter. The focus on social management is a significant departure from the single-minded pursuit of economic growth. A more sophisticated view on development is emerging, as evident in the "Happy Guangdong" and "Five Chongqing" visions. The comprehensive reform packet revealed at the 3rd Plenum of the 18th Party Congress in November 2013 contains substantial elements of both Guangdong and Chongqing models.

5. The Political Foundation of Two Models

The above analysis has revealed the respective *raison d'être* of the two models and their relevance to the overall Chinese development. Neither can be attributed to one individual leader nor dismissed easily. In fact, the Chongqing model has a much deeper root system in the political establishment than the Guangdong model, despite Bo Xilai's fall. It resonates better with the communist cadre corps because it taps into the organizational strength and political toolbox of the CCP. Ultimately, it works to strengthen the party's rule and the *status quo* interests. Its "co-prosperity" message also has great popular appeal. The resurrection of the revolutionary-era songs, dances, and heroes or role models went far beyond Chongqing to many other provinces. The city attracted a string of high profile visitors, including seven of the nine members of the Politburo Standing Committee, and mesmerized international figures such as Henry Kissinger. In contrast, the repeated calls by Premier Wen Jiabao for political reforms, often using Guangdong as his launch pad, met with lukewarm and sometimes hostile responses from the establishment.

The Guangdong model is a departure from the *status quo* — it is mild in form but radical in essence. Guangdong's vision of a small, limited, and service oriented government, a vibrant civil society, an emphasis on the rule of law and more political openness etc. is threatening to the existing order and the many interests vested in it. It is, therefore, inevitable to meet with resistance from the party-state establishment. Zhu Xiaodan, governor of Guangdong, put it this way: "Without the determination to wage a revolution against ourselves, we cannot hope to break up the power-interests structure." The reformers must draw support from the society, especially from the middle class. That is why the Guangdong model emphasizes developing the civil society and advocates more political opening. Guangdong's enlightened approach to the Wukan protest is exactly the kind of society-driven political change needed to break down the cycle of corruption and interest group obstruction.

In comparison, the Chongqing model is effective in the short run but precisely because of its reliance on the existing apparatuses, it reinforces the political structure and may further delay the necessary social and political reforms. As much as some enlightened leaders of the CCP want to push for more liberal reforms, the balance of power in the political establishment is not in their favor. "Chongqing model" is far from dead and resurgence cannot be ruled out in the near future.

ESSAY 5: *STATUS QUO* INTERESTS STALL CHINA'S REFORM

During his second term (2007–2012) Chinese Premier Wen Jiabao openly called for political reforms on 15 occasions, warning against the dangers of further delaying political reforms. His plea, however, was largely ignored by the Chinese political establishment despite that his sense of urgency was shared by many, the left and the right alike. There is this shared fear of a pending crisis as social conditions deteriorate and the economy slows.

The deterioration is manifested in a wide range of social malaises: increasing incidents of senseless violence such as massacre of school children, stabbing of doctors, suicide and self-immolation; rapid increase of mental illnesses among the population; widespread cynicism and apathy;[1] high crime rates; mafia and gangster proliferation, and widespread

3.2 "Letters and Visits Department" is a branch of the government that receives letters of grievances and petitioners and redirects them to appropriate authorities for resolution. It continues a tradition of imperial China in which petitioners from the grassroots could initiate a law suit or arbitration case by beating the drum in front of the office of the magistrate.

In recent years, this system is overwhelmed by the large number of petitioners seeking justice. Local governments have done everything in their power to stop petitioners under their jurisdiction from going to Beijing. They send cadres or hire gangsters to intercept and detain these people illegally, creating the so-called "black jails."

---

[1] In a famous recent incident in Dongguan, Guangdong province, a little girl was run over by a van and lay in the middle of the road, bleeding and dying. Eighteen

counterfeiting and intellectual property rights theft. Not to mention commercial frauds and academic cheating that have almost become the norm; worsening corruption; rising homelessness and an expanding urban underclass; a pervasive sense of injustice that has led to a blind hatred for the rich and the powerful among large segments of the population; mounting social conflicts and mass protests and so on. More fundamentally, there is a lack of basic trust in the Chinese society.

These social malaises have created a precarious situation even for the rich and powerful. The rich are emigrating in droves; corrupt state officials are planning for exit too, secretly moving their money as well as families out of the country.[2] With a constant stream of corruption scandals paraded in the media, the ordinary people are losing confidence as well as trust in the ruling party.

The most troubling of all is however this: There are no clear anchor points in the Chinese system for moral cultivation. Plagued by scandals and drenched in corruption, the state or the ruling party is hardly a moral exemplar for the population, despite decades of peddling communist role models such as Lei Feng and Jiao Yulu.[3] Religion is constrained because the ruling party is avowedly atheist and fearful of organized religion. The civil society that has served as the tutelage of civic virtues in mature democracies is until recently rigorously suppressed by the party-state for fear of losing control over the masses. The single-child family hardly provides the right environment to build character. To a considerable extent, the society is ruled by money and run by power worshiping.

The developmental potential of the current system has been depleted considerably and its drawbacks become clearer every

---

passers-by did nothing to help her. The incident was caught by surveillance camera and the video went viral online.

[2] These are referred to as "naked officials" and subject to intense criticism and ridicule from the population. See Hedging their bets: Officials, Looking for an Exit Strategy, Send Family and Cash Overseas. *The Economist*, May 26, 2012.

[3] Lei Feng, a soldier do-gooder, has been the perennial role model meant for everybody since the early 1960s while Jiao Yulu, a hardworking, thrifty, people-loving, and devoted county-level cadre also of the 1960s, is recently brought back by Xi Jinping, apparently in a naïve attempt to serve as the role model for cadres.

passing day. Inevitable economic slowdown is posing a host of fresh challenges to the regime. The problems China faces are complex, multifaceted but are by no means unusual for a society under rapid transformation. They remind one of the Charles Dickens' England and the era of Robber Barons of the United States. In both cases, those seemingly intractable problems were eventually overcome by progressive forces in society that effectively utilized the legal and democratic institutions available.

But China is no democracy; its rule of law and civil society are both weak. A peaceful and non-revolutionary solution to the mounting problems has to come from the top and within the ruling elite. For a starter, the Chinese state needs to give up the three decade-long Dengist reform approach of "crossing the river by feeling for stepping stones." It needs to resume the political reform of the 1980s that has been suspended for over two decades after the Tiananmen Incident. However, in the Hu-Wen years, all we saw were hesitation and false starts, followed by inaction.

1. The Rise and Consolidation of Status quo Interests

The inaction in the face of societal atrophy stems from the growing dominance of *status quo* interests in areas where new reform initiatives have to originate. *Status quo* interests are those whose very existence tends to preserve the present order. Because they are in advantageous positions in terms of resources allocation and power distribution, they can effectively resist changes that undermine their interests. *Status quo* interests differ from both special interests groups and public interests groups. The former are usually highly organized to pursue their narrowly defined objectives, often at the expense of the general public. Public interest groups attempt to organize but suffer from the collective action problem.[4] *Status quo* interests in contrast do not have as much a need to organize

---

[4]Or the "free-rider" problem. A classic study of this problem was that done by Mancur Olson. 1971. *The Logic of Collective Action; Public Goods and the Theory of Groups.* Cambridge, Mass.: Harvard University Press.

(although some do) as they are based upon or attached to the basic institutions of a nation and enjoy legitimate power and resource control. They are "the establishment."

The main characteristic of *status quo* interests in China is their close integration with state apparatuses. They are the products of the decentralization and marketization reforms of the 1980s and 1990s, which have allowed the component units in the communist system to evolve their own interests in both market and state. The lack of substantive political reform creates a situation in which power-based and market-based interests become intertwined through the existing political structure. In the resultant political economy, power is the most important form of capital, to which political, economic, and intellectual elite tend to converge to form a symbiotic coexistence.

All major *status quo* interests not only have political backing but are also served by the part of the media and the intelligentsia that have fallen under their control or become their collaborators. Some have become well-oiled political machines that can easily foil any reform initiatives not to their liking. They are simultaneously dependent on and corrosive of the current system, hardening its power structure while distorting the functions of its apparatuses. Their resistance to change has helped to foster the regime's dominant strategy of maintaining social stability: to build up a gigantic coercive apparatus to keep things from falling apart.

2. Nine Major Status quo Interests

Nine main clusters of *status quo* interests can be distinguished in China today. They do not have fundamental conflicts of interest, often overlap in membership, and are in symbiotic coexistence or collaboration to form and maintain the *status quo*.

2.1. Local states

Without doubt, local governments have emerged as one of the most powerful economic actors in the reform era. The decentralization reforms in the 1980s, fiscal and tax reforms in particular, established their relative autonomy and hardened their interests. They have since persistently defended their autonomy and fight hard to protect and advance local interests. They have strong incentives to push local economic development. In the 1980s, local governments pioneered the breaking up of the rigid command economy and were a major source of institutional innovations. Decentralization in the absence of privatization devolves power to the local governments and made them dominant economic players in the market. In fact, they were the driving force behind marketization for the purpose of serving their own interests, resulting for a long time in the fragmentation of the Chinese market and the rise of local protectionism (see Essay 1).

Today, local governments continue to control land, natural resources and infrastructure, and wield vast regulatory power. They have reaped great profits from land sales and are largely responsible for the real estate bubble. They are the primary obstacle that has thawed the numerous attempts by the central government to curb property speculation in the last ten years. The institutional arrangements of the local governments maximize the power of the local leaders, the party chiefs in particular. That the lack of checks and balances and effective supervision in the local power structure is the main cause of rampant corruption is well understood by almost everybody but attempts to reform this system have been few and far in between, and altogether ineffective so far. The silent and yet powerful resistance by local party bosses is the primary reason for the lack of progress in political reform in the recent decade.

2.2. Government *bumen*

Bumen (部门, literally "departments") refer to the ministries, commissions, bureaus, departments, agencies etc. of central and local governments. Seven rounds of administration restructuring in the reform era (up to 2013) have all but eliminated the industrial ministries of the planned economy era, and consolidated policy making and regulatory power in the hands of 25 ministries/commissions and 48 other types of agencies in the central government. These central *bumen* have subsidiaries in the localities that are controlled by local governments. *Bumen* usually have their independent sources of revenue in addition to official budget allocation. These sources of income are all associated with the regulatory power vested in their hands.

Their power comes mainly from two sources; first, they screen all major investment projects and local or sectoral development plans or programs. They can approve, reject, delay them, or demand revisions. Such power is so pervasive in China that the Chinese political economy is often nicknamed "economics of screening." *Bumen* and their bureaucrats derive tremendous influence and potential material benefits from the screening process. Second, they draft regulations and laws. They make laws and regulations to enhance their power and consolidate their turfs. They are under intense lobbying efforts by lower level governments, enterprises, and other interests groups and often form strong alliances with the lobbying groups. Their power is frequently unchecked and only weakly supervised by the National People's Congress. Their interests determine that they work to preserve the *status quo*. In particular, they resist privatization and political reforms that redefine and limit the role of the state in the economy and society.

2.3. *State-owned monopolies*

China has never undergone a thorough privatization, nor does it intend to. A large, viable state-owned sector is considered the economic foundation of the Communist Party rule. Large state-owned enterprises (SOEs), mainly the 100 or so central SOEs that control the commanding heights of the economy, are important policy tools of the state and a source of state revenue. Local SOEs are also important vehicles for local economic development. As a result, the state has lavished resources, privileges, and protection upon them, allowing them to reap monopoly profits. To a lesser extent, the same is true of large and successful private enterprises, especially those globally competitive ones or "national champions". The top executives of SOEs are party-state cadres in regular rotation between the enterprises and the government. As a matter of fact, most of China's largest SOEs have evolved from the dismantled former industrial ministries. Some SOEs are entrusted with formulating sectoral industrial policies and drafting relevant laws.

Employees of SOEs are in general better paid, enjoy larger bonuses, fringe benefits, and better retirement plan and job security. In recent years, large SOEs have surpassed foreign multinationals as the second most desired employers, next only to the government. Being in such enviable position in the current system, SOEs naturally favor the *status quo*. So far, they have been very successful in barring the entry of private and foreign capital in sectors they dominate and have expanded with lightening speed into profitable industries to crowd out private businesses.

2.4. Property developers

The property cluster is without doubt the most complex, most tightly knit, and most developed *status quo* interests so far. In a sense, it is also the most powerful and resilient. In the Hu-Wen decade, the State Council introduced successive rounds of measures to cool down the red-hot real estate market but failed each time. Each round was followed by an even sharper rise in property values that have practically priced the majority of the population out of the market. The repeated failures earned the State Council the unenviable reputation of implementing policies that never get out of the gate of Zhongnanhai (the compound that houses both the Communist Party headquarters and the Central Government). This cluster of *status quo* interests have created perhaps the biggest housing bubble in Chinese history, posed the gravest danger to the Chinese economy, and imposed a heavy financial burden on the average households.

Undergirding the extraordinary staying power of the property developers are first and foremost the local governments, whose interests of maximizing revenues from land sales and generating high GDP growth figures are congruent with developers' desire for a long-lasting housing boom. Developers also play an important role in collaborating with the government to build urban infrastructures and shining city skylines that showcase the achievements of local state leaders. In many cities, the biggest developers are SOEs under the local governments. Private developers have to first develop close ties with local state officials for the simple fact that the latter control the land sale, zoning and other regulations, credit, relocation of residents in the areas of redevelopment, the supply of power, water, gas etc. A complicated network of vested interests has evolved among developers, local government officials, commercial banks, the media, some bought-out economists or market analysts whose job is to paint a rosy prospect of the housing market, encouraging speculators and luring home buyers. Even gangsters are in some cases an integral part of this constellation of interests — they usually carry out the dirty job of driving away reluctant families and forcibly demolishing their homes for new building projects. The synergy of their intertwined interests has made the developers one of the most effective lobbyists in China.

2.5. Civil servants

As mentioned earlier, becoming a civil servant is one of the most coveted occupations of younger people in China. Each year, tens of millions participate in the civil service entrance exams; less than 1% get the ticket to the world of officialdom. Once inside this world, civil servants enjoy not only high prestige and one of the best benefit packages but also state power, which can be used to accrue additional income or other benefits in kind. Party-state units often have their own extra-budgetary income and their own secret coffers to finance their lavish consumption — banquets, cars, housing, telecommunications, overseas trips and so on. Many of them have built their own "special supply systems" that supply them with fresh, organic and uncontaminated fruits, meats, vegetables, brand name cigarettes, wines and liquor, and superior medical service etc., so that the cadres are insulated from the fake products flooding the market. Senior bureaucrats live apart from the general masses in walled and guarded compounds, which prevent them from seeing and experiencing the problems of ordinary citizens who are struggling on a daily basis.

2.6. The military-industrial complex

This complex is remarkably quiet and low profile in China. However, its power and influence can be seen from over a decade-long double-digit rate of growth in defense expenditure. The People's Liberation Army (PLA) is still officially the military of the Communist Party instead of the Chinese nation. It is the ultimate source of power of the Party, adhering to Mao's famous dictum: "Political power comes from the barrow of a gun." Like many militaries in the Third World, it feels more comfortable under an authoritarian regime than under a democracy because the latter tends to put additional constraints on it, making its funding less predictable and more complicated. The military has benefited greatly from the surge of nationalism and is at the forefront of boosting China's prestige and international standing. The current system's capability of mobilizing resources suits the PLA particularly well — it enjoys practically unlimited supply of resources and personnel in case of external conflicts. Their role as the last defense of domestic stability and the CCP rule makes them the core interests of the CCP.

2.7. The multinational corporations

Contrary to what is generally believed that MNCs (especially the Western ones) are a force of progress in the developing world, foreign multinationals in China have, in general, benefited tremendously from collaboration with local governments, who are always competing for their investments. Large and prestigious MNCs are extremely attractive to local governments, who routinely offer them cheap land, and tax and regulatory concessions. To boost and upgrade the local economy, local governments often conspire to depress the pay of workers and help to maintain labor discipline and tranquility (see Essay 3). For example, in recent years of labor shortage, they have helped the manufacturing giant Foxconn to recruit workers using their administrative clout.[5] Foreign companies tend to be better organized, and over the years they have groomed a sizable comprador class consisting of well-connected people who are often more effective lobbyists than Chinese domestic firms.

2.8. *Well connected large private enterprises*

Almost without exception, large and successful private businesses are well connected with the government at some levels. They are often headed by the "princelings" (offspring of senior communist leaders) and serve as the vehicle of state officials to secretly cumulate personal wealth. Private entrepreneurs are over-represented in the state compared to other classes; many are deputies of the People's Congress and the People's Political Consultative Conference. Their own trade organizations, All China Industrial and Commercial Association and The Association of Chinese Entrepreneurs are quasi-government organs that enjoy legitimate channels of participating in policy deliberation. Many private entrepreneurs used to be managers of SOEs before the latter were privatized, and in part because of this, one third China's private entrepreneurs are Communist Party members.[6] Close ties with the state breed corruption. The rise of crony capitalism is a hot topic in the Chinese media and academic circles; many regard it as the gravest danger to the Chinese economy and the future of the nation

---

[5] Such as assigning recruiting quotas to townships and villages. It happened in Chongqing, Zhengzhou, and Chengdu. (Author's China interviews, April 2012).

[6] Chen, Jie and Bruce J. Dickson. 2008. Allies of the State: Democratic Support and Regime Support among China's Private Entrepreneurs. *The China Quarterly*, pp. 780–804. Dickson, Bruce. 2003. *Red Capitalists in China: The Party, Private Entrepreneurs and Prospects for Political Change*. New York: Cambridge University Press.

because they breed corruption, create income polarization, distort the market, dampen public morale and close down channels of upward mobility for ordinary citizens.

2.9. *The Communist Party*

The ultimate *status quo* interests, however, are the Chinese Communist Party. As the single ruling party, its interests have penetrated into almost all areas of the state, the society as well as the economy. These interests are entrenched in so many important organs of power that they have become obstacles to reform. More specifically, the time-honored policy of "the party controls the cadres" and the existence of the privileged and rather closed state-owned sector not only limit social mobility but also breed a privileged class of ruling elites. The primacy of Party chiefs in the political system leads to the lack of effective supervision and accountability of power, rampant corruption, and other abuses. The Party's political and legal committee (*zhengfawei*) deprives the judicial system of its independence and prevents the rule of law from taking roots. The insistence on the presence of party organizations in enterprises obstructs the rationalization of business administration. The restrictions on free association prevent the emergence of a healthy civil society, so on and so forth.

3. Impact of Status quo Interests

3.1. *Social impact*

Status quo interests have reaped most of the wealth generated by the country's high economic growth to create one of the most lopsided income distributions in contemporary world. The official gini coefficient is 0.47[7] but the estimates by many independent parties put it well above 0.5. A Credit Suisse sponsored study by China

---

[7] According to the Macroeconomic Institute of the State Reform and Development Commission, cited in *China Daily*, May 12, 2010.

374 Chinese Politics Illustrated

Reform Foundation in Beijing released in 2010 concludes that there were substantially unreported household incomes (the so-called "grey incomes"), estimated at 9.3 trillion *yuan* for 2008, almost equivalent to 30% of China's GDP that year. About 80% of this amount went to the top 20% of high income families and 63% to the top 10% families. When factoring in these "grey incomes," the income gap (per capita disposable income) between the top 10% and bottom 10% urban households was 26 times in comparison to the official figure of 9 times.[8]

Figure 14 shows the decline of total urban wages as percentage of China's GDP in the reform era. In addition, government expenditure on health care, education, and social security has been consistently lower than nations with comparable per capita income. Adding the high housing costs, most families are financially stretched. The growth of the middle class is slow and precarious. Many middle class families are on the verge of falling back into the poor masses.

The rise and consolidation of *status quo* interests are also creating a society of unequal opportunities by ossifying the social structure and diminishing social mobility. They generate widespread corruption, a pervasive sense of injustice and (especially for most of the 250 million peasant workers) hopelessness.[9] Land grabbing and forced demolition of homes have created waves of protests and bloody incidents. People are losing trust in the legal system and public authority. Although material wellbeing has improved

---

[8] See Wang Xiaolu (chief investigator and director of the China Reform Foundation). Analysing China's Grey Income. Available at Credit Suisse website <http://www.scribd.com/doc/35832909/CreditSuisse-Expert-Insights-20100806> (accessed on November 12, 2010).

[9] See Sun Liping. 2003. *The Fault Line: Chinese Society since 1990s*. Beijing: Shehui kexue wenxian chubanshe and 2009. "Fear not the widening income gap; Fear the poor losing hope of upward mobility." *China Report*, No. 6. Chen Guangjin. 2005. "From elite circulation to elite replication. *Study and Exploration*, No. 1. Wu Xiaoling. 2012. "Class reproduction or elite recirculation? An analysis of the impact of higher education on social mobility." *Journal of the National Education Administration College*, No. 3.

for most, relative deprivation makes people less happy.[10] Widespread hatred for the rich and powerful bode ill for social stability. If the economy slows down drastically, China would move closer to the conditions that brought about the Arab Spring.

3.2. Impact on public policy and law making

Because of the obstruction of *status quo* interests, many proposed laws have languished in the bureaucratic maze for years or even decades. The law requiring public officials to disclose their family assets was first proposed in the 1980s but has yet to come to fruition. The highly anticipated compensation law for the public requisition of land and property is still jammed in the law making process. The same is true of the new anti-trust law and the wage act. In China, laws and regulations are usually drafted by state bureaucracies with little or no public input. The People's Congress that passes these laws remains largely a rubber stamp. The *bumen* maximize their own interests and the interests of those groups or industries closely associated with them. They compromise to accommodate each other's interests when jointly drafting a law or regulations. Public policy making becomes a balancing act among the various *status quo* interests.

3.3. Impact on reform

Status quo interests have delayed, deflected, and derailed some of the most needed reforms in areas such as household registration (*huji*); citizens' petition system (the "letters and visits" department); discrimination against migrant workers and peasants; environmental and intellectual property rights protection; SOE monopoly; the financial system; health care and social security; the electoral system; higher education; administrative restructuring; separation of

---

[10] For a recent study of this subject, see Easterlin, Morgan, Switek, and Wang. 2012. China's Life Satisfaction, 1990–2010. Distributed by Department of Economics, University of California, Los Angeles, April 6.

the party from the government and, above all, judicial independence and the excessive concentration of power in the hands of party secretaries.

The inability to forge ahead with reforms has left the regime with only one option: "maintaining stability" (*weiwen*). The costs of *weiwen* have skyrocketed to surpass the defense budget in 2010. In addition, the notion of reform has been losing popular support. Most reform measures since the late 1990s have disproportionately benefited *status quo* interests, often at the expense of the masses: housing, education, health care, and SOE reforms, to name just a few. Popular discontent has given rise to the "new left," threatening party unity and political stability as evidenced by the recent Chongqing incident (Essay 4).

4. Status quo Interests and China's Development Prospects

Status quo interests are products of China's rapid development in the past 30 years. They are not always negative; many have played important roles in the Chinese success story. However, China's gradualist approach to reform has allowed them to become halfway fortresses of vested interests that block further progress. They routinely twist reform initiatives to serve their interests and have trapped China's transition to a mature market economy.[11] The obstacle they impose is acutely felt by reformers such as Premier Li Keqiang, who exclaimed that "Shaking up the *status quo* interests is sometimes more difficult than touching the soul." Wang Yang, then party chief of Guangdong, threatened to join the mass petitioners to go to Beijing to redress his "grievances" of not being allowed to reform the administrative structure.

Building and maintaining a large and comprehensive apparatus of repression are not only costly but also ineffective. As

---

[11] E.g., a report by the Development Research Project Team, Sociology Department, Qinghua University, titled, "Middle-income Trap or Transitional Trap?", March 2012. Pei, Minxin. 2006. *China's Trapped Transition: The Limits of Developmental Autocracy*. Cambridge, Mass.: Harvard University Press.

mentioned earlier, it preserves the *status quo*. It may be able to prevent social unrest from spinning out of control (only in the short run though) but does nothing to arrest societal atrophy, which is a greater danger to the Chinese nation than social instability that mainly threatens the regime. The Chinese system's capacity to reform and renew itself has diminished. Mao could single-handedly turn the entire country upside down; Deng was able to force millions of revolutionary generation cadres into retirement; Jiang Zemin and Zhu Rongji, in reforming the SOEs, dared to lay off tens of millions of urban industrial workers; but the Hu-Wen leadership was incapable of undertaking bold reforms to pursue long term national objectives. It remains to be seen whether the new leadership under Xi Jinping is able to master enough power to overcome the status-quo interests.

Because China's *status quo* interests have evolved inside the political system and are attached to the political structure, political reform is the key to overcome their resistance. Since there are few incentives within the establishment to reform the political system, the support for reform has to be sought elsewhere. Social forces are the only possible counterweight to *status quo* interests in a well entrenched authoritarian system. The progressive forces consist mainly of the middle class, the unconnected entrepreneurs in small and medium-sized enterprises, part of the academia, lawyers, journalists, NGOs and other advocacy groups, opinion leaders active in both old and new media, and enlightened and ambitious politicians. In comparison with *status quo* interests, these forces are disorganized, divided in opinion, and lack effective political instrument. As the ultimate source of energy for reform, the masses can be both constructive and destructive depending on how their energy is channeled. They may well turn out to be a reactionary force under demagogues such as Bo Xilai, who channeled mass discontent with the Maoist populism.

In the short run, bold reforms will be difficult if not impossible as evidenced by Wen Jiabao's failure in ten-year tenure. In the long run, the reformers need to re-engage the broader (and stronger) society. Building a healthy and thriving civil society is the key to stem both social unrests and societal atrophy, as well as to regain the reform momentum. This, however, inevitably undermines *status quo* interests. In this regard, the reform experiments in Guangdong offer some hope (Essay 4). A main focus of the "Guangdong model" is social reforms. It attempts to re-engage the society, utilizing social forces to break up *status quo* interests. Low intensity (controllable) social upheavals are consciously used as an energy source to push for new reforms, as seen in the way Guangdong dealt with several incidents of social unrests in recent years. Although Guangdong's attempts to redefine the relationships between the state, society, and market are constrained by the large political structure, the province has made some headway in administrative reforms, expanding democratic participation, and enhancing the rule of law and rights protection. Guangdong may be able to blaze a trail for political reform in China, but its success is by no means guaranteed, given the resistance from *status quo* interests that are particularly strong in Guangdong.

The ascension of the fifth generation leadership in November 2012 provides a window of opportunity for new reform initiatives to emerge. The stronger than expected leadership of Xi Jinping demonstrated in the first year of his administration offers a glimpse of hope of breaking up the status-quo interests. However, if the new leadership does not shift the regime's dominant strategy from *weiwen* to society building and legal reform, *status quo* interests may be able to perpetuate themselves and further delay the necessary reforms. In any case, China is entering a difficult stage in its development.

ABOUT THE AUTHOR

Dr. Lance L P Gore has taught or held research positions at Bowdoin College, Tufts University and University of Washington in the U.S., Murdoch University in Australia, the National University of Singapore. Currently he is a senior research fellow at the East Asian Institute, National University of Singapore. His teaching and research interests span a wide range of topics on contemporary China. In addition to numerous journal articles he is the author of *Chinese Communist Party and China's Capitalist Revolution: the Political Impact of Market* (Routledge 2011) and *Market Communism: the Institutional Foundations of China's Post-Mao Hyper-Growth* (Oxford University Press 1999).